The Landlord's Handbook

A COMPLETE GUIDE TO MANAGING SMALL RESIDENTIAL PROPERTIES

Second Edition

· · · · · · · · · · · ·

Daniel Goodwin
and
Richard Rusdorf

**Real Estate
Education Company**®
a division of Dearborn Financial Publishing, Inc.

This publication is designed to provide accurate and authoritative information in regard to the subject matter covered. It is sold with the understanding that the publisher is not engaged in rendering legal, accounting, or other professional service. If legal advice or other expert assistance is required, the services of a competent professional person should be sought.

Acquisitions Editor: Danielle Egan-Miller
Managing Editor: Jack Kiburz
Interior Design: Lucy Jenkins
Cover Design: Salvatore Concialdi
Typesetting: Eliot House Productions

Library of Congress Cataloging-in-Publication Data
Goodwin, Daniel (Daniel L.)
    The landlord's handbook: a complete guide to managing small residential properties / Daniel Goodwin and Richard Rusdorf.—2nd ed.
        p.   cm.
    Includes bibliographical references and index.
    ISBN 1-7931-2732-7 (pbk.)
    1. Real estate management. 2. Rental housing. 3. Landlord and tenant. I. Rusdorf, Richard. II. Title.
HD1394.G656 1998   97-37313
647.92'068—dc21   CIP

Contents

Acknowledgments

Many people helped put this book together. We especially would like to thank the staff, officers, and support personnel of The Inland Group for graciously providing us the benefit of their time and knowledge: Sharen Mangiameli (marketing), Darren Jordan (collections), Cathy Bussa (taxes), and Delores Friedman (insurance).

We are grateful for the legal review and suggestions of Scott Clark, Esq., Phoenix, Arizona. We are thankful to J. Russell Lenich, CPA, in Westmont, Illinois, for sharing his knowledge of accounting procedures. We are very grateful to Jim Tuley, General Manager of Apartments For Rent; the Chicago Association of REALTORS®; David Boatwright of Peachtree Business Products; Greg Jacobs and Walley Voight at Risk Analysis & Insurance Services in Phoenix, Arizona; the National Apartment Association; Don Crane at Tenant Screening Center, Inc.; and to Rich Kival at RentGrow, Inc.

About the Authors

Daniel L. Goodwin, chairman and CEO of The Inland Group of real estate companies, has over 30 years of experience in purchasing, selling, financing, and managing more than $3 billion worth of income-producing residential properties in more than 2,300 real estate transactions nationwide.

Richard F. Rusdorf, CPM®, has more than 28 years of experience in property management, marketing, finance, development, and sales. A real estate broker, and a Certified Property Manager, Rusdorf is a past president of the Chicago chapter of the Institute of Real Estate Management. He works as an independent real estate consultant and lives in Phoenix, Arizona.

Managing Income-Producing Properties— An Overview

Don Dressler had a master's degree in education and had been a high school teacher for 15 years, when, in 1966, he bought his first rental property—two four-flats in Schiller Park, Illinois. Within two years he owned 72 units and decided to quit teaching to manage his properties full time. He has owned and managed a variety of rental properties over the years.

I was making more money operating my rental units than I was making as a teacher, and managing 72 units kept me very busy. I've always worked out of my house. My first purchase required about $9,000 down payment. Many of my subsequent purchases were acquired with no money down from savings and loan companies who wanted to get the properties off their delinquent books.

I stay away from buying single-family homes and look mostly for properties that have from four to eight units in order to get a better yield. Financially speaking, the monthly yield on my investment is more important than counting on the possibility of appreciation when the property is sold.

Owning rental properties is a good business and I've made a lot of money. But I would tell anyone who thinks about being a landlord that one of the requirements is having a landlord's mentality. Some people may not be able to handle the everyday duties, such as dealing with the tenants, which I think is the hardest part of the job. It doesn't require a lot of training, but it can be hard work. I never felt the necessity of getting a real estate license, nor did I have any professional training in managing properties, but I did eventually learn how to do everything myself, including doing all my own repairs, bookkeeping, taxes, marketing, and so on. I've come to believe that if you have to hire other people to do some or all these things, you will probably lose money.

Managing Profitable Investment Property

George Benton, 36, lives in a one-bedroom condominium that is ideally located along Chicago's north Lake Shore Drive. Since he bought the condominium, George has changed jobs and now works in a Chicago suburb. He would like to live closer to work in a larger home with a fenced backyard for his collie. However, he does not wish to sell his downtown condominium because he considers it a good long-term investment.

Nancy Oates and Bill Wellbrook are successful entrepreneurs in South Bend, Indiana. Five years ago they developed an insurance service that caters to the specific needs of senior citizens. Now they are considering renovating a turn-of-the-century six-flat along South Bend's Lincoln Way East.

The Hasbrouck, Kiel, and Lippert families of Dallas, Texas, organized the HKL investment club eight years ago. The club investments have proven profitable. Because they now want to conserve profits, HKL is planning to purchase a 40-unit, five-story apartment building on Rodeo Boulevard.

What do these people have in common? Like you, they currently own or are planning to purchase small income-producing properties. And, like you, what they need is a practical handbook, specifically designed for the do-it-yourself landlord. Most real estate books on the shelves deal mainly with acquiring property and structuring real estate deals. Generally, these books do not provide you—the average real estate investor—with practical, usable techniques and suggestions that help you to manage your investment property more profitably on a day-to-day basis.

This book is designed to share property management expertise with you in clear, everyday language. Based on the experiences of successful property owners and managers, this book clearly explains the importance of attracting and keeping good tenants by using good management techniques. It discusses how to form a business relationship with your tenants based on mutual respect.

The techniques, forms, and worksheets were developed and are used by successful real estate investors and managers throughout the country.

Real estate always has been considered a good investment. However, the combination of tax reform and low mortgage rates has made small income-producing properties one of the best investments of the 1990s. Real estate was and is a purchase that stands the dual tests of time and cyclical economies.

Owning and operating small investment properties has made many people financially independent. As a real estate investor, you have the pride of ownership coupled with a hedge against inflation that serves to protect your asset from losing value. As a property manager, your two chief concerns are:

1. Maintain your property.
2. Increase its value.

Regardless of your specific goals, effective management is the key to achieving them.

Simply owning rental property will not guarantee financial independence, because properties do not generate cash flow by themselves.

To make money, you need to know good property management techniques.

You need to know

- how to keep good tenants;
- how to collect the rent on time;
- how to maintain;
- the physical structure of your property, and most importantly;
- how to deal with people.

Owning a Home versus Managing Rental Property

To some extent, owning your home has prepared you for owning other buildings. However, managing rental property is not the same as managing a home. For example, decorating schemes that might be perfect for your home—especially colorful ones—could be a real detriment in trying to rent an apartment if those colors do not go with a prospective tenant's furniture. In apartments, carpeting and wall treatments should be in neutral colors, and in materials that are durable and easy to clean and maintain.

Kitchen appliances also are different for rental properties as compared to home use. You may choose to buy a range with added features for your home, but a tenant who does not cook will not want to pay a premium rental for having it. Also, as a property manager you must be aware of depreciation (see Chapter 12); thus you might choose a different water heater or furnace for a rental property than you would for your own use.

You Don't Need an MBA

Some would-be investors think property management requires a master's degree in management. They have heard horror tales of tenant complaints, problems with collecting rent, mechanical equipment failures, apartment vacancies, and so on. They suspect that unless they have formal training, managing rental property could be a nightmarish experience.

Property management can be a headache if you do not know what you are doing. To maximize your investment property, you must make money while keeping expenses in check. If you let tenants run the property down, if you fail to get regular rent increases, or if you mismanage cash flow, you might not make a profit. Worse, you could even decrease the value of your asset. Certainly, attending managerial and real estate courses and seminars can be helpful. And this book will give you proven methods based on actual experience in dealing with virtually every form of residential property and all types of tenants.

Use Your Management Skills in a New Setting

If you work in corporate management or operate your own business, you already have many of the necessary skills for small property management. However, you probably take them for granted as part of your daily business routine. You do not realize that the same marketing and management skills can be applied to a number of business situations.

Marketing

For example, grocery store management requires attracting regular customers; apartment management requires attracting good renters. To bring customers into the grocery, the manager uses numerous marketing tools, including newspaper advertising, special promotions, and so on. The property manager advertises rental vacancies and highlights special features of the apartment and complex such as carpeting, off-street parking, etc.

Maintenance

Regular maintenance is important to the grocery store and the apartment complex. The grocery store manager may not operate the floor scrubber or wash down the checkout counters, but he or she will check that these jobs are done because customers prefer shopping in a clean environment. The property manager also needs to actively monitor maintenance of apartments, common areas, landscaping, parking areas, and so on.

Accounting

At the end of the business day the grocery store manager tallies receipts for each department and prepares bank deposits. These accounting numbers will be tallied weekly or monthly against costs of inventory, spoilage, overhead, and other factors to monitor the store's profitability. Similar bookkeeping and accounting skills are necessary in property management to make sure rental receipts cover costs while producing a profit. Anyone who can balance a checkbook can quickly learn the accounting procedures used to control income and expenses of a property.

Customer Relations

The grocery store manager needs to have a balanced combination of diplomacy and judgment when dealing with customers. For example, if an irate customer demands a refund for one rotten orange found in a five-pound bag, a smart manager will replace that $2.99 bag of oranges or refund the purchase price to keep that customer buying oranges and other products in the store. It's a good investment in customer relations.

Diplomacy and judgment are also crucial in good property management. For example, an irate tenant may insist that he or she needs a new dead-bolt lock because their apartment is too difficult to open. A smart property manager will promptly and cheerfully apply a little carbon to the keys and locks. This will probably solve the problem, and the cost in time and materials is about the same as for that five-pound bag of oranges.

Managing Time and People

Properly done, the management of small rental properties can be a rewarding experience. Property management does not have to be a full-time job. Obviously the amount of time you will need to manage your rental property depends on your knowledge and resources and the size of your portfolio.

Once you've mastered the techniques offered in this book, you should be able to handle a single condominium unit in 30 minutes a month, while a typical four-flat will require about four hours of your time. Most of this time will be spent dealing with people, so how well you deal with people is one key to effective management.

How the Landlord's Handbook Can Help

The information and forms in this book provide you with valuable tools to help you increase your cash flow and create financial independence. The book walks you through the important management tasks involved from the day you hand over the apartment keys to a new tenant through the day you take them back.

As a new apartment investor and manager you will have to determine the proper rental rate for your property based on local market conditions. We'll show you how to determine rental rates, how to find tenants, and we'll suggest ways to convince them that your rental property specifically meets their needs.

Lease applications and rental agreements can be complicated, but the handbook simplifies them, and even supplies sample applications, leases, and riders to cover special situations. Terminology and contents are defined, along with discussions of prohibited transactions, security deposits, lease distribution, and important caveats. You also learn about apartment inspections, lease renewals and subletting, and reletting agreements.

Other important aspects of property management include rent collections, maintenance, the different types of insurance required, property taxes, and accounting. Each of these is thoroughly addressed, along with sample forms and guidelines.

Managing Residents

*R*on Vanden Bossche has a Ph.D. in clinical psychology and practices in the Veterans Administration. He purchased a three-flat building in 1981.

Tenant phobia is not a true psychiatric entity, but it does appear to be a major reason people avoid owning income property. It is a multi-faceted syndrome, ranging from our childhood training in avoidance of strangers, to anxious anticipation of being imposed on by pushy complainers, and uncertainty about one's ability to handle the power differential between landlord and tenant.

It is easy to exaggerate these fears to the point of total avoidance of the role of landlord. But being a landlord is just that—a role. Roles can be learned. The first step is to accept these interpersonal anxieties as normal in landlord life.

The second step involves practicing assertiveness training. Simply put, assertiveness is stating the reality of a given situation in a clear, certain, but nonaggressive way. The difference between assertion and aggression is that assertiveness is the giving of information, while aggression is pure power play.

Although the lease can be seen as speaking all the necessary words for you, at times you will have to restate them to your tenants due to noise, overdue rent, and other situations. Do not view this assertive behavior as a confrontation with battle lines drawn and full of explosive potential. It is your right to state the fact of the matter. The reasonableness of the tenant's response will be the guide as to whether or not to continue your relationship with this tenant. Keep in mind that the landlord-tenant power differential means that no friendship or social relationship will be at stake. Nor will the assertive person take the behavior of tenants personally.

Finally, do not confuse the role of landlord with the role of parent. Responding to tenants as adults who need information—not as children who need correcting—gives the best chance of having good relations and minimized anxiety.

The Landlord-Tenant Relationship

Many people believe that landlords and tenants are natural enemies. Landlords are sometimes seen as heartless money-grubbers who would trade their mothers for a rent increase; or they are overworked, underpaid drudges who are slaves to their properties and tenants. Tenants are frequently seen as ne'er-do-wells who make unreasonable demands, destroy property, and refuse to pay the rent.

There is some truth in these stereotypes: Bad landlords and bad tenants do exist. But the landlord-tenant relationship is basically a business relationship. If you learn to manage rental property efficiently—and that includes choosing good tenants—then landlord-tenant transactions can be mutually rewarding.

It is well worth learning to deal with residents in a rational, businesslike way. When a property is badly managed it becomes an active drain on all your valued resources: the physical property itself, your time, your energy, and your money.

Landlords and tenants will often have differences of opinion about their mutual responsibilities. Tenants may have the perception that landlords should do everything in their power to make the tenants happy. Certainly you will want your tenants to be satisfied with their dwelling, but you are not obligated to provide them a garden paradise, unless that's what you are specifically marketing. If you know your basic obligations as a landlord, you will be less likely to resent a tenant's legitimate request, and will be able to assertively refuse an unreasonable demand.

Most of your obligations are governed and limited by the express conditions contained in a lease or rental agreement. With or without a written lease, the business of owning and leasing rental property is also subject to state and local municipal statutes and ordinances.

Across the country, local and state governments are beginning to take stronger positions in regard to landlord-tenant relationships. Tenant groups are presenting their cases to city councils everywhere, demanding more favorable treatment from landlords. Landlord/Tenant Ordinances contain the obligations of both parties. As of February 1996, at least 20 states had adopted the Uniform Residential Landlord and Tenant Act, and the entire residential rental industry may soon operate under laws of this type.

Throughout this chapter the words *tenant* and *resident* are used interchangeably. *Tenant* refers to the legal relationship between a lessor and lessee; *resident* refers to a person (or persons) living in a dwelling unit. In communications with lessees you can take some of the formality out of the landlord-tenant relationship and put it on a more personal level, by referring to lessees as residents instead of tenants.

Landlord and *owner* are similarly interchangeable; they always refer to the lessor. Owner is the less formal term.

Landlord Obligations

Landlords must adhere to three widely recognized obligations:

1. *Make Yourself Known*

An owner (or other person who is authorized to enter into a rental agreement on the owner's behalf) should disclose to the resident, in writing, at or before the beginning of the lease:

- The name and address of the owner or agent of the premises
- The person authorized to manage the premises

The tenant needs to know where to send payments, and both tenant and landlord or agent need to know where to receive and document notices and demands.

If tenants are not told who has authority to respond to their requests, they may be able to file a complaint with the local housing authority, withhold rent, or take other measures to keep their units habitable. Further, the owner may face substantial fines.

In many states, an owner must disclose the insurance agent or carrier for the property. In case of fire damage or other emergency, tenants would know whom to call if the owner or agent were unavailable.

2. *Maintain Habitable Premises*

At all times during a tenancy, owners must maintain the premises in a "habitable" condition. A dwelling unit is considered habitable if the following minimum standards are maintained:

- Effective weather protection is provided, including unbroken windows and doors.
- Plumbing facilities are in good working order.
- The unit has a water supply connected to a sewage system. If the water supply is under the control of the resident, it must be capable of producing hot and cold running water; if under the control of the owner, it must produce hot and cold running water furnished to appropriate fixtures.
- Heating units and, if provided, air conditioning and ventilation systems, are in good working order. If these are under the control of the resident, they are capable of producing heat (or cooling and ventilation); if under control of the owner, they produce heat (or cooling and ventilation) in fixtures provided. Minimum temperatures for heat are usually established by municipal code. (A good

rule of thumb is having a heating system capable of maintaining a minimum of 70°F at all times in the unit, regardless of how cold it gets outside.)

- Gas or electrical appliances supplied by the landlord must be in good working order and properly installed with appropriate gas piping and electrical wiring systems according to building codes, and they must be maintained in good working order.
- The building, grounds, and areas under the control of the owner must be in a clean, sanitary, and safe condition, free from all accumulation of debris, filth, rubbish, garbage, rodents, and vermin.
- Adequate and appropriate receptacles for garbage and rubbish must be provided. If these are under the control of the landlord, they must be kept in clean condition and in good repair.
- Floors, stairways, railings, and common areas are in good repair.
- Apartment floors, walls, and ceilings are in good repair and in safe condition.
- Elevators are maintained in good repair and safe condition.

Generally, landlords are not held responsible if interruptions in service, breakdown of equipment, or disrepairs are caused by:

- the tenant or members of tenant's household, guests, or other persons on the premises with the resident's consent, or other residents.
- the resident's unreasonable refusal of, or other interference with, entry of the owner or the owner's workers or contractors into the premises for purposes of correcting any defective conditions.
- a lack of reasonable opportunity for the owner to correct defective conditions.
- conditions beyond the owner's reasonable control, including strikes, lockouts, and unavailability of essential utilities, materials, or services.
- the owner's not having actual knowledge or notice of such defective conditions.

Any exclusion or modification of any part or all of these obligations must be in writing and separately signed by the party against whose interest the modification works. That is the legal way of saying that if the modification appears in the rental agreement, it must also be typed or printed in a conspicuous place. This means that if you and a tenant have an agreement that the tenant will maintain part or all of the property, it must be specifically spelled out in writing. The tenant should sign an acknowledgment of the agreement.

3. Honor Express Warranties

If you make a promise to a tenant about the condition of a specific dwelling unit, or of the overall premises, services or repairs, or replacements to be made, and this promise is part of the reason the tenant signed the lease, you have created an express warranty. This promise is binding whether it was oral or written.

An express warranty may be created even if there is not a specific intention to make one. It is not necessary to use formal words such as "warrant" or "guarantee" in order to create an express warranty. Statements as: "We plan to replace the dishwasher in a few months," or, "We wash the outside of the windows three times a year," or, "You never have to worry about security around here; this is a safe building," all create express warranties. You might be held liable if someone did have a security problem, or if you washed windows only twice, etc. It is best to avoid making statements that create express warranties.

On the other hand, giving your *opinion* of the relative value of the dwelling unit, premises, or services does not create a warranty. For example, you could say, "We have the best maintenance crew around," or, "I think my property is the best building on the block," or, "The view from this apartment is beautiful," without creating a warranty.

If you think you may have created an express warranty, it would be wise to consult your attorney for guidance in this matter.

Additional Services

Tenants expect to receive all of the services and amenities your property offers for their rental dollar. They rightfully expect you to live up to your basic obligations as listed above. But many properties also offer additional services such as a swimming pool, snow removal, and so on.

Before the resident moves in, outline exactly what additional services you provide, such as snow removal, landscaping, garbage removal, utilities, and so on. Then see that these services are provided consistently.

Having the swimming pool closed for repairs on the hottest day of the year or failing to provide snow removal after a blizzard, are both good ways to ruin a landlord-tenant relationship. Residents tend to remember these things when it comes time to renew their leases.

Liabilities of Ownership

Landlords are generally responsible for maintaining the premises and performing the basic services required. They can be held liable for damages caused by negligence. These liabilities generally remain with the owners until a property is sold.

In some cases, liability continues after the sale transaction. Unless otherwise agreed, an owner who sells his or her property subject to existing leases, and who assigns the leases in a good faith sale to a bona fide purchaser, is relieved of liability for events occurring subsequent to written notice to the resident of the sale and assignment. The new owner becomes liable to the residents for events occurring after this notice, and for money to which residents are entitled from security deposits or prepaid rent.

If you've retained a manager under a management contract, unless otherwise agreed, this person is also relieved of liability for events occurring after written notice to the resident of the termination of the manager's contract.

Security and Crime Prevention

There are several ways you can help yourself become more knowledgeable about securing your property, and working toward creating a safer environment for your residents. It may require you to attend a seminar or two from time to time, but the time you spend in these classes is well worth your effort.

One program, called the Crime Free Multi-Housing Program (CFMHP), is now being offered in more than 500 American cities in 37 states. It is designed to help residents, owners, and managers of apartments keep drugs and other illegal activity off their property. It was created by sponsoring members of the National Apartment Association.

Attendees learn about identifying illegal activities, addressing community concerns, and educating residents about crime prevention. Benefits range from increasing your property value to developing better relations with both residents and the surrounding neighborhood.

The program consists of eight hours of training by a local police agency. Afterwards, the police inspect your property from a security viewpoint. Residents are invited to crime-prevention meetings, and are encouraged to form a community Block Watch, whereby neighbors protectively look out for each other.

Part of the program includes receiving a sample Crime Free Lease Addendum (Figure 2.1) that residents sign indicating their agreement not to engage in any illegal activity. If they violate the addendum, the law allows you to serve them with a 24-hour eviction notice.

To find out if such a program is offered in your community, contact your local police department, or local chapter of the National Apartment Association.

Another new program is called FAX NET 1. When a crime happens that has the capacity of impacting anybody in a community, law

Figure 2.1: Crime Free Lease Addendum

In consideration of the execution or renewal of a lease of the dwelling unit identified in the lease, Owner and Resident agree as follows:

1. Resident, any members of the resident's household or a guest or other person under the resident's control shall not engage in criminal activity, including drug-related criminal activity, on or near the said premises. "Drug-related criminal activity" means the illegal manufacture, sale, distribution, use, or possession with intent to manufacture, sell, distribute, or use of a controlled substance (as defined in Section 102 or the Controlled Substance Act [21 U.S.C. 802]).

2. Resident, any member of the resident's household or a guest or other person under the resident's control shall not engage in any act intended to facilitate criminal activity, including drug-related criminal activity, on or near the said premises.

3. Resident or members of the household will not permit the dwelling unit to be used for, or to facilitate criminal activity, including drug-related criminal activity, regardless of whether the individual engaging in such activity is a member of the household, or a guest.

4. Resident, any member of the resident's household or a guest, or another person under the resident's control shall not engage in the unlawful manufacturing, selling, using, storing, keeping, or giving of a controlled substance as defined in A.R.S. 13-3451, at any locations, whether on or near the dwelling unit premises or otherwise.

5. Resident, any member of the resident's household, or a guest or another person under the resident's control shall not engage in any illegal activity, including prostitution as defined in A.R.S. 13-3211, criminal street gang activity as defined in A.R.S. 13-105 and 13-2308, threatening or intimidating as prohibited in A.R.S. 13-1202, assault as prohibited in A.R.S. 13-1203 including but not limited to the unlawful discharge of firearms, on or near the dwelling unit premises, or any breach of the lease agreement that otherwise jeopardizes the health, safety, and welfare of the landlord, his agent or other tenant or involving imminent or actual serious property damage, as defined in A.R.S. 33-1368.

6. VIOLATION OF THE ABOVE PROVISIONS SHALL BE A MATERIAL AND IRREPARABLE VIOLATION OF THE LEASE AND GOOD CAUSE FOR IMMEDIATE TERMINATION OF TENANCY. A single violation of any of the provisions of this added addendum shall be deemed a serious violation and a material and irreparable noncompliance. It is understood that a single violation shall be good cause for immediate termination of the lease under A.R.S. 33-1377, as provided in A.R.S. 33-1368. Unless otherwise provided by law, proof of violation shall not require criminal conviction, but shall be by a preponderance of the evidence.

7. In case of conflict between the provisions of this addendum and any other provisions of the lease, the provisions of the addendum shall govern.

8. This LEASE ADDENDUM is incorporated into the lease executed or renewed this day between Owner and Resident.

_____ Date: _____
Resident Signature

_____ Date: _____
Resident Signature

_____ Date: _____
Resident Signature

_____ Date: _____
Property Manager's Signature

_____ Date: _____
Property

enforcement sends FAX NET 1 a one-page alert, and FAX NET 1 faxes that alert to anyone in the community that crime could impact next. For information about FAX NET 1, call 602-320-4941, or e-mail them at: peggy@faxnet1.org or view their web site at www.faxnet1.org.

Resident Obligations

Tenants are also bound by the lease document and laws governing rental apartments. Unfortunately, most tenants are not knowledgeable or made aware of their obligations. This problem is solved by thoroughly communicating these responsibilities before a tenant moves in.

Standard Tenant Responsibilities

There are six widely recognized tenant obligations. In most states, residents must:

1. Maintain the dwelling unit, furnishings, fixtures, and appliances in a clean, sanitary, and safe condition.
2. Dispose of all rubbish, garbage, and other waste in a clean, sanitary manner in the refuse facilities.
3. Use in a reasonable manner all electrical, plumbing, sanitary, ventilating, air conditioning, and other facilities and appliances, including elevators.
4. Do not place in the dwelling unit or premises any furniture, plants, animals, or any other thing that harbors insects, rodents, or other pests.
5. Do not destroy, deface, damage, impair, or remove any part of the dwelling unit or premises or facilities, equipment, or furnishings, except as necessary when hazardous conditions exist that immediately affect the resident's health or safety.
6. Do not make alterations, additions, or improvements to the dwelling unit without the owner's prior consent.

Tenant Restrictions

Unless otherwise agreed, the resident must occupy the premises solely for residential purposes. Residents must respect the fact that someone else owns the property and they must respect the rights of other tenants. The resident and resident's guests must conduct themselves in a manner that (a) will not disturb other tenants' peaceful enjoyment of the premises; (b) is not illegal; and (c) will not injure the reputation of the building or its residents.

Landlord's Right of Access

In most states, residents cannot unreasonably withhold consent for the owner to enter into the apartment in order to

- inspect the premises;
- make necessary or agreed repairs, decorations, alterations, or improvements;
- supply necessary or agreed services; or
- exhibit the property to prospective or actual purchasers, mortgagees, residents, workers, and contractors.

Common courtesy dictates that owners should not abuse this right nor use it to harass residents.

In the event of an apparent or actual emergency, the owner may enter the apartment at any time without notice.

A lease may state that at any time within 90 days prior to the end of the lease term, the owner may, as often as necessary and upon reasonable notice, show the apartment for rent between the hours of 7 AM and 8 PM. In some states (for example, Oklahoma and Texas) you must have this right stated within the lease, while in other states, the right is granted to you by statute.

At other times the owner should enter only after notice of not less than 48 hours and only between the hours of 7 AM and 8 PM.

Of course you need to have a key to get into the unit. The owner should be provided with and retain in a safe place all keys necessary for access to the dwelling unit. If a tenant changes the lock to his or her unit, you should insist on obtaining a new key.

A landlord has no other right of access except the following:

- Pursuant to court order
- During the absence of the resident in excess of 14 days (states vary on the exact number of days)
- To remedy hazardous conditions
- When the resident has abandoned or surrendered the premises

Starting Out Right

From the moment you meet prospective residents until the day you refund their security deposit upon termination of the lease, you are faced with maintaining good resident relations. The kind of relationship you develop with your residents will dictate how much peace of mind and profit you derive from your investment property.

Your first meeting with a prospective tenant is crucial to the success of the landlord-tenant relationship. You want the tenant to respect you and the property, while keeping your relationship strictly on a business level. The image you want to project is one of a professional property owner who is congenial, friendly, and welcoming. Above all, you want to maintain control of the relationship at all times.

Remember, you own the property and they want to rent from you. If you let them think they are doing you a favor by renting your apartment, you may find yourself as the underdog in the relationship. Of course, they are your customers, and you should thank them for renting. You can certainly be appreciative. But remember, you're in business and you must exercise control over who rents your property.

In maintaining positive relationships with all your residents, keep your communications with any problem tenants on a strictly professional business level. You can be sympathetic to their problems, but do not let these problems interfere with your sound judgment or become personal. Landlords have been labeled as the villain throughout history and you do not need to aggravate a situation by playing that role.

If you take pride in your property, you will want the tenants to treat your property with respect. The way to this respect is to create a positive image in the tenants' minds. Let them know how you feel about the apartment. Tell them you want them to make it their home. It is in your best interest if the tenants share your pride and maintain the property as if it were their own.

Keeping Good Tenants

Just about every business involves working with people, and being a landlord is no exception. Smart property owners recognize the importance of the human factor in a successful business. If all you had to deal with was leaky plumbing, electrical wiring, and recordkeeping, the job would be simple.

But, all businesses need customers, and in the apartment business your customers are the tenants. Successful businesses manage to keep their customers satisfied. In the rental business, when you lose customers, you must replace them with others as soon as possible. And when the old customers were especially good, it may not always be possible to replace them with equals. Thus it is much better to keep your good existing customers than to constantly be seeking new ones.

Resident turnover is costly. National surveys estimate that a landlord can lose an amount equal to two months' rent every time a resident moves out. This amount is based on the possibilities of losing money from:

- Cleaning and redecorating for new tenants
- Advertising expenses
- Processing paperwork

- Damage to common area walls, doors, halls and so on by movers
- Time spent showing vacant apartments
- Lost income from vacant apartments
- Commissions to apartment referral services

As an owner you won't be able to eliminate turnover completely, but you can minimize it by maintaining a good relationship with your residents. Here is a checklist on developing strong tenant relationships and keeping your residents satisfied:

- Show a little interest in their lifestyle and needs during the rental interview.
- Follow through on your promises about repairs and decorating. Do not offer something you cannot deliver.
- Give residents your work and home phone numbers to use in case of emergencies. Provide them with a list of other important phone numbers for emergency repairs or services.
- Respond promptly to requests for service. Even if you cannot meet their demands, let them know where you stand on the issue. Communication is the key to maintaining good relationships.
- Let the residents know in advance what you expect from them and what they can expect from you on such items as rent payment due dates, lease provisions, pets, complaints, services, and so on.
- Respect their privacy and their right to peaceful possession of their home during their lease period. (*Peaceful possession* is a legal term that means the right to use the premises without harassment or interruption.)
- If circumstances force you to enter an apartment when the tenants are not at home, and without prior notice, always leave a note stating that you were there and why. You would not like someone coming into your home during your absence and neither do your residents. It is always a stressful situation. In general, make it your personal policy to never enter a resident's apartment without giving at least 48 hours' notice.

Dealing with Tenant Complaints

Handle complaints quickly and discreetly. If a resident complains about another resident, your best response is to ascertain as many facts as possible. Contact the other resident to find out if there is any validity to the allegation. If it's a matter of loud, disturbing noises, you can politely ask the offending resident to be more courteous to his or her neighbors. Most tenants will handle this type of problem without contacting the

---

Figure 2.2: Sample Lease Rules and Regulations Violation Letter

Date

Dear:

We have been informed that there have been complaints about an unusual amount of noise coming from your apartment. This is in violation of paragraph____of your lease.

We realize it is often difficult to keep sounds in an apartment at a level that is not disturbing to neighbors. However, we would greatly appreciate your cooperation in this matter. In particular, please make every effort to play your stereo equipment at a reasonable volume after 10:00 PM. [Or refer to particular complaint that was made.]

We trust that there will be no more complaints about noise. However, be aware that if the disturbances continue, we will seek remedies as provided by law.

If you have any questions, please call. Thank you for your consideration in this matter.

Very truly yours,

---

owner, but if a resident does contact you, do not try to avoid getting involved by telling them to handle it themselves. Having to deal with customer complaints comes with the territory of being a landlord.

If you encounter difficulty with one tenant, do not allow it to escalate to a level that might involve other residents. Never discuss the situation with noninvolved residents, and of course, don't spread gossip.

If there is a valid resident complaint, and the complained-about resident does not respond to your requests to correct the situation, your next step is to send the resident a Lease Rules and Regulations Violation Letter (Figure 2.2) advising the resident of the lease provision. This letter should also state your legal options if the problem persists.

Maintenance complaints should be handled as quickly as possible. If the repair or replacement cannot be completed in a few days, you must tell the resident when you expect it to be done. This eases any anxiety and tension between you and your residents.

Handling Claims and Disputes

There will be times when you and your tenants will not be able to agree on matters concerning physical conditions or operating policies and procedures. In extreme cases, you may have to serve a termination notice, or even carry out an eviction. In such cases, it is wise to consult a lawyer. Following are a number of general guidelines.

Legal counsel. It is wise to consult with an attorney before initiating any action against a tenant that could have the consequence of canceling or enforcing a lease.

If a resident is not in compliance with the lease, or is the source of complaints from neighbors, a letter written on your attorney's stationery usually influences the tenant to correct the problem. Even if the letter is not effective, you'll have the documentation necessary to proceed with an eviction.

Many states have adopted the Revised Model Landlord-Tenant Act and in 1998 every state will have some form of landlord-tenant law. When it comes to who is right and who is wrong, do not assume that common sense will apply. If you are not absolutely sure of the applicable law for a situation, always check with your attorney.

Most states prevent a manager from acting as an agent for an owner to represent the owner in court without being accompanied by an attorney, unless the owner actually appears in court.

General Guidelines

In the adjustment of claims or disputes, use the following general guidelines:

- Both you and your tenant, on reasonable notice to the other and for the purpose of ascertaining the facts and preserving evidence, should have the right to inspect the dwelling unit and common area premises.
- You and your tenant may agree at the time of any claim or dispute to allow a third-party inspection or survey to determine the conformity or condition of the dwelling unit or premises, and may agree that the findings shall be binding in any subsequent litigation or adjustment.
- If arbitration by a third party is unavailable or impractical, it may be possible, if the dispute involves monetary damages, for one or the other party to file a suit in small claims court.
- You may elect to voluntarily vacate a tenant's lease; that is, you might allow the tenant to terminate the lease early if you cannot reach a compromise or satisfactorily settle a dispute.

As an example, one particular tenant registered a strong complaint stating that her kitchen faucet did not have cold water. Normally, you would expect a complaint about hot water, but in this case the tenant expected to have ice cold water running from the tap.

Because the water was supplied to the building from the city and went directly into the apartments, there was little that could be done to make her water colder than anyone else's. She persisted and it became obvious that nothing could be done to satisfy her in this matter. This left two possibilities: The first was to force her to honor the lease and stay in the apartment. The second was to cancel her lease. Since the rental market was strong, and the apartment could be easily rerented, a decision was made to let her move out under the condition that she would pay rent until another tenant was found, which, as it turned out, took less than a month.

Most states allow a form of *constructive eviction*. A constructive eviction occurs when a tenant voluntarily vacates an apartment due to a defect in the condition of the unit, for example, a leaking roof, no heat, no hot water, and so on. For a constructive eviction to be valid, the tenant must actually move out of the apartment. If you sue the tenant for breaking the lease, and the tenant's defense is that you did not cure a problem you were properly notified of, the judge may rule in favor of the tenant, finding that it was a constructive eviction.

If a tenant is in violation of the lease, other than not paying the rent, and you have not been able to settle the dispute, you may have to proceed with a termination notice.

Termination Notice

When a resident is breaking the rules and regulations outlined in the lease, and the owner's communications, either verbally or in writing do not result in cooperation, it may be necessary to begin eviction proceedings. In this case, the Notice of Termination form (Figure 2.3) is used. This kind of form applies to all types of lease violations other than nonpayment of rent, including unauthorized pets, overoccupancy, or excessive noise.

The Notice of Termination form must be filled out correctly. The chances of winning a case in court for this type of eviction are less than when you are suing for rent because the lease violations must be well documented.

In Section (A) of the termination form, quote the actual paragraph or clause in the lease that the resident is breaking. Do not simply use the lease paragraph number.

Figure 2.3: Notice of Termination

NOTICE OF TERMINATION

BLDG. _____ UNIT _____

FOR USE WITH CREB FORM 15 APT. LEASE ONLY

You are hereby notified that your tenancy or lease of the premises situated in _____ _____ County of _____, and State of Illinois and known and described as follows. to wit: _____ _____ together with all buildings, storage areas, recreational facilities, parking spaces and garages used in connection with said premises, will be terminated as follows:

(A) You have breached or are in default of the terms of your lease for said premises, as follows:

_____

_____

The owner has elected to terminate your right of possession under the lease, and you are hereby notified to quit and deliver up possession of the same to the owner within *ten* (10) days after service of this notice.

(B) The undersigned elects to terminate your tenancy of said premises, such termination will be effective on the _____ day of _____, 19 _____, and you are hereby notified to quit and deliver up possession at that time.

To _____

_____

_____

_____

OWNER

_____

AGENT OR ATTORNEY

Dated this _____ day of _____, 19 _____

1. Box (A) is not to be used as a demand for rent; for that purpose. use the form entitled, "Owner's Five Day Notice."
2. Box (B) is for use when tenancy is not to continue after expiration of the current lease term. Give:
   (a) 60 days notice for terminating year to year tenancy, but do not give notice more than 4 months before the last 60 days of the lease,
   (b) 30 days notice for terminating month to month tenancy, or any other tenancy for a term less than one year, except week to week.
   (c) 7 days notice for terminating week to week tenancy.

FOLD

STATE OF ILLINOIS } SS.   **AFFIDAVIT OF SERVICE**
COUNTY OF _____

_____, being duly sworn, on oath deposes and says

(Served by)

that on the _____ day of _____, 19 ___ he served the above notice on the tenant named above, as follows:*

- ☐ (1) by delivering a copy thereof to the above named tenant, _____.
- ☐ (2) by delivering a copy thereof to _____, a person above the age of twelve years, residing on or in charge of the above described premises.
- ☐ (3) by sending a copy thereof to said tenant by both (a) U.S. regular AND (b) certified or registered mail, postage pre-paid, at the address for tenant at the beginning of tenant's lease or such other address as tenant may previously have designated by written notice.
- ☐ (4) (in the event of apparent abandonment only) by posting a copy thereof on the main door of the above described premises, no one being in actual possession thereof.

Subscribed and sworn to before me this _____ day of
_____, 19 _____.

X _____

Identify the method of service used by placing a check in the proper box. Sign on line marked X.

_____ Notary Public

DO NOT USE WITH OTHER LEASE FORMS OR ORAL LEASES

4708

Source: Chicago Association of REALTORS®. Used with permission.

Section (B) of the termination form is used only when you are terminating a resident who does not have a lease. In some states, the law dictates that for a month-to-month tenancy you must allow a full calendar month, and not just 30 days, for eviction. For example, if the notice is served on July 15, the effective date in this space must be the end of the following month, or August 31. Other states, Oklahoma for example, allow you to terminate a tenancy at 30 days, even if that is in the middle of the month.

Deliver the original Notice of Termination to the tenant and keep a copy. The Affidavit of Service section is self-explanatory. Be sure to have the document notarized. Note that in many states you must deliver a Termination Notice to a resident or occupant older than 12 years of age. Certain states (for example, Kansas) recognize a notice that was posted or taped on the outside of the apartment door.

Evictions

This is certainly an unpleasant process that no one wants to be involved in. It is not easy for the landlord, and of course the tenant is not looking forward to that day. But unfortunately, evictions are a normal, if infrequent, part of managing property. The more you know about them, the more comfortable you will be, and the more efficiently you will handle the situation.

There are two reasons why you would need to evict someone:

1. Nonpayment of rent
2. Noncompliance of a lease provision

Some general forms for dealing with an eviction are covered in Chapter 8.

Eviction procedures vary slightly from state to state. It is best to consult with your attorney prior to initiating any action. Usually some legal fees can be assessed, and you may be able to recover your out-of-pocket expenses as well.

Keep in mind the Fair Housing Laws that must be obeyed when evicting someone. While you may not think you are discriminating against a certain resident, it may appear so in the eyes of the law when compared to how you treat another tenant.

According to an article in the April 1997 edition of *Apartment News*, written by attorney Andrew Hull of Phoenix, Arizona, "If you evict one resident for nonpayment of rent but, after a court judgment, let the individual sign a repayment agreement and stay, you should do the same for all tenants in a similar situation.

"A landlord should consider establishing strict policies regarding tenant evictions, with an eye toward fair housing concerns. You cannot treat tenants differently because of race, color, religion, sex, family status, physical, or mental disability."

Marketing

CHAPTER 3

Penny Tally is an administrative assistant for a marketing company. She start-
ed buying income properties a few years ago and performs most of the maintenance work herself. She collects the rent in person by going door to door.
Her properties produce a substantial cash flow and currently provide a 12 percent return on her initial investments.

When I made my first leap into income real estate, I was working
as an office manager and was a single mother of two. I owned a four-
bedroom townhome, and I was struggling with a $600 per month
mortgage payment. I needed supplemental income, and I didn't want
to work two jobs. On the advice of a friend, I invested in real estate
and now, four years later, I own 20 apartment units in the city and
south suburbs.

Marketing my apartments has been a process of trial and error. At
the beginning, I depended a lot on word-of-mouth from my friends
and relatives, and I distributed photocopied flyers in the neighborhood. Then I learned to check the newspapers to determine my rent
figures, and began placing more sophisticated ads. My tenants—and
my methods of attracting them—have improved.

Marketing Tasks

In marketing rental apartments, your task is to present the unit in such a way that a prospect will want to rent and an existing resident will want to renew. You can become quite effective at marketing your units without going back to school to earn a marketing degree. All it takes is a little knowledge and some time to sell your product.

The process of marketing entails six elements:

1. Understanding the marketplace and determining a rental rate
2. Finding and selecting good tenants
3. Qualifying prospects
4. Advertising the product
5. Selling the product
6. Following up on leads

Understanding the Marketplace

How you market your property will depend on the demand for apartments in your neighborhood. Market conditions change every six months or so. If the market is strong with very few vacancies in your neighborhood it would indicate a "sellers' market." You'll be able to rent at a good price with a minimum amount of effort. But if the market is soft, with many vacancies in the area (a "buyers' market"), you'll have to be more creative in your approach.

For example, in a buyers' market you may have to place larger ads with additional selling points about what makes your property appealing. You may have to offer a discount or rent concession. It might be necessary to advertise in more than one newspaper.

Determining a Rental Rate

Before you embark on a search for a tenant, you must first determine how much rent to charge. If you buy a property that has existing tenants you will not have to immediately face the problem of determining rents, but you will have to calculate how much to increase the rent when it comes time to renew the leases. A detailed discussion of renewal increases is contained in Chapter 6.

Determining how much rent to charge is based on two key factors:

1. Return on investment (yield)
2. Market analysis

Return on Investment (Yield)

First, you have to look at the math involved in owning the property. You will want to generate enough income to cover expenses, debt payments, taxes and insurance, and profit. If you project annual operating expenses per unit to be $1,200, your mortgage and taxes are $2,400, and you want an annual 8 percent profit on your initial $15,000 down payment, you will need to generate an income of $4,800 to break even (not taking into account income tax savings through depreciation, etc. (see Chapter 12).

$1,200 Annual operating expenses
+ $2,400 Annual mortgage, principal, and taxes
= $3,600 Total outlay of cash
+ $1,200 Return on investment (profit)
= $4,800 Income to be generated
$4,800 divided by 12 months equals $400 per month
Monthly rent = $400 (yield amount)

Make every effort to purchase a property whose size, amenities, condition, and location warrant a rental rate close to your desired yield. The first year or two of operating a rental property may produce a negative cash flow in which total income does not equal expenses, but the deficiency and losses are made up through tax savings. Each year, as increases in rents outpace increases in expenses, the investment gets closer to producing a positive cash return, and your desired yield.

Market Analysis

In addition to using the income/expense approach, you also have to consider what the market will bear or the law of supply and demand.

Market rent is determined by comparing what similar apartments in comparable locations are getting, and then making adjustments for local vacancy factors.

It is not difficult to find out the current market rent. Some time spent responding to "for rent" advertisements, visiting other properties, and reading your local newspaper classified section will give you a fair idea of what other properties are charging.

You do not have to know absolutely everything about every property, but you should be thoroughly familiar with your competition. How much are other apartments renting for in the same area? Compare your property to competing properties and adjust for the major differences. For example, are your rooms larger or smaller? Does your unit have a balcony or patio? How close is your property to schools, shopping, and major transportation routes? You must be thoroughly familiar with each of the competing properties and the features of each. With this knowledge, you'll be able to set an accurate rental rate and be ready to respond to prospects' questions as to why your rent may be higher or lower than other properties in the immediate area.

If similar one-bedroom apartments offering similar amenities in your vicinity are renting for $750 a month, you will have a hard time trying to get $1,000. On the other hand, if your property has nicer qualities, or is better situated, you may be able to command $800 to $850. If the vacancy rate in the neighborhood is low, with few apartments similar to yours being available, then you will be in a position to raise the rent in accordance with specific demand. However, if your apartments are smaller or lower in quality than the competition, you will have to adjust your rent downward; but again, this adjustment may be offset by a low vacancy rate. You may be able to get the higher rent if you offer a longer lease.

Rental rates vary greatly from city to city, from neighborhood to neighborhood, and from street to street. They even vary substantially between high and low floors, and according to views in a high-rise building. There are too many factors affecting rents to scientifically arrive at an optimum figure. The approach most owners take is to ascertain the general market rent for the area and set a price that is somewhat higher, reducing it slightly if they encounter too much resistance. While this may not be scientific, it does take into consideration competition and the merchandising and sales ability of the landlord.

Finding and Selecting Good Tenants

It is difficult to precisely describe an ideal tenant; however, good tenants have at least five things in common:

1. They pay their rent on time.
2. They care for the property as if it were their own.
3. They are stable and tend to renew their leases.
4. They will leave the premises in as good condition as they found it, or better.
5. They do not cause problems for their neighbors.

Therefore, you want a responsible tenant who is and has been steadily employed, earning enough income to pay the rent. Your first choice would not be someone with a long history of credit problems, although a bad credit history by itself may not be indicative of a bad tenant. Couples with newborn infants often make good tenants. These young families may not be able to buy a house, yet they are upwardly mobile and will want to make your property a home they can be proud to show off to their family and friends. Moreover, they usually move to a larger unit in your building in a year or two.

The elderly also make good tenants. They often have fixed incomes and do not move frequently.

Contrary to popular belief, people having pets, especially cats, can be good tenants, as long as the pet is well trained. A pet owner will not want to move because of the difficulty of finding a building that will accept pets. Sometimes these people have been turned down by so many buildings that they are willing to pay a premium, and will maintain a good relationship with the landlord for the privilege of living in a unit that accepts pets (see Figure 4.10).

Through experience, you will gain some knowledge on how to distinguish good tenants from bad ones, but you will still make an occasional mistake. Consider that the success ratio of people picking marriage partners is only 50 percent. If more than 60 percent of your tenants turn out to be good, you are far ahead of the game.

Tenant screening companies. For added protection or convenience, you may want to consider using a credit-reporting, or tenant screening company to run credit, character and criminal checks. One such company, *Tenant Screening Center, Inc.* (140 Wikiup Drive, Santa Rosa, CA 95403, 800-523-2381), info@tsci.com, runs a 24-hour-a-day, 7-days-a-week national credit reporting business. They charge a $25 membership fee, plus fees ranging from $10 for a mini report, to $25 for a full report. Clients use the company's Consumer History Application forms, and a Tenant Information Card to report any negative information about a tenant.

Another national company is *Rent Grow*, headquartered in Boston with offices throughout the United States, serving all 50 states including Alaska and Hawaii (800-736-8476). They have no upfront membership fee, and their reporting service fees vary from state to state. In addition to providing credit reporting services, they specialize in fair housing compliance, and the rules and regulations surrounding fair housing in each state.

To obtain further recommendations on finding a good tenant screening company, contact the *National Apartment Association* at 703-518-6141. They will give you the name and number of the closest affiliated association in your area who should be able to provide a good recommendation.

It is a very common practice to ask applicants for their previous landlord's address and phone number. If they refuse to provide this information or have not rented before, you'll have to weigh the risks against other factors. It is also common to request a letter from the prospect's employer verifying employment and income.

Fair Housing and Discrimination

There have been recent cases of high-dollar awards for discrimination against handicapped prospects that make us want to focus our attention on the appropriate means of serving prospective residents who are disabled.

The Federal Housing Act of 1988, coupled with legislation in most states, make it illegal to discriminate against the handicapped. The ADA (Americans with Disabilities Act) requires that all public accommodations be accessible to the disabled. Apartment communities must make every reasonable effort to have facilities accessible to disabled persons regardless of when the community was built.

Physically challenged individuals must be able to park and enter the property without facing any physical barriers. Wheelchair users need minimum standards just to enter a property. Even if the costs of modifying an existing property are prohibitive, the property owner is required by law to "reasonably accommodate" the disabled.

You must be an Equal Housing Opportunity landlord. Throughout your discussions and interviews with prospective tenants, remember to adhere to antidiscrimination laws, particularly the Civil Rights Act of 1968, which prohibits discrimination in seven protected categories:

1. Race
2. Color
3. Religion
4. Sex
5. National origin
6. Family status
7. Physical or mental disabilities

Do not volunteer information or comment about the race, religion, color, nationality, sex, family status, or handicaps of residents, even when asked about it directly or indirectly by a prospect. If prospects ask you questions that you cannot answer because of fair housing laws, tell them that it is your policy to consider any qualified applicants, and that it is against fair housing laws for you to answer questions about protected categories of your current tenant population.

Do not make recommendations about specific locations, and/or buildings that you think the resident may like because of a potential discriminatory factor. For example, it is discriminatory to recommend that a family with children be on the first floor, or in a special building with other families.

A few states and municipalities have enacted laws prohibiting adult-only rental policies. Such policies are still permissible in some states (for example, Florida, Arizona, and Texas). In other states, a requirement by owners that prospective residents shall have no children under the age of 14 years is prohibited. Any owner who attempts to enforce such requirements in a state that prohibits it shall be subject to remedies as set forth by law. Before instituting an adults-only policy, check with your local real estate board to make sure it is legal in your state.

You can contact *HUD* at 800-669-9777 to get updated information on any fair housing or discrimination issue.

Qualifying the Prospect

Qualifying prospects is both about marketing your product to a specific customer and about determining if a customer is right for your product. It is a conversation used to establish a rapport with prospects and to put them at ease, while inquiring about their backgrounds and needs. This information will help you in marketing your property. (To learn how to determine if a prospective resident is "income-qualified" to rent your apartment, see Chapter 4.)

Begin qualifying prospective tenants over the telephone when they respond to your advertising. In this preliminary interview, find out as much as you can about their lifestyle and apartment expectations. Strike up a friendly conversation. Ask a lot of questions. The more you know about your prospects' needs and desires, the easier it will be to match them with an apartment. One way to get prospects to elaborate on what they like is to ask them what they do not like about their present living quarters. Based on their answers, you can point out the particular advantages of your apartment.

Some important questions to ask include:

- When do you need the apartment?
- What do you do for a living?
- What kind of apartment are you looking for?
- Do you have a pet? If so, what kind?
- How far do you (and other residents) commute to work?
- What features of apartment living are important: large rooms, large kitchen, balcony or patio, privacy, quiet, high or low floor in a high-rise, and so on.
- What is wrong, if anything, with your present dwelling unit?
- Why do you want/need to move?
- How many people will occupy the apartment?

With answers to these questions, you can determine whether to go on to subsequent steps. For instance, if you have only a one-bedroom apartment available, there is no reason to attempt to rent that apartment to prospects with large families. It is up to you to identify what the prospects need. If you do not have a suitable apartment available, you can offer to put the prospects on a waiting list.

The prospects have been qualified when the following details are worked out and/or requirements fulfilled:

- An apartment of the appropriate type and size is available.
- The prospects are of legal age to sign contracts.
- The prospects are employed or otherwise earning a qualifying income.
- The prospects have the appropriate family size for the particular unit.
- The prospects are moving out of their present accommodations legally.

All, or most of this information can be obtained during your initial conversation.

Advertising the Product

There are several ways to reach prospective suitable tenants, all involving some form of advertising. You may have the best property in the world, but it will not rent itself. You must make your property's availability known.

Apartment Rental Agencies

If you do not have the time to advertise and show your units, you can use an apartment rental agency or referral service. You should still learn a little about what types of advertising to use, but these companies work on a contingency basis with many different owners, and they will screen all prospective residents. They complete all the groundwork, show the unit as many times as it takes, complete the negotiations, and then present you with a signed lease.

Their fees are usually based on a percentage of the rent, which varies between 50 percent and 100 percent of one month's rent. For example, suppose you retain an agency to rent a vacant apartment for October 1 at a rental of $500 a month. You agree to pay a 50 percent commission for a bona fide signed lease. The agency will locate, qualify, and execute a lease with a suitable tenant, usually collecting the first month's rent and a security deposit equal to a month's rent. In most cases, the agency will deduct its fee from these funds and give you the balance, along with the signed documents. In this example, the fee would be $250. Some agencies add miscellaneous fees for advertising, but this is not a common practice. The agency's commission should cover its out-of-pocket expenses.

Using an apartment referral service can save you time. One drawback however, is that professional rental agencies work for many different owners simultaneously, and thus offer prospective tenants a wide variety of units. Because of the large volume and selection of apartments they represent, it may take longer to rent your apartment if it is a lot less desirable than others in their portfolio.

To find an apartment rental agency, look in the local Yellow Pages™ in your area. Some firms do not accept clients that own fewer than 50 units. If you decide to use an agency, be sure to get at least three bids, and always ask for references. It is doubtful that any company will give you a guarantee that your vacant apartments will rent. You can ask for their track record, and inquire how long it takes them on average to rent units similar to yours.

Types of Advertisements

Your first order of business is to consider a written ad. You can advertise in the classified section of your local newspaper or in an apartment rental guide magazine. You can put fliers or signs around the apartment building or complex. Keep in mind when considering the timing of an ad that prospective tenants usually start looking for an apartment two to three months in advance of when they need it.

Apartment Rental Magazines

We have all seen them in grocery and convenience stores—the apartment rental guides or magazines that list dozens and dozens of apartments throughout a region.

Jim Tuley, general manager of *Apartments For Rent* (800-845-0800) says most of its clients are owners/managers of large apartment communities, but it also regularly has quite a few customers who own smaller buildings and take advantage of the enormous distribution and appeal of these magazines. If you have only two or three units to rent per year, this medium might be too expensive to give you the best value. If you have a 24-unit building, or four six-flats, and have at least a 40 percent annual turnover, you may want to consider advertising in one of these magazines.

Apartments For Rent offers at least five different preset formats designed for the small community. Cost is around $100 per issue, and the magazine is published and distributed every other week. For that price, the small-time landlord gets a quarter-page—room for a photograph and small map, plus about 35 words. The company also offers regularly scheduled seminars on advertising and marketing as an extra benefit to its clients.

The other national magazine is the *Apartment Guide*, published by Haas Publishing Company (800-551-2787). Created in 1975, they print about 18 million annual copies of 66 different magazines covering 61 metropolitan areas in 26 states. Their publications, containing over 12,000 apartment communities, are distributed in approximately 128,000 locations. Advertising prices are comparable to *Apartments For Rent*. They also publish a newsletter and maintain an internet web site.

Newspapers

Almost all prospective tenants look at newspaper ads. A good newspaper ad should include all the necessary information to attract good prospects, including:

- Location
- Monthly rent
- Apartment size
- Major amenities
- Contact name and phone number

If the property is currently occupied, you should also mention the availability date. Emphasize important selling features such as good views, a high floor in a high-rise building, backyards, patios, playgrounds, nearby shopping, schools, and transportation.

All advertising is highly competitive. And this is true even more so on the classified page, where there are literally hundreds of ads vying for the reader's attention. In order to get the message across, you want your ad to:

- Gain the reader's attention.
- Hold the reader's interest.
- Stimulate a desire for your property.
- Persuade the reader to act on your rental.

In order to be successful at this, it is important to remember that the property you are writing about cannot be all things to all people. For your ad to get action, you must direct your advertising to a specific market. Before you write the ad, always ask yourself: Who is a likely customer for this property?

To pinpoint the market, you must consider the demographics of the renter.

Determine:

- Household income
- Size of household

Figure 3.1: Sample Newspaper Ads

EVANSTON 8825 ALBANY

DELUXE 6 LARGE RMS $886 Across from Lincoln Schl. Near beach, shops, subway, commuter train. 555-3456 June 1st 555-7890

GARDEN APARTMENT

31/2 rms., stove & frig. Utilities incl. 8100 W./7600 N. $350 + 2 mos. sec. 555-1136

Lrg. 4 rm., 1 BR in English Tudor bldg. Very classy, very bright. Walk-in closets & more. No pets please. Managed by owner. Avail. 5/1. 5543 N. Washington (4300W). $425. Eves. 555-3765

NEWLY REMOD.—Near 63rd & Ashland. 5 rms., 3 bdrms., living room, large cabinet kitchen, tile bath. $450 + utilities. 644-4441

6 ROOMS—2nd. flr., heated, 2 blocks west of Dan Ryan on 105th St. No pets. Working. $475 + sec. Days 555-2686 or Eves. 555-4974

Newly renovated Victorian. 2 BR, owner occ. Walk to train. Immediately avail. $650/mo.
555-2093

HARVEY—2 bedrooms. Apt. newly dec. Tenants pay util. $400 + 1 mo. sec. Sect. 8 welcome.   731-2049

HAMPTON/MILWAUKEE

6 rms., clean, quiet, stv./refg., firepl. $535 mo., htd. 555-7878

Avail. May 1—Kimball/ Sawyer. 2 Flat, 5 Rm., 2 Br. Mod. Kit. $475 + sec. 555-6110

HYDE PARK—7500 E. 54th Pl. 1st fl., 4 rms., decor., $535. Avail. now. Excellent transp. 555-4192

Nearing Irving & Western. 2 bdrms, 2nd flr, 2 flat. Available May 1st. Cable. Will decorate & carpet. Htd. No pets. $425/mo. + dep. 555-2144 afternoons & eves.

SKOKIE—Spacious Garden Apt., near train, all utilities paid. $420 mo. Call 555-4467

2 blks from Jeff Pk terminal. 2 br apt. Oak flrs. 2nd flr of quiet bldg. No pets. Nonsmokr pref. $500 + sec. 555-5167

DesPlaines—HUGE dlx. 1BR. Quiet 4 unit bldg. New dec., appls. Pkg., ht. incl. Near train. $525.   555-3004

- Age, occupation and education of target market

Then write your ad for that particular group. An effective ad will answer the question: How does the property fulfill the potential renter's needs?

The sample ads in Figure 3.1 are examples of effective copy that would produce the desired results.

Fliers

Professional-looking fliers can be designed on many home computers, or typed on regular typewriters, and reproduced inexpensively. Because a flier provides more space than an ad, you can include more information, such as a floor plan, or a photo of the property. You can distribute fliers throughout the neighborhood (where permitted by law), and, with permission, in grocery stores, churches, coin laundries, and other establishments where there are bulletin boards. Fliers can also be distributed to tenants of other apartment buildings in the area—not with the intent to solicit your competition's residents directly, but rather to make them aware of an apartment available in your building just in case they have a friend or relative who needs one.

Note: The United States Postal Authority prohibits placing fliers inside mailboxes unless they are stamped.

Signs

Because most people have a preconceived notion about the neighborhood where they wish to live, one of the most effective and cost-efficient means of advertising is a sign. Often, potential tenants will drive or walk around the area they wish to live in, and a simple sign advertising your apartment is the least expensive way to attract a customer.

A small handwritten or typed sign (Figure 3.2) can be taped on the door of the building highlighting basic rental information in a neat, legible manner.

A larger and more expensive, professionally painted, permanent portable, wooden or metal sign on the building or in the front of the property can also be used. Frequently the placement, size, and type of signs are regulated by zoning codes. To play it safe, visit your local city zoning department and ask about sign regulations before putting up your sign. Temporary signs are usually exempt from the zoning regulations.

Because of its larger size and overall appearance, a wooden or metal sign will attract more attention than a paper sign. This sign should state only the type of units available and a contact phone number. Depending on the street traffic pattern, the sign can be either double-sided or single-faced in an appropriate size to allow easy readability from the street.

Depending on the number of units you own, a sign may be installed permanently, subject to local sign codes. If there are no vacancies at one particular property, the sign can still be useful—serving as a referral to other locations where you may have vacancies. Or it can invite prospective tenants to be on a waiting list.

A sign should always be fresh, clean, and professional-looking. A poorly lettered, weather-beaten sign gives a poor first impression.

Figure 3.2: Sample Doorway Sign

APARTMENTS
FOR RENT
In This Building

FLOOR	ROOMS	RENTAL
2nd	3½	$525.00 month
	Sunny, one-bedroom, parquet floors, fully applianced kitchen, one month security deposit. Utilities not included.	

Apply to: Mr. J. Neits
555-1616 Days
555-1212 Evenings

The Internet

The authors have been actively using the Internet for several years, and we have seen it become one of the most useful tools to reach an audience. "Surfing the Net" has become a very popular pastime, as well as an easy way to find out lots of information about relocating within a city or a different city. Do not overlook its potential as a marketing tool to advertise your product. There are several companies that have sophisticated web pages advertising hundreds of apartments in almost every major city in the U.S. They will list your units for a small fee.

Most of the people who use the Internet to search for housing want relocation information. But the data is also reviewed by locals as well who want to save time by scanning the web. Because the Internet is improving faster than we can write, it is safe to say that no one can predict today how effective it will be as an electronic marketing tool in two to five years. We suspect that soon after the turn of the century, most Americans will have some form of access to it.

Imagine a prospective tenant accessing information about your property electronically, viewing photos or a video of the unit and the surrounding neighborhood, then clicking a button for more information, or better still, to begin the rental application process. This technology is happening right now with the marketing of single-family homes, and rental apartment communities will not be far off.

Referrals

Your most effective, and certainly the least expensive method of finding new tenants is through referrals from existing residents. If people like where they live, they are prone to tell others about the positive aspects. In fact, over the long run, your best source for valuable new leads will probably be other satisfied tenants. Most residents will make referrals voluntarily, but if you want to help motivate them to bring you possible referrals, you can offer a referral fee of anywhere between 25–50 percent of a month's rent.

Selling the Product

Once you have located a prospective tenant, you must sell your product to him or her. This is a complex task. It involves preparing the apartment for showing, doing preliminary interviews to determine the prospect's needs, and making a good first impression when greeting the prospect in person. You then need to present the apartment in the best possible light, handle objections diplomatically, and finally, ask for the closing.

Preparing the Apartment

Before letting prospective tenants see your building or apartments, you must first make certain that the property is sparkling clean, freshly painted, and in good operating condition. First impressions are lasting ones. Do not show an apartment if it is not ready to be seen. Many people lack imagination, and cannot easily envision a filthy apartment being cleaned up and looking good in the future. You may be able to "see it" in your mind, but rest assured, they will not. If, while you are showing the unit, you have to say things like, "We are going to paint," or "we are going to replace the carpeting," or "we will be fixing the entryway," you will be making your marketing job a lot harder. For more information on this subject, refer to Chapter 10: Maintenance.

Greeting the Prospective Tenant

A prospective resident is any person who either calls or walks in to inquire about an apartment. Every prospect should be treated as a future resident who will provide the income to sustain your business. See Figures 3.3 and 3.4 for detailed reviews of effective presentation techniques.

Figure 3.3: How to Greet a Prospect

When greeting a prospect:

1. Stand up and greet the customer as soon as they enter.
2. Introduce yourself and ask for their names. Shake their hands.
3. Ask them, "How may I help you?"
4. Talk to the customers and find out what they are interested in. LISTEN.
5. Tell them about the apartments that meet their needs and offer to show them each apartment.
6. Show them clean apartments.
7. Ask them if any apartment meets their needs. LISTEN. Then ask what specifically they wanted. LISTEN.
8. Ask them if they would like to reserve an apartment.
   Ask them to fill out an application.
   Ask them when they would like to move in.
   Ask them to rent the apartment.
9. Ask for a deposit.
10. Thank them for visiting.

Convincing the Prospect

Once you have qualified the prospects, you then must convince them that you have the best apartment available.

Here are a few useful techniques to help convince prospects to rent: Talk to the prospects. Show a genuine interest in them. People will sometimes rent an apartment even if it is not as perfectly suited to their needs as others they have seen. Why? Because the rental agent or owner gave them a warm, welcome feeling and showed sincerity when talking to them. On the other hand, if you leave the prospects feeling cold and unwelcome or treat them indifferently, they may not rent even if the apartment is perfect and the rent is less than others. Your personal and professional image is all-important in making or breaking a potential rental. In other words, the dwelling unit will not "rent itself," no matter how perfect or appealing it is.

Figure 3.4: Checklist of Presentation Techniques

- ❑ Did I introduce myself?
- ❑ Did I ask their names?
- ❑ Did I offer them chairs and cold drinks/coffee?
- ❑ Did I ask about their family size and composition?
- ❑ Did I ask when they expected to move?
- ❑ Did I ask why they are moving and how long they expect to stay in their new apartment?
- ❑ Did I ask what type of apartment and what facilities they are looking for?
- ❑ Did I ask where they are working?
- ❑ Did I point out the convenience and accessibility of this apartment complex?
- ❑ Did I discuss neighborhood advantages, shopping, schools, recreational facilities?
- ❑ Did I exhibit a "spic and span," completely prepared apartment that was suitable to their needs?
- ❑ Did I describe apartment benefits and offer proof? (Example: "After you move into this apartment it will feel just like your own home because the rooms are unusually spacious.")
- ❑ Did I build enthusiasm by eliciting "yes" (positive) responses?
- ❑ Did I attempt to close the sale?
- ❑ Did I offer an application to be completed?
- ❑ Did I ask for a deposit?
- ❑ Did I use a persuasive "close"? ("Would you prefer to leave your deposit by cash or check?")
- ❑ Did I continue to sell even after they indicated uncertainty?
- ❑ Did I try to close a second time after reviewing the key benefits?
- ❑ Did I appear sincere and interested in their needs?
- ❑ Did I discuss the number of vacant apartments available?

Ask questions about the prospects' lifestyle and gear your presentation to this lifestyle. You must appeal to both the intellect and emotions of your prospects; it is on both levels that they will make a decision. Remember, prospects see only walls, floors, and ceilings. You must create an image, allowing them to envision and to desire the apartment, and the community, as a home. As an example, instead of making obvious statements such as "This is the living room," or "This is the kitchen," let the prospects make these observations while you point out the benefits of your unit. You can say, "Doesn't this view give you a peaceful feeling?" or "The neutral color of the carpet will go well with your furniture."

Accentuate the positive. Offset negative aspects with positive comments. You can anticipate getting objections and hesitations. If you have studied the marketplace you will know all about your competition, enabling you to emphasize your strong points.

If there are many vacant apartments in the area, do not point this out to the prospects. Good salespeople demonstrate that their product is in great demand, thereby creating a sense of urgency that helps close the sale. Most prospects want to be sold and they only get confused if the salesperson points out dozens of other alternatives. They want you to help them make up their minds.

If the available apartment does not show well because it is dirty or needs decorating, you can show a similar unit. Point out how it meets their exact needs as discovered in the interview. Even if the prospect does not insist, you should make every effort to show the actual unit before a lease is signed. This will avoid an unhappy tenant who fell in love with some aspect of the shown unit that the actual unit lacks.

In fact, certain states require the actual apartment be shown to prospective tenants, but this can be accomplished after they have decided to rent. In these jurisdictions, failure to show the actual unit can result in a cancellation, possibly requiring you to return all monies collected. Quite a few apartments have been rented through showing only a model unit. Quite often the actual apartment may not have been built yet. Remember that lease provisions should permit access to occupied units; thus you can show an occupied apartment as a model.

Handling Objections

Prospects often will point out objections to the apartment. It might be either a legitimate concern, or they might be bickering to get a rent reduction or other concession. Whatever the underlying reason, they do always expect a response. Learn how to respond positively, avoiding anything that resembles an apology, a defensive statement, or leaning towards agreeing to a concession. For example, if someone comments, "The kitchen is very small," your positive response could be, "Yes, it is; cleaning it will be a snap, and look at the spacious, well-lit dining room you have."

Following is a list of some common objections with suggested responses.

The rent is too high. This statement does not always mean that they cannot afford it. Point out that the rent is comparable to similar units in the area. The amount of rent you are asking is adjusted to the market for the type of apartment and amenities offered. You can control the rental rate, however, and you may elect to lower it for other considerations (but don't be hasty).

The view is bad. Some "bad" views are privacy views. Not everybody is looking for the spectacular scenic skyline view. The amount of rent for the unit has been adjusted accordingly. You may not be able to change the view, but you can suggest a variety of window treatments to offset a poor view.

The rooms are too small. Mention that efficient room sizes are good for energy savings. You cannot make the rooms bigger, but you may be able to counter the objection if you have large closets or other amenities such as storage lockers, a bike room, and so on.

The apartment is dirty. A dirty apartment should never be shown. If you must show an occupied apartment that is dirty, explain that it will be cleaned and redecorated. This is the type of objection you can take action on.

The closets are too small. Point out to your prospects that smaller closets take up less square footage space allowing for more living space. It is pretty difficult to add more closet space, but you can suggest having the closets more efficiently reorganized using new shelving and rods specifically designed for this purpose.

The kitchen is too small. Smaller kitchens are usually step-saver kitchens with less floor area and cabinetry to clean. While you usually cannot make the kitchen larger, you can point out the larger living room, bedroom, or bathroom and show how the kitchen layout is very efficient. If the kitchen is very small, let the prospects enter it first; don't walk into it and ask them to come in after you.

We do not like an electric stove. Electric stoves are modern and usually trouble-free. Unless all the tenants agree to switch to gas stoves it will be difficult to change just one. Everyone adapts to electric cooking after a few weeks. More benefits: Electric cooking is cleaner; less odor; cooking vapor residue does not build up; gas fumes can sometimes fade clothes, furniture, drapes and get things dirty.

An all-electric apartment is expensive. Many all-electric heating and cooling systems allow for individually controlled thermostats located in the apartment, allowing the tenants to selectively control the temperature in each room. Electric is controlled by the tenants, who pay only for what they use. Where utilities are included in the rent, the landlord must charge more to offset these costs, and the tenants then pay not only for what they use but also for what their neighbors use. You may not be able to change the system, but you can point out energy-saving tips for using the heating and air-conditioning units. In tenant-heated buildings, tenants often forget that their electric bill includes electricity for lights, appliances, a microwave, a stove, etc. The portion of the electric bill spent on electric heat is usually less than it appears.

There is no lobby door attendant (doorman). A smaller building with a few units will not warrant having a door attendant. A larger condominium property where you own and rent out an investment unit may benefit from having an attendant to help maintain privacy. Providing 24-hour coverage can cost a building upwards of $125,000 and this expense is added into the assessments forcing the landlord to increase the rent. Attendants do not provide security and only serve as a convenience to tenants. If you think having the entrance staffed is necessary, you can suggest it to the Board of Directors of your condominium association.

The carpet is the wrong color. Carpeting cannot usually be replaced to suit each new resident's color choice. Instead, suggest using an area rug. Explain that once furniture is put in place there will not be much perimeter carpet showing. Carpeting can be dyed; however, a dark-colored carpet cannot be dyed a lighter color.

The carpeting is old. Carpets are replaced periodically due to tears or bad stains. New carpeting would increase the monthly rent if replaced unnecessarily. However if a prospect insists on having a serviceable carpet replaced, suggest putting it in if the prospect agrees to pay for it amortized over the lease period. The tenants must agree to pay any outstanding balance should they terminate the lease early.

The appliances are old (or the wrong color). Appliances should be replaced if they are not in good working order. Appliances cannot be replaced to suit each new resident's color choice. Suggest that the prospects either pay for new appliances or amortize them over the lease period.

There is no parking garage. Apartments with garages cost a lot more to rent. In some cases, street parking is available. You have no control over this factor, but you can provide information about public garages or parking lots in the area. Many residents in downtown areas use public transportation and many do not own cars.

There is no balcony or patio. Tenants seldom use their balconies or patios, which frequently serve only as storage areas for bicycles and miscellaneous debris. You cannot add a balcony, but you can provide information on where public storage facilities are, and you may suggest sunbathing at the pool, rooftop sundeck, or nearest public facility. Tenants can barbecue in the park or nearby picnic grounds.

We do not like the layout of rooms. You cannot change the floor plan, but you can point out the advantages of your floor plan. As an example, if the bedrooms are side by side, down the hall from the living room, point out how this arrangement is suited for entertaining while allowing privacy and quiet in the sleeping areas. If the bedrooms are on opposite sides of the living room, point out how this facilitates privacy between roommates or parents and children.

We do not like hardwood floors. Mention that they are easier to keep clean, the tenants will not need a vacuum cleaner, and hardwood floors do not create dust. You can carpet the floor (raising the rent). Suggest an area rug as an option.

There is no swimming pool. Properties with pools usually demand higher rents. Tell the prospects the locations of the nearest public pools and/or beaches.

There is no security. The word security should never be used, since you really should not be responsible for their security. You are providing a place to live for a fair rent. State that a building has controlled access (not "security doors"). Do not say you have security guards but that the building is controlled. Security is a function of the residents themselves. Whatever security management does provide is for the building and the building property—not the residents. You may want to suggest that they install other locking devices on their entry doors, or windows, but that you will need to have copies of all keys.

There are no storage facilities. Properties without separate storage facilities usually have bigger apartments with larger closets. If lack of storage space is a common objection, you could provide information about the closest self-storage facility.

There are not enough bathrooms. This is another situation you cannot change, although you might point out that previous residents lived there satisfactorily with the existing bath arrangement.

The apartment needs decorating. The apartment will be decorated as far as being cleaned, painted, carpet cleaned, and so on. Make the residents aware that they can decorate the apartment themselves, according to the lease or your management policies.

The apartment needs repairs. If you must show an apartment in need of repairs, explain that the owner will have all repairs completed before move-in. Sometimes you can allow the resident to do the repairs in exchange for a rent deduction, but this is generally not a good practice.

There is no dishwasher. Many people prefer washing dishes by hand because they feel they get them much cleaner. A dishwasher will increase the electric bill. Depending on kitchen size and layout, there might be room to install either a double sink, or a compact-sized dishwasher, or the tenants may want to use their own portable unit.

There is no health club. When a property offers a health club, the rents are higher and all tenants pay for it whether they use it or not. Provide information on the nearest available facility. Try to obtain a promotional introductory membership to the nearest local health club for your new residents.

Remember, it is the prospects who will be paying the rent and not you, so do not let your personal opinions of the apartment influence the customers' decision. Just because you may not like some aspect of the apartment does not mean they will feel the same way.

Do not let prospective tenants wander around an apartment unit unattended. Always remain at a discreet distance, yet close enough to hear and observe any negative comments that may arise. Familiarize yourself with the surrounding community and be prepared to answer questions about schools, shopping, commuting, local laws, and nearby services.

Ask for the Sale

Many people in the property management business are excellent at greeting and qualifying prospects and showing apartments, yet they produce few actual rentals. The reason for this is that they fail to ask for the close.

Ask for a signature on the application and a security deposit while the prospects are still with you. Discourage people from saying, "We want to think about it," or, "We'll be back." It is worth being a little pushy at this point. Indicate that your units rent quickly; if the prospects hesitate, they may lose the apartment. Press to get a commitment, a deposit, and a signature.

Follow Up

Not every prospect will agree to rent the first time she or he is shown a unit. This does not mean that you have lost the prospect, or that you should give up. Keeping in touch with prospects can be productive.

Assuming that you have obtained the prospect's address and phone number, you can send a post card the day after the prospect visits the property. The card should be handwritten and should politely encourage further questions and visits.

Telephone the prospect 24 hours after showing the unit. Be prepared to give the prospects some new piece of information that was not covered previously. Be enthusiastic. Impress the prospects with your desire to see them living in your apartment property.

Applications, Leases, and Rental Agreements

CHAPTER 4

Steve Holowicki is an accountant and has been employed in the real estate industry for six years.

It has been my goal for about three years to own and manage income-producing real estate, but the main stumbling block that kept me from reaching that goal was a lack of time to devote to the property and my limited knowledge of maintenance. I recently overcame these limitations by forming a partnership with four friends to acquire and manage a six-flat building. We share the workload and pool our abilities.

The most important point about leases and applications is to have a standard form and to know the terms of that form backward and forward. However, I never limit my negotiating options to the terms of the standard form. The standard lease or application is presented as an initial offer of tenancy. If the applicant takes exception to a particular clause of the lease or application, I negotiate to modify or delete that clause.

Lease modification is usually not an issue with initial move-ins. It is most useful when dealing with tenants who want to renew their lease for a period of less than one year, or who are not certain of when they wish to move out; for example, if they are building a house and do not know when it will be ready for occupancy.

I have a standard lease cancellation rider and modify it according to circumstances involving the tenant. Good tenant relations will, of course, reflect favorably on lease cancellation terms.

Application for Lease (Rental Agreement)

When prospects apply for an apartment, they should fill out an application for lease form (Figure 4.2). Have the prospects complete the form in your presence. Never take an application over the telephone. You should always meet the prospects and discuss the lease terms in person. You want to be sure that they understand and agree to the rules and regulations that pertain to the property before they sign a lease. Also, this is the time to ask for their security deposit and credit-check funds.

A married couple can fill out a joint application using only one form, but roommates or co-tenants should fill out individual applications. Check the credit and verify employment for all joint tenants, including a husband and wife if they are listed together on the lease as being jointly and severally responsible. All applicants should be asked to fill out the pertinent areas indicated and to sign the form while in your presence.

When the prospective residents have completed and signed the form, review the application for any incomplete or missing information. Question the prospects to obtain the information and record a brief explanation in any blanks where the information cannot be provided or completed. It is a very common practice to ask applicants for their previous landlord's address and phone number. If they refuse to provide this information, or haven't rented before, you'll have to weigh the risks against other factors.

At the time of signing the rental application, explain to the applicants that they will receive a refund of the security deposit if the application is not accepted, but that the entire deposit will be forfeited if they cancel. When an applicant submits a security deposit and is later rejected, he or she should expect to wait a few days for a refund unless the payment was in cash or a canceled check is submitted. This time is required to ensure that the check or money order is backed by sufficient funds.

Approving the Application

Tell applicants that you will verify income and other items listed on the application, after which you will contact them as soon as possible. It is imperative that prospective residents be notified immediately of acceptance or rejection. Get a telephone number where the prospects can be reached, or where you may leave a message. If the process of verification takes too long, your apartment may become vacant or the residents may find other suitable housing.

Income Requirements

Check the applicants' income against the income requirements table (Figure 4.1). The applicants should earn above the gross income listed. If the applicants earn an amount that falls within the parentheses, you may want to request more of a double security deposit, if permitted by law (see double deposit clause in this chapter), or you might ask the prospects to have a qualified cosigner fill out an application and sign the lease also.

If applicants earn less than the lowest figure within the parentheses, you can reject the prospects or demand to have the lease put in a qualified cosigner's name with the prospects listed as additional residents.

Verifying Employment and Other Sources of Income

If you want to do this work yourself, instead of using a tenant screening company (see Chapter 3), you can use the information a prospect has provided on the Application for Lease (see Figure 4.2) to call his or her current employer and explain why you want to verify employment. If the employer insists you make the request in writing, ask to speak to the "person to contact" named by the prospect on the application. If you cannot get verification over the telephone, you will have to send the employer a verification request letter. Prospects should be asked to expedite a prompt response from their employers in order to speed up the approval process.

If the employer reports lower gross earnings than the applicant indicated, the income requirements chart must be rechecked to be sure the applicant still qualifies for the apartment. If the employer will not verify any information, the applicant should be asked to provide a letter, on company stationery, verifying length of employment and amount of income.

If the applicant is self-employed, you can request copies of his or her latest tax returns that would show gross earnings. In lieu of this, a prospect can provide a financial statement verified by a bank. A letter of reference or recommendation from an officer of a banking or other financial institution is a reasonable request. Although such a letter will not demonstrate an applicant's credit history, it may give you a better idea of his or her general overall credit-worthiness. Your primary goal is to ascertain that the prospect earns enough income to qualify for the apartment.

Rental Agreements and Lease Forms

The lease is the primary legal document that specifies the terms of the rental agreement binding the owner and the resident. A lease is a contract between an owner of real property and a tenant for the possession and use of lands and improvements in return for payment in rent. The lease defines the formal relationship between the landlord and tenant. In addition to what common sense and state laws dictate about tenant-landlord obligations, the lease spells out specific agreements that bind both parties.

Figure 4.1: Income Requirements Table

Mid-America Management Corp. Income Requirements Effective December 1997

Monthly Rent	Weekly Income	Weekly Income with Security Deposit Equal to 2 Month's Rent From To		Monthly Income	Monthly Income with Security Deposit Equal to 2 Month's Rent From To		Yearly Income	Yearly Income with Security Deposit Equal to 2 Month's Rent From To	
300	198	(173 -	197)	857	(750 -	856)	10286	(9000 -	10285)
305	201	(176 -	200)	871	(763 -	870)	10457	(9150 -	10456)
310	204	(179 -	203)	886	(775 -	885)	10629	(9300 -	10628)
315	208	(182 -	207)	900	(788 -	899)	10800	(9450 -	10799)
320	211	(185 -	210)	914	(800 -	913)	10971	(9600 -	10970)
325	214	(188 -	213)	929	(813 -	928)	11143	(9750 -	11142)
330	218	(190 -	217)	943	(825 -	942)	11314	(9900 -	11313)
335	221	(193 -	220)	957	(838 -	956)	11486	(10050 -	11485)
340	224	(196 -	223)	971	(850 -	970)	11657	(10200 -	11656)
345	227	(199 -	226)	986	(863 -	985)	11829	(10350 -	11828)
350	231	(202 -	230)	1000	(875 -	999)	12000	(10500 -	11999)
355	234	(205 -	233)	1014	(888 -	1013)	12171	(10650 -	12170)
360	237	(208 -	236)	1029	(900 -	1028)	12343	(10800 -	12342)
365	241	(211 -	240)	1043	(913 -	1042)	12514	(10950 -	12513)
370	244	(213 -	243)	1057	(925 -	1056)	12686	(11100 -	12685)
375	247	(216 -	246)	1071	(938 -	1070)	12857	(11250 -	12856)
380	251	(219 -	250)	1086	(950 -	1085)	13029	(11400 -	13028)
385	254	(222 -	253)	1100	(963 -	1099)	13200	(11550 -	13199)
390	257	(225 -	256)	1114	(975 -	1113)	13371	(11700 -	13370)
395	260	(228 -	259)	1129	(988 -	1128)	13543	(11850 -	13542)
400	264	(231 -	263)	1143	(1000 -	1142)	13714	(12000 -	13713)
405	267	(234 -	266)	1157	(1013 -	1156)	13886	(12150 -	13885)
410	270	(237 -	269)	1171	(1025 -	1170)	14057	(12300 -	14056)
415	274	(239 -	273)	1186	(1038 -	1185)	14229	(12450 -	14228)
420	277	(242 -	276)	1200	(1050 -	1199)	14400	(12600 -	14399)
425	280	(245 -	279)	1214	(1063 -	1213)	14571	(12750 -	14570)
430	284	(248 -	283)	1229	(1075 -	1228)	14743	(12900 -	14742)
435	287	(251 -	286)	1243	(1088 -	1242)	14914	(13050 -	14913)
440	290	(254 -	289)	1257	(1100 -	1256)	15086	(13200 -	15085)
445	293	(257 -	292)	1271	(1113 -	1270)	15257	(13350 -	15256)
450	297	(260 -	296)	1286	(1125 -	1285)	15429	(13500 -	15428)
455	300	(263 -	299)	1300	(1138 -	1299)	15600	(13650 -	15599)
460	303	(265 -	302)	1314	(1150 -	1313)	15771	(13800 -	15770)
465	307	(268 -	306)	1329	(1163 -	1328)	15943	(13950 -	15942)
470	310	(271 -	309)	1343	(1175 -	1342)	16114	(14100 -	16113)
475	313	(274 -	312)	1357	(1188 -	1356)	16286	(14250 -	16285)
480	316	(277 -	315)	1371	(1200 -	1370)	16457	(14400 -	16456)
485	320	(280 -	319)	1386	(1213 -	1385)	16629	(14550 -	16628)
490	323	(283 -	322)	1400	(1225 -	1399)	16800	(14700 -	16799)

Figure 4.1: Income Requirements Table, continued

Mid-America Management Corp. Income Requirements Effective December 1997

Monthly Rent	Weekly Income	Weekly Income with Security Deposit Equal to 2 Month's Rent From To	Monthly Income	Monthly Income with Security Deposit Equal to 2 Month's Rent From To	Yearly Income	Yearly Income with Security Deposit Equal to 2 Month's Rent From To
495	326	(286 - 325)	1414	(1238 - 1413)	16971	(14850 - 16970)
500	330	(288 - 329)	1429	(1250 - 1428)	17143	(15000 - 17142)
505	333	(291 - 332)	1443	(1263 - 1442)	17314	(15150 - 17313)
510	336	(294 - 335)	1457	(1275 - 1456)	17486	(15300 - 17485)
515	340	(297 - 339)	1471	(1288 - 1470)	17657	(15450 - 17656)
520	343	(300 - 342)	1486	(1300 - 1485)	17829	(15600 - 17828)
525	346	(303 - 345)	1500	(1313 - 1499)	18000	(15750 - 17999)
530	349	(306 - 348)	1514	(1325 - 1513)	18171	(15900 - 18170)
535	353	(309 - 352)	1529	(1338 - 1528)	18343	(16050 - 18342)
540	356	(312 - 355)	1543	(1350 - 1542)	18514	(16200 - 18513)
545	359	(314 - 358)	1557	(1363 - 1556)	18686	(16350 - 18685)
550	363	(317 - 362)	1571	(1375 - 1570)	18857	(16500 - 18856)
555	366	(320 - 365)	1586	(1388 - 1585)	19029	(16650 - 19028)
560	369	(323 - 368)	1600	(1400 - 1599)	19200	(16800 - 19199)
565	373	(326 - 372)	1614	(1413 - 1613)	19371	(16950 - 19370)
570	376	(329 - 375)	1629	(1425 - 1628)	19543	(17100 - 19542)
575	379	(332 - 378)	1643	(1438 - 1642)	19714	(17250 - 19713)
580	382	(335 - 381)	1657	(1450 - 1656)	19886	(17400 - 19885)
585	386	(338 - 385)	1671	(1463 - 1670)	20057	(17550 - 20056)
590	389	(340 - 388)	1686	(1475 - 1685)	20229	(17700 - 20228)
595	392	(343 - 391)	1700	(1488 - 1699)	20400	(17850 - 20399)
600	396	(346 - 395)	1714	(1500 - 1713)	20571	(18000 - 20570)
605	399	(349 - 398)	1729	(1513 - 1728)	20743	(18150 - 20742)
610	402	(352 - 401)	1743	(1525 - 1742)	20914	(18300 - 20913)
615	405	(355 - 404)	1757	(1538 - 1756)	21086	(18450 - 21085)
620	409	(358 - 408)	1771	(1550 - 1770)	21257	(18600 - 21256)
625	412	(361 - 411)	1786	(1563 - 1785)	21429	(18750 - 21428)
630	415	(363 - 414)	1800	(1575 - 1799)	21600	(18900 - 21599)
635	419	(366 - 418)	1814	(1588 - 1813)	21771	(19050 - 21770)
640	422	(369 - 421)	1829	(1600 - 1828)	21943	(19200 - 21942)
645	425	(372 - 424)	1843	(1613 - 1842)	22114	(19350 - 22113)
650	429	(375 - 428)	1857	(1625 - 1856)	22286	(19500 - 22285)
655	432	(378 - 431)	1871	(1638 - 1870)	22457	(19650 - 22456)
660	435	(381 - 434)	1886	(1650 - 1885)	22629	(19800 - 22628)
665	438	(384 - 437)	1900	(l663 - 1899)	22800	(19950 - 22799)
670	442	(387 - 441)	1914	(1675 - 1913)	22971	(20100 - 22970)
675	445	(389 - 444)	1929	(1688 - 1928)	23143	(20250 - 23142)
680	448	(392 - 447)	1943	(1700 - 1942)	23314	(20400 - 23313)
685	452	(395 - 451)	1957	(1713 - 1956)	23486	(20550 - 23485)

Figure 4.1: Income Requirements Table, continued

Mid-America Management Corp. Income Requirements Effective December 1997

Monthly Rent	Weekly Income	Weekly Income with Security Deposit Equal to 2 Month's Rent From	To	Monthly Income	Monthly Income with Security Deposit Equal to 2 Month's Rent From	To	Yearly Income	Yearly Income with Security Deposit Equal to 2 Month's Rent From	To
690	455	(398 -	454)	1971	(1725 -	1970)	23657	(20700 -	23656)
695	458	(401 -	457)	1986	(1738 -	1985)	23829	(20850 -	23828)
700	462	(404 -	461)	2000	(1750 -	1999)	24000	(21000 -	23999)
705	465	(407 -	464)	2014	(1763 -	2013)	24171	(21150 -	24170)
710	468	(410 -	467)	2029	(1775 -	2028)	24343	(21300 -	24342)
715	471	(413 -	470)	2043	(1788 -	2042)	24514	(21450 -	24513)
720	475	(415 -	474)	2057	(1800 -	2056)	24686	(21600 -	24685)
725	478	(418 -	477)	2071	(1813 -	2070)	24857	(21750 -	24856)
730	481	(421 -	480)	2086	(1825 -	2085)	25029	(21900 -	25028)
735	485	(424 -	484)	2100	(1838 -	2099)	25200	(22050 -	25199)
740	488	(427 -	487)	2114	(1850 -	2113)	25371	(22200 -	25370)
745	491	(430 -	490)	2129	(1863 -	2128)	25543	(22350 -	25542)
750	495	(433 -	494)	2143	(1875 -	2142)	25714	(22500 -	25713)
755	498	(436 -	497)	2157	(1888 -	2156)	25886	(22650 -	25885)
760	501	(438 -	500)	2171	(1900 -	2170)	26057	(22800 -	26056)
765	504	(441 -	503)	2186	(1913 -	2185)	26229	(22950 -	26228)
770	508	(444 -	507)	2200	(1925 -	2199)	26400	(23100 -	26399)
775	511	(447 -	510)	2214	(1938 -	2213)	26571	(23250 -	26570)
780	514	(450 -	513)	2229	(1950 -	2228)	26743	(23400 -	26742)
785	518	(453 -	517)	2243	(1963 -	2242)	26914	(23550 -	26913)
790	521	(456 -	520)	2257	(1975 -	2256)	27086	(23700 -	27085)
795	524	(459 -	523)	2271	(1988 -	2270)	27257	(23850 -	27256)
800	527	(462 -	526)	2286	(2000 -	2285)	27429	(24000 -	27428)
805	531	(464 -	530)	2300	(2013 -	2299)	27600	(24150 -	27599)
810	534	(467 -	533)	2314	(2025 -	2313)	27771	(24300 -	27770)
815	537	(470 -	536)	2329	(2038 -	2328)	27943	(24450 -	27942)
820	541	(473 -	540)	2343	(2050 -	2342)	28114	(24600 -	28113)
825	544	(475 -	543)	2357	(2063 -	2356)	28286	(24750 -	28285)
830	547	(479 -	546)	2371	(2075 -	2370)	28457	(24900 -	28456)
835	551	(482 -	550)	2386	(2088 -	2385)	28629	(25050 -	28628)
840	554	(485 -	553)	2400	(2100 -	2399)	28800	(25200 -	28799)
845	557	(488 -	556)	2414	(2113 -	2413)	28971	(25350 -	28970)
850	560	(490 -	559)	2429	(2125 -	2428)	29143	(25500 -	29142)
855	564	(493 -	563)	2443	(2138 -	2442)	29314	(25650 -	29313)
870	574	(502 -	573)	2486	(2175 -	2485)	29829	(26100 -	29828)
875	577	(505 -	576)	2500	(2188 -	2499)	30000	(26250 -	29999)
880	580	(508 -	579)	2514	(2200 -	2513)	30171	(26400 -	30170)
885	584	(511 -	583)	2529	(2213 -	2528)	30343	(26550 -	30342)
890	587	(513 -	586)	2543	(2225 -	2542)	30514	(26700 -	30513)

Figure 4.1: Income Requirements Table, continued

Mid-America Management Corp. Income Requirements Effective December 1997

Monthly Rent	Weekly Income	Weekly Income with Security Deposit Equal to 2 Month's Rent From	To	Monthly Income	Monthly Income with Security Deposit Equal to 2 Month's Rent From	To	Yearly Income	Yearly Income with Security Deposit Equal to 2 Month's Rent From	To
895	590	(516 -	589)	2557	(2238 -	2556)	30686	(26850 -	30685)
900	593	(519 -	592)	2571	(2250 -	2570)	30857	(27000 -	30856)
905	597	(522 -	596)	2586	(2263 -	2585)	31029	(27150 -	31028)
910	600	(525 -	599)	2600	(2275 -	2599)	31200	(27300 -	31199)
915	603	(528 -	602)	2614	(2288 -	2613)	31371	(27450 -	31370)
920	607	(531 -	606)	2629	(2300 -	2628)	31543	(27600 -	31542)
925	610	(534 -	609)	2643	(2313 -	2642)	31714	(27750 -	31713)
930	613	(537 -	612)	2657	(2325 -	2656)	31886	(27900 -	31885)
935	616	(539 -	615)	2671	(2338 -	2670)	32057	(28050 -	32056)
940	620	(542 -	619)	2686	(2350 -	2685)	32229	(28200 -	32228)
945	623	(545 -	622)	2700	(2363 -	2699)	32400	(28350 -	32399)
950	626	(548 -	625)	2714	(2375 -	2713)	32571	(28500 -	32570)
955	630	(551 -	629)	2729	(2388 -	2728)	32743	(28650 -	32742)
960	633	(554 -	632)	2743	(2400 -	2742)	32914	(28800 -	32913)
965	636	(557 -	635)	2757	(2413 -	2756)	33086	(28950 -	33085)
970	640	(560 -	639)	2771	(2425 -	2770)	33257	(29100 -	33256)
975	643	(563 -	642)	2786	(2438 -	2785)	33429	(29250 -	33428)
980	646	(565 -	645)	2800	(2450 -	2799)	33600	(29400 -	33599)
985	649	(568 -	648)	2814	(2463 -	2813)	33771	(29550 -	33770)
990	653	(571 -	652)	2829	(2475 -	2828)	33943	(29700 -	33942)
995	656	(574 -	655)	2843	(2488 -	2842)	34114	(29850 -	34113)
1000	659	(577 -	658)	2857	(2500 -	2856)	34286	(30000 -	34285)
1005	663	(580 -	662)	2871	(2513 -	2870)	34457	(30150 -	34456)
1010	666	(583 -	665)	2886	(2525 -	2885)	34629	(30300 -	34628)
1015	669	(586 -	668)	2900	(2538 -	2899)	34800	(30450 -	34799)
1020	673	(588 -	672)	2914	(2550 -	2913)	34971	(30600 -	34970)
1025	676	(591 -	675)	2929	(2563 -	2928)	35143	(30750 -	35142)
1030	679	(594 -	678)	2943	(2575 -	2942)	35314	(30900 -	35313)
1035	682	(597 -	681)	2957	(2588 -	2956)	35486	(31050 -	35485)
1040	686	(600 -	685)	2971	(2600 -	2970)	35657	(31200 -	35656)
1045	689	(603 -	688)	2986	(2613 -	2985)	35829	(31350 -	35828)
1050	692	(606 -	691)	3000	(2625 -	2999)	36000	(31500 -	35999)
1055	696	(609 -	695)	3014	(2638 -	3013)	36171	(31650 -	36170)
1060	699	(612 -	698)	3029	(2650 -	3028)	36343	(31800 -	36342)
1065	702	(614 -	701)	3043	(2663 -	3042)	36514	(31950 -	36513)
1070	705	(617 -	704)	3057	(2675 -	3056)	36686	(32100 -	36685)
1075	709	(620 -	708)	3071	(2688 -	3070)	36857	(32250 -	36856)
1080	712	(623 -	711)	3086	(2700 -	3085)	37029	(32400 -	37028)
1085	715	(626 -	714)	3100	(2713 -	3099)	37200	(32550 -	37199)

Figure 4.1: Income Requirements Table, continued

Mid-America Management Corp. Income Requirements Effective December 1997

Monthly Rent	Weekly Income	Weekly Income with Security Deposit Equal to 2 Month's Rent From — To		Monthly Income	Monthly Income with Security Deposit Equal to 2 Month's Rent From — To		Yearly Income	Yearly Income with Security Deposit Equal to 2 Month's Rent From — To	
1090	719	(629	- 718)	3114	(2725	- 3113)	37371	(32700	- 37370)
1095	722	(632	- 721)	3129	(2738	- 3128)	37543	(32850	- 37542)
1100	725	(635	- 72~)	3143	(2750	- 3142)	37714	(33000	- 37713)
1105	729	(638	- 728)	3157	(2763	- 3156)	37886	(33150	- 37885)
1110	732	(640	- 731)	3171	(2775	- 3170)	38057	(33300	- 38056)
1115	735	(643	- 734)	3186	(2788	- 3185)	38229	(33450	- 38228)
1120	738	(646	- 737)	3200	(2800	- 3199)	38400	(33600	- 38399)
1125	742	(649	- 741)	3214	(2813	- 3213)	38571	(33750	- 38570)
1130	745	(652	- 744)	3229	(2825	- 3228)	38743	(33900	- 38742)
1135	748	(655	- 747)	3243	(2838	- 3242)	38914	(34050	- 38913)
1140	752	(658	- 751)	3257	(2850	- 3256)	390B6	(34200	- 39085)
1145	755	(661	- 754)	3271	(2863	- 3270)	39257	(34350	- 39256)
1150	758	(663	- 757)	3286	(2875	- 3285)	39429	(34500	- 39428)
1155	762	(666	- 761)	3300	(2888	- 3299)	39600	(34650	- 39599)
1160	765	(669	- 764)	3314	(2900	- 3313)	39771	(34800	- 39770)
1165	768	(672	- 767)	3329	(2913	- 3328)	39943	(34950	- 39942)
1170	771	(675	- 770)	3343	(2925	- 3342)	40114	(35100	- 40113)
1175	775	(678	- 774)	3357	(2938	- 3356)	40286	(35250	- 40285)
1180	778	(681	- 777)	3371	(2950	- 3370)	40457	(35400	- 40456)
1185	781	(684	- 780)	3386	(2963	- 3385)	40629	(35550	- 40628)
1190	785	(687	- 784)	3400	(2975	- 3399)	40800	(35700	- 40799)
1195	788	(689	- 787)	3414	(2988	- 3413)	40971	(35850	- 40970)
1200	791	(692	- 790)	3429	(3000	- 3428)	41143	(36000	- 41142)
1205	795	(695	- 794)	3443	(3013	- 3442)	41314	(36150	- 41313)
1210	798	(698	- 797)	3457	(3025	- 3456)	41486	(36300	- 41485)
1215	801	(701	- 800)	3471	(3038	- 3470)	41657	(36450	- 41656)
1220	804	(704	- 803)	3486	(3050	- 3485)	41829	(36600	- 41828)
1225	808	(707	- 807)	3500	(3063	- 3499)	42000	(36750	- 41999)
1230	811	(710	- 810)	3514	(3075	- 3513)	42171	(36900	- 42170)
1235	814	(713	- 813)	3529	(3088	- 3528)	42343	(37050	- 42342)
1240	818	(715	- 817)	3543	(3100	- 3542)	42514	(37200	- 42513)
1245	821	(718	- 820)	3557	(3113	- 3556)	42686	(37350	- 42685)
1250	824	(721	- 823)	3571	(3125	- 3570)	42857	(37500	- 42856)
1255	827	(724	- 826)	3586	(3138	- 3585)	43029	(37650	- 43028)
1260	831	(727	- 830)	3600	(3150	- 3599)	43200	(37800	- 43199)
1265	834	(730	- 833)	3614	(3163	- 3613)	43371	(37950	- 43370)
1270	837	(733	- 836)	3629	(3175	- 3628)	43543	(38100	- 43542)
1275	841	(736	- 840)	3643	(3188	- 3642)	43714	(38250	- 43713)
1280	844	(738	- 843)	3657	(3200	- 3656)	43886	(38400	- 43885)

Figure 4.1: Income Requirements Table, continued

Mid-America Management Corp. Income Requirements Effective December 1997

Monthly Rent	Weekly Income	Weekly Income with Security Deposit Equal to 2 Month's Rent From To		Monthly Income	Monthly Income with Security Deposit Equal to 2 Month's Rent From To		Yearly Income	Yearly Income with Security Deposit Equal to 2 Month's Rent From To	
1285	847	(741	846)	3671	(3213	3670)	44057	(38550	44056)
1290	851	(744	850)	3686	(3225	3685)	44229	(38700	44228)
1295	854	(747	853)	3700	(3238	3699)	44400	(38850	44399)
1300	857	(750	856)	3714	(3250	3713)	44571	(39000	44570)
1305	860	(753	859)	3729	(3263	3728)	44743	(39150	44742)
1310	864	(756	863)	3743	(3275	3742)	44914	(39300	44913)
1315	867	(759	866)	3757	(3288	3756)	45086	(39450	45085)
1320	870	(762	869)	3771	(3300	3770)	45257	(39600	45256)
1325	874	(764	873)	3786	(3313	3785)	45429	(39750	45428)
1330	877	(767	876)	3800	(3325	3799)	45600	(39900	45599)
1335	880	(770	879)	3814	(3338	3813)	45771	(40050	45770)
1340	884	(773	883)	3829	(3350	3828)	45943	(40200	45942)
1345	887	(776	886)	3843	(3363	3842)	46114	(40350	46113)
1350	890	(779	889)	3857	(3375	3856)	46286	(40500	46285)
1355	893	(782	892)	3871	(3388	3870)	46457	(40650	46456)
1360	897	(785	896)	3886	(3400	3885)	46629	(40800	46628)
1365	900	(788	899)	3900	(3413	3899)	46800	(40950	46799)
1370	903	(790	902)	3914	(3425	3913)	46971	(41100	46970)
1375	907	(793	906)	3929	(3438	3928)	47143	(41250	47142)
1380	910	(796	909)	3943	(3450	3942)	47314	(41400	47313)
1385	913	(799	912)	3957	(3463	3956)	47486	(41550	47485)
1390	916	(802	915)	3971	(3475	3970)	47657	(41700	47656)
1395	920	(805	919)	3986	(3488	3985)	47829	(41850	47828)
1400	923	(808	922)	4000	(3500	3999)	48000	(42000	47999)
1405	926	(811	925)	4014	(3513	4013)	48171	(42150	48170)
1410	930	(813	929)	4029	(3525	4028)	48343	(42300	48342)
1415	933	(816	932)	4043	(3538	4042)	48514	(42450	48513)
1420	936	(819	935)	4057	(3550	4056)	48686	(42600	48685)
1425	940	(822	939)	4071	(3563	4070)	48857	(42750	48856)
1430	943	(825	942)	4086	(3575	4085)	49029	(42900	49028)
1435	946	(828	945)	4100	(3588	4099)	49200	(43050	49199)
1440	949	(831	948)	4114	(3600	4113)	49371	(43200	49370)
1445	953	(834	952)	4129	(3613	4128)	49543	(43350	49542)
1450	956	(837	955)	4143	(3625	4142)	49714	(43500	49713)
1455	959	(839	958)	4157	(3638	4156)	49886	(43650	49885)
1460	963	(842	962)	4171	(3650	4170)	50057	(43800	50056)
1465	966	(845	965)5	4186	(3663	4185)	50229	(43950	50228)
1470	969	(848	968)	4200	(3675	4199)	50400	(44100	50399)
1475	973	(851	972)	4214	(3688	4213)	50571	(44250	50570)

Figure 4.1: Income Requirements Table, continued

Mid-America Management Corp. Income Requirements Effective December 1997

Monthly Rent	Weekly Income	Weekly Income with Security Deposit Equal to 2 Month's Rent		Monthly Income	Monthly Income with Security Deposit Equal to 2 Month's Rent		Yearly Income	Yearly Income with Security Deposit Equal to 2 Month's Rent	
		From	To		From	To		From	To
1480	976	(854	- 975)	4229	(3700	- 4228)	50743	(44400	- 50742)
1485	979	(857	- 978)	4243	(3713	- 4242)	50914	(44550	- 50913)
1490	982	(860	- 981)	4257	(3725	- 4256)	51086	(44700	- 51085)
1495	986	(863	- 985)	4271	(3738	- 4270)	51257	(44850	- 51256)
1500	989	(865	- 988)	4286	(3750	- 4285)	51429	(45000	- 51428)
1505	992	(868	- 991)	4300	(3763	- 4299)	51600	(45150	- 51599)
1510	996	(871	- 995)	4314	(3775	- 4313)	51771	(45300	- 51770)
1515	999	(874	- 998)	4329	(3788	- 4328)	51943	(45450	- 51942)
1520	1022	(877-	- 1001)	4343	(3800	- 4342)	52114	(45600	- 52113)
1525	1005	(880	- 1004)	4357	(3813	- 4356)	52286	(45750	- 52285)
1530	1009	(883	- 1008)	4371	(3825	- 4370)	52457	(45900	- 52456)
1535	1012	(886	- 1011)	4386	(3838	- 4385)	52629	(46050	- 52628)
1540	1015	(888	- 1014)	4400	(3850	- 4399)	52800	(46200	- 52799)
1545	1019	(891	- 1018)	4414	(3863	- 4413)	52971	(46350	- 52970)
1550	1022	(894	- 1021)	4429	(3875	- 4428)	53143	(46500	- 53142)
1555	1025	(897	- 1024)	4443	(3888	- 4442)	53314	(46650	- 53313)
1560	1029	(900	- 1028)	4457	(3900	- 4456)	53486	(46800	- 53485)
1565	1032	(903	- 1031)	4471	(3913	- 4470)	53657	(46950	- 53656)
1570	1035	(906	- 1034)	4486	(3925	- 4485)	53829	(47100	- 53828)
1575	1038	(909	- 1037)	4500	(3938	- 4499)	54000	(47250	- 53999)
1580	1042	(912	- 1041)	4514	(3950	- 4513)	54171	(47400	- 54170)
1585	1045	(914	- 1044)	4529	(3963	- 4528)	54343	(47550	- 54342)
1590	1048	(917	- 1047)	4543	(3975	- 4542)	54514	(47700	- 54513)
1595	1052	(920	- 1051)	4557	(3988	- 4556)	54686	(47850	- 54685)
1600	1055	(923	- 1054)	4571	(4000	- 4570)	54857	(48000	- 54856)
1605	1058	(926	- 1057)	4586	(4013	- 4585)	55029	(48150	- 55028)
1610	1062	(929	- 1061)	4600	(4025	- 4599)	55200	(48300	- 55199)
1615	1065	(932	- 1064)	4614	(4038	- 4613)	55371	(48450	- 55370)
1620	1068	(935	- 1067)	4629	(4050	- 4628)	55543	(48600	- 55542)
1625	1071	(938	- 1070)	4643	(4063	- 4642)	55714	(48750	- 55713)
1630	1075	(940	- 1074)	4657	(4075	- 4656)	55886	(48900	- 55885)
1635	1078	(943	- 1077)	4671	(4088	- 4670)	56057	(49050	- 56056)
1640	1081	(946	- 1080)	4686	(4100	- 4685)	56229	(49200	- 56228)
1645	1085	(949	- 1084)	4700	(4113	- 4699)	56400	(49350	- 56399)
1650	1088	(952	- 1087)	4714	(4125	- 4713)	56571	(49500	- 56570)
1655	1091	(955	- 1090)	4729	(4138	- 4728)	56743	(49650	- 56742)

Figure 4.2: Application for Lease

☐ NEW RENTAL:
☐ PRERENT FOR:
☐ RELET FROM:
☐ ROOMMATE WITH:
☐ BUYOUT/CANCELLATION:
☐ CO-SIGNER:
REFERRED BY _____

MID-AMERICA MANAGEMENT CORP.

APPLICATION FOR LEASE
_____

CIC # _____

BLDG # _____ UNIT # _____

TERMS OF LEASE:
From: _____ To: _____
Move in date: _____
Rent: _____ / Addl. Rent _____
Sec. Dep.: _____
Addl. Sec. Dep.: _____
Pet Fee: _____
Address: _____ Apt. # _____
Concession: _____
Bedrooms: 0   1   2   3   (Circle one)

S/D Pd: _____
C/C Pd: _____
Rent Pd: _____
Bal. Due: _____
Riders: _____

S/D Recd: _____
C/C Recd: _____
Rent Recd: _____
Date: _____
By: _____

——— COMPLEX ———   ——— MAIN OFFICE ———

APPLICANT: SPOUSE:
SS # _____   SS # _____
DRIV. LIC. # _____   DRIV. LIC. # _____

PLEASE DO NOT WRITE ABOVE THIS LINE

APPLICANT

NAME _____ AGE _____ DATE OF BIRTH _____
CURRENT ADDRESS _____ CITY _____ ZIP CODE _____ PHONE _____
LANDLORD NAME _____ PHONE _____ HOW LONG _____ DATE VERIFIED _____
PREVIOUS ADDRESS _____ CITY _____ ZIP CODE _____ PHONE _____
LANDLORD NAME _____ PHONE _____ HOW LONG _____
CURRENT EMPLOYER _____ PERSON TO CONTACT _____
EMPLOYMENT ADDRESS _____ CITY _____ PHONE _____ DATE VERIFIED _____
POSITION _____ YEARS SERVICE _____ WEEKLY GROSS EARNINGS _____
PREVIOUS EMPLOYER _____ PERSON TO CONTACT _____
PREVIOUS EMPL. ADDRESS _____ CITY _____ PHONE _____
POSITION _____ YEARS SERVICE _____ WEEKLY GROSS EARNINGS _____
ADDITIONAL INCOME $_____ EXPLAIN _____

SPOUSE

NAME _____ AGE _____ DATE OF BIRTH _____
CURRENT EMPLOYER _____ PERSON TO CONTACT _____
EMPLOYMENT ADDRESS _____ CITY _____ PHONE _____ DATE VERIFIED _____
POSITION _____ YEARS SERVICE _____ WEEKLY GROSS EARNINGS _____
ADDITIONAL INCOME $_____ EXPLAIN _____

CREDIT

CREDIT   1. _____ # _____   3. _____ # _____
ACCOUNTS   2. _____ # _____   4. _____ # _____
CHECKING ACCT. AT: _____ # _____ HOW LONG _____
SAVINGS ACCT. AT: _____ # _____ HOW LONG _____

MISCELLANEOUS

HOW MANY PEOPLE WILL OCCUPY THIS APARTMENT? _____
DO YOU HAVE ANY PETS? _____ Yes _____ No   IF YES, TYPE _____ WEIGHT _____
IN EMERGENCY NOTIFY _____ RELATIONSHIP _____
ADDRESS _____ CITY _____ PHONE _____
CAR MAKE(S) _____ YEAR(S) _____ LICENSE NO(S) _____ FINANCED BY _____

DATE APPROVED: _____ MANAGER'S SIGNATURE: _____
DATE RESIDENT NOTIFIED: _____ PERSON CONTACTED: _____ BY: _____

FAIR HOUSING STATEMENT. Mid-America Management Corp. is an equal-opportunity housing manager. It is the policy of Mid-America Management Corp. for it and its employees and agents not to discriminate on the basis of race, color, religion, national origin, ancestry, physical or mental disability, familial status, age, marital status, sex or unfavorable discharge from military service in the offering of rental apartments or in the terms, conditions or privileges of rental. You have the right to be offered and to choose any rental apartment that we have available that meets your budgetary requirements. We will offer any available rental apartment to you, subject to our standard confirmation of your credit history, income and housing references. If you believe that you have been treated unfairly or discriminated against by any employee or agent of Mid-America Management Corp., please contact the compliance officer at (708) 574-2400.

I represent to you that I have read this entire application and that all of the above information hereon is true and correct. I further represent that my rental and credit records are in good standing with no judgements or liens against me. If any of the above information is false, I hereby agree that my entire deposit may be forfeited to you. I also agree that if I am accepted and fail to complete this transaction by signing your lease, my entire deposit will be forfeited to you. I understand that this application is subject to your approval, and if my application is not accepted, my deposit will be returned in full. I understand that my $35.00 credit check fee is nonrefundable. I also understand that this is not a lease and should my application be accepted, I agree to sign your lease form currently in use. If for any reason whatsoever you are unable to make the apartment which is the subject of this application available at the beginning of the lease term, I hereby waive any and all rights to seek to recover any damages whatsoever against you, including without limitation, actual, punitive or consequential damages.

_____
APPLICANT

_____
RECEIVED BY

_____
APPLICANT

_____
DATE

4301 REV. 2/93   ORIGINAL

Oral Leases

Oral leases are generally not recommended unless you want month-to-month tenants. It is extremely important to use a written lease, and there are plenty of good standard forms available; oral leases are not recommended. Years ago, it may have been to the landlord's advantage not to give a tenant a written lease. The tenant was then at the mercy of the landlord, who could raise rents at will and give short termination notices. The problems are that oral leases run on a month-to-month basis, cannot be substantiated, and may not always be enforceable. A written lease is a binding contract on both parties and it is usually upheld in court.

Commercially Available Lease Forms

Many good preprinted lease forms are available. Some of the best are offered through local REALTOR® associations, the *Peachtree Business Products Company* (800-241-4623), and local chapters of the *National Apartment Association* (703-518-6141). These organizations keep their forms updated to reflect current landlord-tenant laws.

If you cannot find what you want through one of the above organizations, go to a local stationery store. Forms purchased in a local store must be carefully reviewed to see that they are up-to-date and that they will work for you.

Owners and residents may add to a preprinted form lease any terms and conditions that are not prohibited by state or local ordinances or other rules of law. Additions to a lease document may include: additional rent, additional terms of agreement, additional rules and regulations, lease riders, and other provisions governing the rights and obligations of the parties. Explanations of these additions follow below.

Terms and Conditions of Leases

The following brief summary discusses the terms and conditions of most standard apartment rental agreements (leases). Riders to a lease, and additional lease clauses will be discussed later in this chapter.

Filling Out the Lease

Many states now indicate in their statues that all blank spaces on the lease must be completed or the lease may be voidable. You may be familiar with some of the basic lease language and definitions. Pay special attention to the following areas where you will be inserting the specific details concerning your property and prospective tenants. **NOTE:** Some of the forms presented as figures in this book can be adapted for your personal use. However, this is not true of the lease forms. Always purchase and use original blank leases.

Lessor is you, the landlord.

Lessee is the tenant. Enter the full names of all occupants 18 years or older on the lease. If there is a *cosigner*, this name is added under the occupant's name and the word cosigner should appear.

The date the lease begins is the date the resident starts paying rent. This could be a different date than the actual move-in date. For example, you may be offering a concession such as one month's free rent (see prorated or free rent programs later in this chapter).

The date the lease ends should be the last day of a month.

Unless the rental agreement fixes a definite term, the tenancy is week-to-week in the case of a resident who pays weekly rent and, in all other cases, month-to-month.

Monthly rent is the dollar amount the resident will pay for rent of the unit each month. Additional monthly payments for a parking space, garage, pet, furniture rental, or other applicable charges can be reflected on the appropriate lease clause or rider.

The security deposit is normally equal to one or two months' rent, though some landlords charge a flat fee. Other required deposits are additional deposits for pets, furniture rental, or other extraordinary security deposit fees. In soft rental markets a smaller security deposit might serve as an added inducement to a potential renter. There is no legal requirement to charge a security deposit, however you may be required to pay interest on the security deposit.

Premises is the complete address of the apartment being leased.

The special provisions section of the lease is for documentation of any additional riders to the lease such as pet, garage and furniture riders, and so on, or of any special provisions that require additional security deposits.

Prohibited Provisions in Rental Agreements

Many states have restrictions on the language and agreements in leases. For example, in Illinois the following provisions would be prohibited:

- An agreement to waive or to forego any rights or remedies granted by law
- A provision that authorizes any person to confess judgment on a claim arising out of the rental agreement
- An agreement to exculpate or limit any liability of the other party arising as a result of the other party's willful misconduct

Figure 4.3: Chicago Apartment Lease

UNIVERSITY PRINTING COMPANY
CHICAGO, IL

NO. 15C

NOT FURNISHED **CHICAGO APARTMENT LEASE**

REV 1992

©CHICAGO ASSOCIATION OF REALTORS®
COPYRIGHT 1992
ALL RIGHTS RESERVED

DATE OF LEASE	TERM OF LEASE		MONTHLY RENT	SECURITY DEPOSIT*
	BEGINNING	ENDING		

ADDITIONAL CHARGES AND FEES

Late Charge $_____   Returned Check Charge $_____   Reletting Charge $_____   Parking Fee $_____   Laundry Room Fee $_____

Social Security No. _____ - _____ - _____   Storage Fee $_____ $_____ $_____

IF NONE, WRITE "NONE." Paragraph 5 of Lease Agreements and Covenants then INAPPLICABLE.

(Owner or agent authorized to manage the Apartment and to act for or on behalf of the Owner for the purpose of service of process and for the purpose of receiving and receipting for notices and demands.)

TENANT		**LESSOR**	
TENANT ●		NAME ●	
APARTMENT ●		ADDRESS ●	
BUILDING ●		CITY ●	
CITY ●		PHONE ● ( )	

In consideration of the mutual agreements and covenants set forth below and on the reverse side hereof (the same being fully included as part of this Lease) Lessor hereby leases to Tenant and Tenant hereby leases from Lessor for use in accordance with paragraph 8 hereof the Apartment designated above, together with the fixtures and accessories belonging thereto, for the above Term. All parties listed above as Lessor and Tenant are herein referred to individually and collectively as Lessor and Tenant respectively.

5-12-100   Building Code Violations

Tenant is hereby notified that, during the 12 month period prior to the date of execution of this Lease, the following code violations have been cited for the Apartment and or the Building and the following notices have been received from the City of Chicago or any utility provider regarding termination of utility services (If none write "none"; if enforcement litigation is pending, also state the case number):

ADDITIONAL AGREEMENTS AND COVENANTS (including DECORATING AND REPAIRS), if any.

Figure 4.3: Chicago Apartment Lease, continued

| TENANT(S) | SIGNATURES | LESSOR(S) |

_____(SEAL)   _____(SEAL)

_____(SEAL)   _____(SEAL)

LEASE AGREEMENTS AND COVENANTS

1. RENT: Tenant shall pay to Lessor at the above address (or such other address as Lessor may designate in writing) the monthly rent set forth above on or before the first day of each month in advance. **The time of each and every payment of rent is of the essence of this Lease. To cover Lessor's added costs for late payments, the monthly rent set forth above shall be increased by the amount set forth above as "Late Charge" if paid after the 5th of the month. To cover Lessor's added costs for processing of checks that are dishonored or are returned due to insufficient funds in the account, the monthly rent shall be increased by the amount set forth above as "Returned Check Charge." Rent mailed in shall be deemed paid on date of receipt by Lessor.**

2. POSSESSION: At the commencement of this Lease, Lessor shall deliver possession of the apartment to Tenant. Possession shall be deemed to have been delivered to Tenant on the day that Lessor either (A) actually delivers to Tenant keys to the Apartment or (B) makes available to Tenant at the office of the Building or at such other place as designated by Lessor keys to the Apartment. If Lessor cannot deliver possession of the Apartment to Tenant on the date set for commencement of the Term, this Lease shall remain in full force and effect with rent abated until such time as the Apartment is available for Tenant's occupancy, unless Tenant elects to maintain an action for possession of the Apartment or, upon written notice to Lessor, elects to terminate this Lease.

3. APPLICATION: The application for this Lease and all representations and promises contained therein are hereby made a part of this Lease. Tenant warrants that the information given by Tenant in the application is true. If such information is false, Lessor may at Lessor's option terminate this Lease by giving Tenant not less than 10 days prior written notice, which shall be Lessor's sole remedy.

4. PROMISES OF THE PARTIES: The terms and conditions contained herein shall be conclusively deemed the agreement between Tenant and Lessor and no modification, waiver or amendment of this Lease or any of its terms, conditions or covenants shall be binding upon the parties unless made in writing and signed by the party sought to be bound.

5. SECURITY DEPOSIT: Tenant has deposited with Lessor the Security Deposit in the amount set forth above for the performance of each and every covenant and agreement to be performed by Tenant under this Lease. Lessor shall have the right, but not the obligation, to apply the Security Deposit in whole or in part as payment of such amounts as are reasonably necessary to remedy Tenant's defaults in the payment of rent or in the performance of the covenants or agreements contained herein. Lessor's right to possession of the Apartment for non-payment of rent or any other reason shall not be affected by the fact that Lessor holds security. Tenant's liability is not limited to the amount of the Security Deposit.

Lessor shall give Tenant written notice of the application of the Security Deposit or any part thereof within thirty (30) days of said application. If the application is on account of maintenance, repairs or replacements necessitated by Tenant, said notice shall include the estimated or actual cost of the same, attaching estimates or paid receipts. Upon receipt of said notice, Tenant shall at once pay to Lessor an amount sufficient to restore the Security Deposit in full. Upon termination of this Lease, full payment of all amounts due and performance of all Tenant's covenants and agreements (including surrender of the Apartment in accordance with Paragraph 15), the Security Deposit or any portion thereof remaining unapplied shall be returned to Tenant in accordance with applicable law.

The Security Deposit shall not be deemed, construed or allocated by Tenant as payment of rent for any month of the lease term.

6. LESSOR TO MAINTAIN:
A. Tenant hereby declares that Tenant has inspected the Apartment, the Building and all related areas and grounds and that Tenant is satisfied with the physical condition thereof. **Tenant agrees that no representations, warranties (expressed or implied) or covenants with respect to the condition, maintenance or improvements of the Apartment, Building, or other areas have been made to Tenant except (1) those contained in this Lease, the application, or otherwise in writing signed by Lessor and (2) those provided under applicable law.**
B. Lessor agrees that Lessor will perform work set forth in this Lease within a reasonable time not to exceed 30 days from the commencement of the Term hereof.
C. Lessor covenants that at all times during the Term hereof, Lessor shall maintain the Apartment and the Building to the following minimum standards:
  (1) Effective weather protection, including unbroken windows and doors;
  (2) Plumbing facilities in good working order;
  (3) A water supply which either under the control of Tenant is capable of producing hot and cold running water, or under the control of Lessor produces hot and cold running water, furnished to appropriate fixtures, and connected to a sewerage system;
  (4) Heating (and, if furnished, air conditioning and ventilation) facilities in good working order which, if under the control of Tenant, are capable of producing, or, if under the control of Lessor, produce heat (and if furnished, air conditioning and ventilation) in fixtures provided (and no other) within reasonable accepted tolerances and during reasonable hours. (In the case of heat, minimum tolerances shall be those established by municipal code);
  (5) Gas and/or electrical appliances which are supplied by Lessor in good working order, and appropriate gas piping and electrical wiring system to the extent existing in the Building maintained in good working order and safe condition;
  (6) Building, grounds and areas under the control of Lessor in clean, sanitary and safe condition free from all accumulations of debris, filth, rubbish, garbage, rodents and vermin;
  (7) Adequate and appropriate receptacle(s) for garbage and rubbish, and, if under the control of Lessor, in clean condition and good repair;
  (8) Floors, stairways, walls and railings and common areas in good repair;
  (9) Apartment floors, walls and ceilings in good repair and safe condition; and
  (10) Elevators (if existing) in good repair and safe condition.
D. It is, however understood and agreed that buildings are physical structures subject to aging, wear, tear, abuse, inherent defects, and numerous forces causing disrepair or breakdown beyond Lessor's reasonable control, and that components and skilled workmen are not always immediately available. Lessor's costs of operation are fixed and unavoidable and to permit rent abatement or damages to Tenant would create an intolerable burden on Lessor, other tenants and surrounding neighborhood. It is, therefore, understood and agreed that breakdowns of equipment or disrepair caused by (1) conditions caused by Tenant, members of Tenant's household, guests or other persons on the premises with Tenant's consent; (2) Tenant's unreasonable refusal of or other interference with entry of Lessor or Lessor's workmen or contractors into the Apartment or Building for purposes of correcting defective conditions; (3) lack of reasonable opportunity for Lessor to correct defective conditions; (4) conditions beyond Lessor's reasonable control, including strikes or lockouts; or (5) Lessor's not having actual knowledge of such defective conditions may be asserted by Lessor as a defense in any action against Lessor for breach of covenant based upon the duties of Lessor to maintain the Apartment or Building.

Source: Chicago Association of REALTORS®. Used with permission.

Figure 4.4: Apartment Lease

New Lease	☐ $ _____	Transfer Lease	☐	**APARTMENT LEASE**
Renewal Lease	☐ $ _____	Replacement Lease	☐	
Lease Extension	☐	Relet/Rerent	☐	S.C. NO. _____ BLDG. _____ UNIT _____

LEASE TERM		MONTHLY RENT	REQUIRED SECURITY DEPOSIT	OTHER REQUIRED RENT**	REQUIRED PET DEPOSIT**	OTHER REQUIRED DEPOSIT
Begins	Ends					

LESSOR: MID-AMERICA MANAGEMENT CORP.   **LESSEE:** NAME

Managing Agent

2901 Butterfield Road   NAME

Oak Brook, Illinois 60521

                            NAME

** See Rider attached hereto and made a part hereof.

PREMISES: ADDRESS _____ **APT NO.** _____

Special Provisions:

Lessor and Lessee have read and hereby agree to all the covenants, conditions and provisions contained in this lease on the face of this page, the reverse side of this page and in any Rider(s) attached hereto.

_____ (SEAL)   **MID-AMERICA MANAGEMENT CORP.** , Managing Agent

LESSEE

_____ (SEAL)   By _____ (SEAL)

LESSEE

_____ (SEAL)

LESSEE

Dated: _____ , 19 ____   Dated: _____ , 19 ____

Fair Housing Statement: Mid-America Management Corp. is an equal-opportunity housing manager. It is the policy of Mid-America Management Corp. for it and its employees and agents not to discriminate on the basis of race, color, religion, national origin, ancestry, physical or mental disability, familial status, age, marital status, sex or unfavorable discharge from military service in the offering of rental apartments or in the terms, conditions or privileges of rental. You have the right to be offered and to choose any rental apartment that we have available that meets your budgetary requirements. We will offer any available rental apartment to you, subject to our standard confirmation of your credit history, income and housing references. If you believe that you have been treated unfairly or discriminated against by any employee or agent of Mid-America Management Corp., please contact the compliance officer at (630) 574-2400.

In consideration of the execution or renewal of this lease, Lessee and Lessor agree as follows:

1. Lessee, any member of the Lessee's household or a guest or visitor shall not engage in criminal activity, including drug related criminal activity, with or without Lessee's knowledge on or near the Premises. "Drug-related criminal activity" means the illegal manufacture, sale, distribution, use, or possession with intent to manufacture, sell, distribute, or use of a controlled substance (as defined in Illinois Compiled Statutes Chapter 720)

2. Lessee, any member of the Lessee's household or a guest or visitor shall not engage in any act intended to facilitate criminal activity, including drug-related criminal activity, with or without Lessee's knowledge on or near the Premises.

3. Lessee, any member of the Lessee's household or a guest or visitor will not permit the dwelling unit to be used for or to facilitate criminal activity, including drug-related criminal activity regardless of whether the individual engaging in such activity is a member of the household, a guest, or a visitor.

4. Lessee, any member of the Lessee's household or a guest or visitor will not engage in the manufacture, sale, or distribution of illegal drugs at any locations, whether on or near the dwelling unit Premises or otherwise.

5. Lessee, any member of the Lessee's household or a guest or visitor shall not engage in acts of violence or threats of violence, including but not limited to the unlawful discharge of firearms, with or without Lessee's knowledge on or near the dwelling unit Premises.

6. VIOLATION OF THE ABOVE PROVISIONS SHALL BE A MATERIAL VIOLATION OF THE LEASE AND GOOD CAUSE FOR TERMINATION OF TENANCY. A single violation of any of the provisions of this added clause shall be deemed a serious violation and material non-compliance with the lease. It is understood and agreed that a single violation shall be good cause for termination of the lease. Unless otherwise provided by law, proof of violation shall not require criminal conviction, but shall be by a preponderance of the evidence.

7. In case of conflict between the provisions of this clause and any other provisions of the lease, the provisions of the clause shall govern.

Lessor, in consideration of the covenants, conditions and agreements herein contained on the part of the parties hereto, hereby leases the Premises to the Lessee to be occupied as a private dwelling for use of Lessee and other persons as stated in the lease application, and to no other person, and for no other purpose for the above stated Lease Term. In consideration thereof, Lessee agrees to pay Lessor the above stated Monthly Rent, in advance throughout the Lease Term, and without notice or demand, on the **FIRST DAY** of each calendar month of the Lease Term at the Lessor's address as set forth above or wherever designated in writing by Lessor from time to time. It is agreed by the parties hereto that the time of each and all such payments is of the essence of this agreement. Lessee acknowledges that Lessor reports Lessee's payment activity to credit agencies.

1. SECURITY DEPOSIT. Lessee shall deposit with Lessor the above-described security deposit to secure the faithful and timely performance of each and every covenant and provision of this lease, and covenants to maintain said entire security deposit with the Lessor until the termination of this lease. Provided Lessee has satisfied and complied with all the conditions of the release of security deposit as set forth on the reverse side of this lease, said deposit will be returned to Lessee after the termination of this lease in accordance with applicable law; it being understood that Lessee will remain liable for any loss or damage sustained by Lessor arising out of Lessee's failure to fully and faithfully perform hereunder. Lessee agrees that the security deposit shall not be considered an advance payment of rent and that Lessee shall at no time apply said deposit to payment of any rent becoming due hereunder. Should the Lessee violate this paragraph by using the security deposit as the last month's rent, Lessee herein agrees to a special handling charge of $50.00 in addition to damages, if any, said charge to be deemed so much additional rent due and payable to Lessor immediately without notice or demand.

2. SPECIAL CONDITIONS. It is mutually agreed that in the event the rent payment is not made on the **FIRST DAY** of each calendar month of the Term, a charge of two dollars ($2.00) per day for each day overdue shall become due and payable, which charge shall constitute so much additional rent hereunder, payable on demand. Lessee herein agrees to a $10.00 per day charge should he violate any restriction against pets, which charge shall constitute so much additional rent hereunder, payable on demand. Lessor shall have the right, but not the obligation, to apply any payment received from Lessee towards the payment of any additional rent or charges that remain unpaid at the time of receipt of any such payment, and the balance of Lessee's payment, if any, shall than be applied towards current monthly rent due hereunder. The Premises, the building in which the Premises are situated, the facilities and public areas

same, himself or by his agents, and put the same in good condition, and Lessee agrees to pay Lessor in addition to the rent hereby reserved, the expense of Lessor in so doing, the amount of which such expense may be incurred, as so much additional rent. Lessee hereby assumes full and complete liability and responsibility for any and all loss, costs or damages, including, but not limited to, fire damage, resulting from Lessee's negligent or intentional acts or any other act or omission of Lessee or anyone acting on Lessee's behalf or any invitee of Lessee. Lessee will carry liability insurance to insure Lessor for all of the aforementioned negligent or intentional acts and omissions. In no instance, including, but not limited to, the payment of rent, shall Lessee, or Lessee's agents or invitees, be considered an insured, as a co-insured or an additional insured or otherwise under Lessor's property or casualty insurance policies or under Lessor's self-funded risk management programs, if any. Lessee also agrees to see to it that none of the foregoing persons violate any of the terms or provisions of this lease or the rules and regulations that are a part hereof or cause damage or disrepair to any part of the Premises, the building of which the Premises is a part, or any other property on or adjacent thereto.

8. ACCESS. Lessee agrees to give the Lessor or persons designated by Lessor, free access to the Premises, at all reasonable times, to inspect, alter, repair, or exhibit the Premises for sale or for rent or to exterminate vermin, rodents and insects from the Premises or to permit the Lessor to display a "For Rent" sign in any window during any sixty (60) day period prior to the expiration of the Term and agrees not to move or remove such a sign. For each breach of this paragraph, the Lessee agrees to pay the Lessor twice the amount of one month's rent as liquidated damages for such action, the same constituting so much additional rent hereunder, payable upon demand.

Figure 4.4: Apartment Lease, continued

shall be used by the Lessee at his own risk. Drinking of alcoholic beverages in public places is strictly prohibited. No person other than the person(s) signing this lease and other persons described in Lessee's lease application may occupy or live in said Premises without the prior written consent of Lessor. Lessee warrants and represents to Lessor that all information in the lease application for this lease is true. In the event any of the information supplied by the Lessee in the lease application is false or inaccurate, this lease shall be deemed to be materially breached by Lessee at its inception, and at the Lessor's option, the Lessee's occupancy shall be deemed a forcible entry and detainer.

3. CONDITIONS OF PREMISES. Lessee has examined the Premises before signing this lease, and is satisfied with the physical condition thereof, and his signing shall be conclusive evidence of this acknowledgement except as otherwise specified herein. Lessee agrees that no representation or warranty as to condition or repair has been made by Lessor or Lessor's Agent except as contained herein, and that no promise to decorate, alter, repair or improve the Premises has been made by Lessor or Lessor's Agent, either before or at the signing hereof. Lessee also acknowledges that no representation or warranty as to security at the Premises or at the building or apartment complex of which the Premises are a part has been made by Lessor.

4. NO ASSIGNMENT OR SUBLETTING. Lessee shall not sublet the Premises or any part thereof, nor assign this lease, nor permit to take place by any act or default of himself or any person, any transfer by operation of Law of Lessee's interest created hereby; nor offer the Premises or any portion thereof for lease or sublease.

5. USE OF PREMISES. No part of the Premises shall be used or occupied for a boarding or lodging house, for rooming or school purposes, to give instructions of any kind, for any trade, business or entertainment, for any purpose that will increase the rate of insurance thereon, nor shall there be kept on or used in or around the Premises or in any place contiguous thereto any flammable fluids or explosives. Neither Lessee nor any other person with or without Lessee's permission shall commit or permit any unlawful or immoral practice, nor any act, nor any practice that will injure the reputation of the Premises or the building of which the Premises are a part, or that disturbs other tenants or occupants of the building, or any other building within the apartment complex of which the Premises are a part, or that violates any local ordinance applicable to the Premises, or that is injurious to the Premises, the building or the apartment complex of which the Premises are a part, or the operation thereof. Lessee shall be fully responsible for the conduct of all persons residing with, or visiting Lessee. Lessor has the right to bar individuals from the Premises, or the apartment complex of which the Premises are a part. Lessee must inform his guests of the terms of this lease, and all rules and regulations as contained herein. If any of the terms of this lease or any of the rules or regulations are violated by Lessee's guests, they may be barred and/or arrested for criminal trespassing.

6. RADIOS, TV, ETC. Lessee, or any guest of Lessee, shall not operate any audio or visual equipment, radios, televisions, musical instruments, citizens band radios or other equipment or device on the Premises, or in or on any part of the apartment complex of which the Premises are a part, which disturbs an occupant or occupants of any building in the apartment complex of which the Premises are a part.

7. UPKEEP. Neither the Lessee nor any other person permitted to occupy the Premises nor any guests of Lessee shall suffer or commit any waste in and about the Premises or in and about the building of which they are a part, and shall keep the Premises, together with the fixtures therein and appurtenances, in a clean, sightly and sanitary condition and in good repair and free from vermin, rodents, and insects, all at his own expense, and shall yield the same back to the Lessor upon termination of the lease or of Lessee's right of possession, by expiration of the Term or in any other manner, in the same condition as at the date of the signing hereof, except as repaired or altered by Lessor and except loss from reasonable wear and tear. If, however, the Premises shall not thus be kept by the Lessee as aforesaid, Lessor may enter the

4305 Rev. 11-96

9. SECURITY. At its election Lessor, its agents and employees may, but is not obligated, to retain an' independent contractor to provide protective services for the proper security and safeguard of the property of which the Premises are a part. Where Lessor has elected to furnish such security service, it is expressly understood and agreed that security personnel, in rendering any of the services provided or otherwise, shall not under any circumstances whatsoever be considered employees of Lessor. It is further understood and agreed that the providing of said security confers neither rights upon Lessee nor corresponding obligations upon Lessor. Lessor may withdraw said service at anytime without notice to Lessee. This provision is not a basis of the bargain and Lessee is not responsible for any proportionate share of any costs and expenses incurred by Lessor in providing security. Lessee acknowledges that no representations have been expressed or implied by Lessor regarding the security or safety of the Lessee or Lessee's property.

10. NO SIGNS, ETC. Without Lessor's prior written consent, Lessee shall not cause or permit the display of any sign or advertising material upon or about the Premises or the building of which they are a part.

11. NO ALTERATIONS. Lessee shall make no alterations or additions without the prior written consent of Lessor. All alterations and additions shall remain as part of the Premises, unless the Lessor shall otherwise elect, including without limitation, locks, bolts, antennas, carpeting and all fixtures.

12. NO INSTALLATION WITHOUT PERMISSION. Lessee shall not install in, on or about the Premises nor attach to or affix to any interior or exterior part of the building of which the Premises are a part including without limitation, any air conditioning unit, dishwasher, humidifier, dehumidifier, laundry equipment, refrigerator, or antenna or any other mechanical device or appliance of any kind or nature in whole or in part, without the prior written consent of Lessor or Lessor's agent, and any such consent shall be wholly and solely upon the terms and conditions specified in such consent.

13. HEAT AND UTILITIES. Lessor agrees, if the building is equipped for the purpose and there is no separate system or meter servicing the Premises, to furnish, during the Term of this lease, sufficient heat to comply with the minimum requirements set forth in the applicable laws of the municipality in which the Premises are situated, gas, electricity and/or water. Lessor shall not be held liable for any injury or damage whatsoever which may arise or accrue from its failure to furnish any of the above items, regardless of the cause of such failure, all claims for such injury or damage being hereby expressly waived by Lessee. In the event the Premises are equipped with a self-contained furnace system and/or are separately metered for gas, hot water for heat, electricity and/or water, Lessee covenants and agrees to be responsible for all charges for same and/or establish and maintain in its own name accounts with the appropriate utilities and timely make all required deposits and utility payments for such items; and the Lessee further covenants and agrees to operate the system at a temperature sufficient to prevent damage to the Premises or any portion of the building in which the Premises are located; and Lessee further covenants and agrees to be fully liable and responsible for any damage to the Premises and the building resulting due to a breach of this subparagraph. Lessor shall also have the right, but not the obligation, to make any such utility payments when due and pay any arrearages of such payments, which amount shall immediately become due to Lessor from Lessee as additional rent hereunder. Lessor shall also have the right to apply payments received from Lessee first to payment of additional rent under this subparagraph, and then to monthly rent and other amounts due from Lessee under this lease. Lessee hereby indemnifies and holds Lessor and the owner of the Premises harmless from and against any and all claims of nonpayment for utility services, including, without limitation, all amounts paid by Lessor in satisfaction of such claims and all costs, expenses and attorney's fees which may be incurred.

or negligence; or to indemnify the other party for that liability or the cost connected therewith

- An agreement to waive attorney's fees as provided by state or local ordinance, or to pay the attorney's fees of the other party except as may be required by law
- A provision that the rental agreement shall be terminated if there are, or shall be, any children under the age of 14 years in resident's family

If any of the above provisions are included in a rental agreement, the provision would be unenforceable while the rest of the lease would remain valid, provided there is a clause that states this provision.

If a party is injured by a prohibited provision in a rental agreement initiated by the other party and such injury results in damages, the injured party may bring suit to recover actual damages and reasonable attorney's fees. If the inclusion was deliberate and with knowledge, an additional monetary amount may be awarded.

Security Deposits

An owner may, pursuant to a written rental agreement, require a security deposit from the resident, in an amount that generally should not be in excess of two months' rent. However, nothing prevents an owner from requiring prepaid rent in any amount.

If the resident does prepay rent, the money cannot be applied as security, but only to the payment of rent as it becomes due. A security deposit shall not be used nor applied as rent except as provided by law.

Applicants should pay you the full required security deposit upon signing the lease and always prior to moving into the property. Avoid taking a partial payment. Apartments should not be taken off the market unless the full security deposit has been paid.

Most form-lease provisions pertaining to security deposits provide that the lessor has the right, but not the obligation, to apply the security deposit in payment of any unpaid delinquent rent or other moneys due from the tenant. Some leases also provide that the lessor's right to possession of the apartment for nonpayment of rent or any other reason is not affected by the fact that the lessor holds a security deposit.

In some states, if you apply a security deposit to the payment of unpaid rent due, or to compensate for damages caused by the resident's noncompliance with the rental agreement, you must notify the resident within a reasonable time period, usually 15 to 20 days. In the case of compensation for damages, include an itemized statement of the damage allegedly caused to the dwelling unit or the premises and the estimated or actual cost for repairing or replacing each item on that statement, with estimates or paid invoices or copies attached. If estimated costs are given on this statement, owners should furnish the resident with copies of paid invoices within 30 days from the date of the statement. Security deposits may not be used by owner to repair or replace for normal wear and tear.

Tenants have a specified time limit, normally 15 days, after receiving notice that the security deposit has been applied to rent or damages, to pay the owner an amount sufficient to restore the security deposit in full.

Security deposit laws in most states dictate that within a certain amount of time of termination of the tenancy (usually 14 to 45 days), owners must refund the security deposit or any portion thereof remaining unapplied. Each state differs on the exact number of days; check with your local real estate association to find out how much time you have. Failure to return a security deposit within the legal time limit may result in additional monetary fines.

Owners should not withhold any portion of the security deposit because of the resident's failure to give the owner advance notice of vacating the dwelling unit, unless the requirement of advance notice is stated on the face of the rental agreement and the resident fails to give such notice, the dwelling unit is vacant for a subsequent period, and local laws permit the same.

In the event of a sale, lease, or other transfer of the property, owners have to transfer or assign any security deposit funds to the new owner (purchaser, lessee, assignee, mortgagee). When the owner notifies each resident affected by a transfer, the new owner assumes the obligations with respect to security deposits and is bound by law to perform. If a new owner comes into possession of a premises and has not in fact received the security deposit moneys, he or she would not be liable to the residents for the return of the security deposits unless otherwise agreed to in advance.

States have different rules governing the handling of security deposit funds. In Illinois, for example, security deposits for residential properties containing six or more units must be deposited in a bank or savings and loan association chartered by the state or a federal agency. Deposits are not subject to claims of creditors of the owner. Interest paid on the account is paid to the owner. This number of units may be reduced in future legislation; other states have no exemption.

Even if your state does not require it, security deposit money should be kept in a separate interest-bearing bank account instead of mingling it with your personal funds. Many states now require landlords to pay semi-annual interest to the tenant on the security deposit amount.

If owners fail to comply with a security deposit provision of their state statutes, residents can sue to recover the property or money due them, and in some cases can be awarded punitive damages and reasonable attorney's fees.

Restrictions on Use

Many leases contain specific rules and regulations that limit the use of a dwelling unit and the common areas of the apartment building. Common restrictions include prohibiting pets, water beds, and cooking on a barbecue; they often govern the use of air conditioners and the replacement of locks. These restrictions are legal in most cases; however, if there is an ambiguity in the meaning of the restriction, the language would be construed in favor of the tenant against the landlord.

Owners can adopt new rules or regulations concerning the resident's use and occupancy of the premises, but such new rules are generally enforceable against the resident only if they meet the following criteria:

- Their purpose must be to promote the convenience, safety, or welfare of all the residents on the premises; preserve the owner's property from abusive use; or make a fair distribution of services and facilities offered to residents in general.
- They must be reasonable in relation to the purpose for which they are adopted.
- They must apply to all residents on the premises in a fair manner.
- They must be sufficiently explicit in their prohibition, direction, or limitation to fairly inform the resident of what the resident must or must not do to comply.
- They are not for the purpose of evading the obligations of the owner.
- The resident must be notified of the rules and regulations at the time the resident enters into the rental agreement.

A rule or regulation incorporated after the resident enters into the rental agreement is enforceable against the resident only if reasonable notice of its adoption is given to the resident and it does not bring about a substantial reduction of the resident's value in renting the apartment.

For example, if someone rented an apartment in your property because you allowed them to keep a pet and you subsequently adopted a new rule outlawing pets, or if someone rented because your property had a swimming pool that was free and open until 10 PM and then you decided to charge a fee or reduce the hours the pool was open, these would be reductions in value to the tenant.

Riders and Additions to the Lease

The standard apartment rental agreement covers most but not all aspects of the landlord-tenant relationship. You may want to add clauses and riders to the document to cover such matters as garage rent, pets, agreements to extend or cut short the term of the lease, furniture rental, and so on. Clauses are typed onto the lease; riders are separate sheets that are attached to the lease.

Following are some commonly used riders and clauses.

Lead-Based Paint Disclosure Form

Housing built before 1978 may contain lead-based paint. Lead from paint, paint chips, and dust can pose health hazards if not managed properly. Lead exposure is especially harmful to young children and pregnant women. A federal law effective December 1996, affecting rental housing built before 1978, requires lessors to disclose the presence of known lead-based paint and/or lead-based paint hazards in the dwelling, before the lease takes effect. Lessees must also receive a federally approved pamphlet on preventing lead poisoning prevention.

The Environmental Protection Agency (EPA) pamphlets and disclosure form (Figure 4.5) must be attached to the lease and signed by the Lessor and the Lessee(s). They are available through your local EPA or health agency (see state phone numbers in Figure 4.6).

Security Deposit Agreement

This form (Figure 4.7) specifies the conditions under which a security deposit will be returned. It should be signed by all parties signing the lease and attached to the lease form. The second page lists charges for various repairs. You can modify the schedule and prices to suit your specific situation. The amount of the required security deposit should correspond with the amount indicated on the lease.

Garage and Vehicle Riders

If your property has carports, garages, or designated parking spaces available for rent and your resident elects to lease a space, you should execute a garage rider form (Figure 4.8). The form spells out the terms and conditions under which a space is rented.

If you want the garage rental term to coincide with the apartment lease, be sure the resident understands that the garage rental agreement applies to every month covered by the lease.

Pet Rider

If you allow pets on your property and a resident chooses to keep one, you can use a pet rider (Figure 4.9), which dictates the terms and con-

Figure 4.5: Lead-Based Paint Disclosure Form

CHICAGO ASSOCIATION OF REALTORS®/MLS

DISCLOSURE FORMAT FOR PRE-1978 HOUSING RENTAL AND LEASES
DISCLOSURE OF INFORMATION
LEAD-BASED PAINT AND/OR LEAD-BASED PAINT HAZARDS

Lead Warning Statement

Housing built before 1978 may contain lead-based paint. Lead from paint, paint chips, and dust can pose health hazards if not managed properly. Lead exposure is especially harmful to young children and pregnant women. Before renting pre-1978 housing, Lessors must disclose the presence of known lead-based paint and/or lead-based paint hazards in the dwelling. Lessees must also receive a federally approved pamphlet on lead poisoning prevention.

Lessor's Disclosure (initial)

_____(a)   Presence of lead-based paint and/or lead-based paint hazards (check one below):

☐   Known lead-based paint and/or lead-based paint hazards are present in the housing (explain):

_____

_____

☐   Lessor has no knowledge of lead-based paint and/or lead-based paint hazards in the housing.

_____(b)   Records and Reports available to the Lessor (check one below):

☐   Lessor has provided the Lessee with all available records and reports pertaining to lead-based paint and/or lead-based hazards in the housing (list documents below):

_____

_____

☐   Lessor has no reports or records pertaining to lead-based paint and/or lead-based paint hazards in the housing.

Lessee's Acknowledgement (initial) (All Lessees should initial)

_____(c)   Lessee has received copies of all information listed above.

_____(d)   Lessee has received the pamphlet *Protect Your Family From Lead in Your Home.*

Agent's Acknowledgement (initial) (Lessor's Agent)

_____(e)   Agent has informed the Lessor of the Lessor's obligations under 42 U.S.C. 4852 d and is aware of his/her/its responsibility to ensure compliance.

Certification of Accuracy

The following parties have reviewed the information above and certify, to the best of their knowledge, that the information they have provided is true and accurate.

Lessor _____ Date / /   Lessor _____ Date / /

Lessee _____ Date / /   Lessee _____ Date / /

Agent _____ Date / /   Agent _____ Date / /

Keep a fully executed copy of this document for three (3) years from the date hereof.

This Disclosure Form should be attached to the Lease.

[62796\bddoc\leadpnt2.dis]

Source: Chicago Association of REALTORS®. Used with permission.

Figure 4.6: State Health and Environmental Agencies

Some cities and states have their own laws for lead-based paint activities. Check with your state agency to see if state or local laws apply to you. Most state agencies also can provide information on finding a lead abatement firm in your area, and on possible sources of financial aid of reducing lead hazards.

State/Region	Phone Number	State/Region	Phone Number
Alabama	205-242-5661	Montana	406-444-3671
Alaska	907-465-5152	Nebraska	402-471-2451
Arkansas	501-661-2534	Nevada	702-687-6615
Arizona	602-542-7307	New Hampshire	603-271-4507
California	510-450-2424	New Jersey	609-633-2043
Colorado	303-692-3012	New Mexico	505-841-8024
Connecticut	203-566-5808	New York	800-458-1158
Washington, DC	202-727-9850	North Carolina	919-715-3293
Delaware	302-739-4735	North Dakota	701-328-5188
Florida	904-488-3385	Ohio	614-466-1450
Georgia	404-657-6514	Oklahoma	405-271-5220
Hawaii	808-832-5860	Oregon	503-248-5240
Idaho	208-332-5544	Pennsylvania	717-782-2884
Illinois	800-545-2200	Rhode Island	401-277-3424
Indiana	317-382-6662	South Carolina	803-935-7945
Iowa	800-972-2026	South Dakota	605-773-3153
Kansas	913-296-0189	Tennessee	615-741-5683
Kentucky	502-564-2154	Texas	512-834-6600
Louisiana	504-765-0219	Utah	801-536-4000
Massachusetts	800-532-9571	Vermont	802-863-7231
Maryland	410-631-3859	Virginia	800-523-4019
Maine	207-287-4311	Washington	206-753-2556
Michigan	517-335-8885	West Virginia	304-558-2981
Minnesota	612-627-5498	Wisconsin	608-266-5885
Mississippi	601-960-7463	Wyoming	307-777-7391
Missouri	314-526-4911		

ditions of maintaining pets on your property. It has become fairly common to require a pet deposit for each pet; some owners also charge a fixed monthly rent or other nonrefundable fees for pets. A pet rider can be executed and made a part of the lease at any time during the lease term.

As with all other riders, you should indicate the existence of this rider and record any deposit or rental amount on the face of the lease.

Condominium Apartment and Lease Rider

If you own investment condominiums you can use a special condominium lease or a condominium apartment lease rider (Figure 4.10) attached to a regular apartment lease. If you elect to use the rider, the word "condominium" should be typed on all copies of the lease, and the following statement should be typed in the special provisions section of the lease: "See rider to lease attached hereto and made a part thereof."

Many condominium associations have rules and special procedures with regard to renting apartments. Contacting the management office or association president will give you the information you need. Sometimes an association will require your tenant to sign additional forms and agreements, such as a separate agreement to abide by the condominium's specific rules and regulations. Some associations levy move-in fees, key deposits, and so on, and some owners pass these fees on to the tenant, making sure to collect the money before the tenant moves in. The larger associations usually have a manager who will add the fees to the assessment statement if they are not paid in advance.

You may elect to use a separate condominium unit apartment lease form (Figure 4.11) that has been specifically designed and written for condominiums. This document contains much of the language condominium associations require of their investor owners and contains enough blank space to add a clause that allows you to cancel the lease in the event you sell the unit to a buyer who wants to take possession and occupy the unit.

Indicate the rental amount and deposit in the spaces marked "other required rent" and "other required deposit" on the lease. If your lease does not contain this blank space, write the information on the top of the form. On the rider, indicate the deposit and the monthly rental amount.

The resident should also complete a vehicle information form (Figure 4.12), listing all pertinent information concerning the vehicles that will use the facility.

Lease Extension Agreement

When renewing a lease, you can do one of two things. One option is to present the resident with a brand-new lease, typed on a regular lease

Figure 4.7: Security Deposit Agreement

Security Deposit Agreement

Due from _____ (Lessee) $_____ Dollars
as Security Deposit for _____ (Address)
Apartment # _____ in _____, _____.
                                      City/Village   State

Release of Security Deposit is Subject to the Following Provisions

1. Full term of lease has expired and all provisions herein complied with.
2. Should lessee desire to RERENT (sublet or assign) under the provisions of the lease, a "one-half month's rent" service charge will be assessed.
   a. Approval must be obtained from lessor prior to initiating a rerent or sublet.
   b. Notice in writing must be given to management by certified mail prior to initiating a rerent or sublet.
3. For company transfers, comply with No. 2 above, with notice given on Company letterhead.
4. Entire apartment including range, oven, refrigerator, bathroom, closets, cabinets, windows, carpet, balcony, etc., cleaned.
5. No damage to apartment beyond normal wear and tear.
6. No unpaid late charges or delinquent rents.
7. Forwarding address left with management.
8. No indentations or scratches in wood or resilient floor caused by furniture or other means. Floor must be restored to the original condition if tack down or wall-to-wall carpeting was installed by lessee.
9. No wallcoverings, stickers, scratches, or large holes on walls.
10. All keys including those from mailboxes must be returned.
11. All debris, rubbish, and discards to be placed in proper rubbish containers in designated area.
12. All building-owned carpeting must be professionally cleaned.

IF THE PREREQUISITE CONDITIONS ARE NOT COMPLIED WITH, LESSEE WILL BE CHARGED THE CURRENT RATES LESSOR IS PAYING TO HAVE ITEMS REPAIRED AND/OR CLEANED.

The cost of labor and materials for cleaning, repairs, removals, and replacements, where applicable, or rent loss due to necessary repair time, and numerous other charges based on actual damages will be deducted from the security deposit. See reverse side for charges.

Lessor agrees that subject to the conditions listed above, this Security Deposit will be refunded in full.	Lessee agrees that this Security Deposit may NOT be applied as rent and is fully aware of the provision set forth on this agreement. Lessee further agrees that he will be present for final inspection of apartment.

By: _____

Date: _____

_____
Lessee

_____
Lessee

_____
Lessee

_____
_____
_____

Figure 4.7: Security Deposit Agreement, continued

Minimum Charges

Cleaning
1. Trash removal $10.00 per hour
2. Kitchen:

Stove		$25.00
Refrigerator		15.00
Cabinets and Countertops		15.00
Floor		15.00

3. Bathrooms (each)

Toilet		$5.00
Shower and Tub		20.00
Medicine Cabinet		5.00
Vanity		5.00
Floor		5.00

4. Closets   10.00
5. Windows   5.00
6. Floors

Vacuum		$5.00
Tile Cleaning	1 Bedroom	40.00
	2 Bedroom	50.00
Carpet Cleaning	1 Bedroom	35.00
	2 Bedroom	45.00

7. Excessive Cleaning $10.00 per hour

Decorating
1. Patching Holes: ½" to 2" $10.00 each
2. Double Coating   10.00 each wall
3. Removal of wall coverings   16.00 per hour

Maintenance
1. Materials plus labor at $16.00 per hour
2. Light bulb replacement   1.50 each

---

form. If you decide to use a new lease, you should type the words First Renewal, Second Renewal, and so on at the top of the form. This will remind you that your tenant has been in occupancy for longer than one year when it comes time to renew the following year.

Another option is to use a lease extension agreement (Figure 4.13) that can be used instead of a regular lease form. It also may be used for lease renewals for periods of less than a full year. Indicate the existence of this rider by making a notation on the original lease.

Refer to Chapter 6 for further information on the procedures to follow and the forms to use in executing renewals.

Figure 4.8: Garage Rider Form

BLDG. No. _____ UNIT No. _____

MID-AMERICA MANAGEMENT CORP.
2901 Butterfield Road
Oak Brook, Illinois 60521

GARAGE RIDER

THIS RIDER is hereby made a part of and incorporated as part of a certain lease agreement ("Lease") dated _____ , 19 _____ , for an apartment located at_____ in _____ ("Premises), by and between **MID-AMERICA MANAGEMENT CORP.** as Managing Agent ("Lessor") and _____

_____

_____ ("Lessee").

TO THE EXTENT OF ANY CONFLICT IN TERMS, THE TERMS AND CONDITIONS OF THIS RIDER SHALL GOVERN OVER THE TERMS AND CONDITIONS OF THE AFORESAID LEASE.

In consideration of the deposit of the sum of _____ ($_____) DOLLARS to be paid by Lessee to Lessor upon the execution hereof, the parties hereto agree to the following:

1. Lessor shall permit Lessee to use _____ parking space(s) designated as space number(s) _____ at the Premises for the term of the Lease.

2. Lessee agrees to maintain the space(s) in a clean and sanitary condition at all times.

3. Lessee agrees to utilize the space(s) only for the purpose of parking the assigned vehicle(s).

4. Lessee agrees to remove any vehicle deemed unsightly or in non-working condition by Lessor within five (5) days of notification.

5. Lessee agrees that in the event of any violation of the terms and conditions set forth above, the Lessor shall have the right to make a demand for immediate possession of said space(s). Any refusal by Lessee to comply with such demand by Lessor to return said space(s) shall be material breach of the Lease, and Lessor shall be entitled to retain aforementioned deposit as well as be entitled to any and all other remedies provided by law or equity. However, if Lessee returns said space(s) upon such demand, the deposit shall be returned less damages, if any, caused by violation hereof and said Lease shall continue in effect, except that this rider shall be deemed null and void.

IN WITNESS WHEREOF, the Lessor and Lessee have executed this document on the _____ day of _____ , 19 _____ .

MID-AMERICA MANAGEMENT CORP.
Managing Agent

By:_____
              Agent

_____
LESSEE

_____
LESSEE

$ _____ is required deposit for each garage transmitter.

$ _____ is the required monthly rental amount.

4307 / 3-93

Figure 4.9: Pet Agreement

PET AGREEMENT

In the event of a violation of any of the following terms and conditions, the owner/management shall have the right to immediately cancel this agreement and require the pet owner/tenant to immediately remove the pet from the premises. Cancellation of this agreement will not imply a waiver of the tenant's responsibility for any damages.

ELMWOOD VILLAGE APARTMENTS
472 NORTH SPRUCE AVENUE
ATLANTA, GEORGIA 30324
(404) 351-2070

Tenant's Name _____ Address _____

Owner/Management agrees to waive the pet restrictions of the rental agreement/lease provided that the tenant and pet owner agree to and meet the following terms and conditions:

1. Only the pet/pets listed and described below are authorized under this pet agreement. Additional or other pets must be approved by the owner/management.

2. Pet/pets will not cause: danger, damage, nuisance, noise, health hazard, or soil the apartment/unit, premises, grounds, common areas, walks, parking areas, landscaping or gardens. Tenant agrees to clean up after the pet and agrees to accept full responsibility and liability for any damage, injury, or actions arising from or caused by his/her pets.

3. Tenant agrees to register the pet/pets in accordance with local laws and requirements. Tenant agrees to immunize the pet/pets in accordance with local laws and requirements.

4. Tenant warrants that the pet/pets is housebroken. Tenant warrants that the pet/pets has no history of causing physical harm to persons or property, such as biting, scratching, chewing, etc., and further warrants that the pet/pets has no vicious history or tendencies.

5. The tenant agrees to observe the following regulations:

Dogs and Cats: Must be controlled at all times. Must be kept on a short leash while in common areas or on the grounds. Barking will not be tolerated in that it is considered to be a nuisance to other tenants. Proper disposal of cat litter (securely bagged) will be done on a frequent basis. Odors arising from cat litter will not be tolerated.

Birds: Birds will be properly caged. Seeds and droppings will be shielded or caught to prevent accumulation and/or damage to carpeting/floors.

Fish: Aquariums will not leak and will be cleaned regularly to prevent foul water and/or odors.

Other Terms: _____
_____
_____

Pet Description:

Kind	Type or Breed:	Color	Name	Age	Weight

Pet Fee/Deposit:

Tenant agrees to pay the following non-refundable pet fee... $_____
Tenant agrees to pay the following pet deposit.. $_____
Other.. $_____

NOTICE: ANY FEE OR DEPOSIT ABOVE SHALL NOT LIMIT THE TENANT'S OBLIGATION

TOTAL $_____

Date _____ _____ _____
Owner/Management Signature   Tenant Signature

Source: Peachtree Business Products. Used with permission. (To order this form or a catalog, call 800-241-4623.)

Lease Cancellation Rider

A lease cancellation rider (Figure 4.15) is a useful form that can be offered to new or renewal residents who are not able to fully complete their lease term. For complete details on terminating or canceling a lease, see Chapter 7. An owner may agree to this rider because the resident has an upcoming job transfer or is in the market to purchase a home. It is not intended for use when the tenant requests to break a lease during the

Figure 4.10: Condominium Apartment Lease Rider

RIDER TO
CONDOMINIUM APARTMENT LEASE

THIS RIDER is made this_____day of_____, 19____, and is incorporated into and shall be deemed to amend and supplement that certain Condominium Apartment Lease dated of even date herewith ("Lease") between _____

_____("Lessor") and_____

_____("Lessee"),

demising the condominium apartment described as Unit No._____at_____

_____("Premises").

CONDOMINIUM COVENANTS: In addition to the covenants, conditions and agreements made in the Lease, Lessor and Lessee further covenant and agree as follows:

Lessee shall abide by all covenants and restrictions (excepting the requirement to pay monthly condominium common expense assessments) running with the title to the Premises contained in the declaration of condominium for the Condominium ("Declaration"), and the by-laws ("By-Laws") thereto, as amended, together with all rules and regulations promulgated from time to time by the unit owners' association ("Association") responsible for the overall administration of the Condominium property of which the Premises are a part.

In addition to all the rights and remedies contained in the Lease, Lessee shall be subject to all of the rights and remedies of the Association for breach of any covenants or restrictions contained in the Declaration, By-Laws, or rules and regulations of the Association from time to time, and Lessee agrees to indemnify and hold Lessor harmless from any damages, costs, expenses or attorney's fees incurred by Lessor, or any fines, penalties, or assessments levied against the Premises by the Association in connection with Lessee's use of the same, any such amount being payable by Lessee upon demand by Lessor as additional rent under the Lease. Failure to abide by any covenant or restriction contained in the Declaration, by any By-Law, or rules or regulations of the Association shall constitute a material breach of the Lease, and such default shall entitle Lessor to exercise any and all remedies as set forth in the Lease.

Lessee agrees to park in only such parking space or spaces as are designated in the Lease, if any, and that the use of the same shall be subject to the terms and provisions of the Declaration, By-Laws and rules and regulations of the Association from time to time.

In the event the Declaration and/or By-Laws contain any "right of first refusal" or "right of first option" providing that the Association shall have the first right or option to lease the Premises under the same terms and provisions contained in the Lease (notwithstanding Lessee's execution of the same), then Lessee agrees that (i) the terms and provisions of the Lease shall be subject to the Association's "right of first refusal" or "right of first option", (ii) that Lessor shall be under no obligation to cause the termination or waiver of such "right of first refusal" or "right of first option", and (iii) in the event that the Association elects to exercise any such "right of first refusal" or "right of first option", Lessor shall not be responsible for any costs, damages or expenses to Lessee, whether direct or indirect, resulting therefrom.

Lessee acknowledges that, under the Declaration, the responsibility for the maintenance and repair of certain portions of the Condominium and for the provision of certain services Lessee may expect to enjoy is the responsibility of the Association and not of Lessor. Accordingly, Lessor shall have no obligation to provide, maintain, or repair those facilities and services under the control of and the responsibility for which lies with the Association.

Lessee shall promptly forward to Lessor any notice received by Lessee from the Association or relating to Association meetings or business or complaints about Lessee's or Lessor's actions or omissions.

_____   LESSOR
(Lessee)

_____   By:_____
(Lessee)

_____
(Lessee)

DATE:_____, 19____   DATE:_____, 19____

Figure 4.11: Condominium Unit Apartment Lease

UNIT LEASE

1. PARTIES

LANDLORD ("I") _____

Tel: _____

TENANT ("YOU") _____

2. AGREEMENT TO LEASE: PROPERTY DESCRIPTION

I, as Landlord, lease to you, _____, as Tenant, Unit No. _____ and Garage Unit No. _____ in [PROJ], [Town], [State] (called the "Unit"). The building and the land on which the building is located known as [PROJ] will be called the "Common Interest Community." The portion outside the Unit including sidewalks, entrances, and passages will be called the "Common Elements." You are also being leased the ownership interest of the Unit in the Common Elements. This lease includes responsibilities toward [ASSN], the association of Unit Owners of [PROJ] ("Association").

3. TERM OF LEASE

The term of this Lease is _____. The term begins on _____ and ends at 12:00 noon on _____.

4. RENT

You agree to pay me the total rent of _____. Rent is due in advance in monthly installments of _____, on the first day of each month, starting _____.
The first month's rent is paid upon signing this lease. I will not have to make a demand or send you a bill for payment of rent. If I elect to send rent bills, they will be for convenience only and not a condition of your payment. Payments must be sent to _____
unless I notify you otherwise in writing. You will directly pay to the Association as additional rent, any increase in monthly Common Expense Assessments assessed by the Association against the Unit, above the monthly Common Expense Assessments presently assessed, mending all times late charges. Attorney fees and costs and charges attributed to your tenancy or your default in your obligations under this lease. Also, if this lease, or any options to extend this lease, are for over a year, you will pay as increased monthly rent, one-twelfth of the increase in taxes, insurance and interest payment on my mortgage attributable to the Unit, over those expenses which are currently paid by the Landlord. You will also pay one fifth of any special assessment for capital improvements levied by the association for budget shortfalls or expense items. You will also pay, as additional rent, the cost of electricity billed to the unit, when such bill is sent to you.

5. SECURITY DEPOSIT

You agree to pay me a security deposit of _____ on or before _____. The security deposit will be held in escrow. It will be returned to you, with interest as required by law, if you fully perform your promises in this Lease. If you breach this Lease, I may apply the security deposit to offset all or part of my damages. The security deposit is not a payment of rent. If I spend some or all of the security deposit for any legal purpose attributable to your tenancy during the term of this Lease, then you will restore it to the full amount on demand.

If I sell the Unit to a new owner, I may assign your security deposit to the new owner. If the security deposit is assigned, I will have no further liability to you with respect to the security deposit.

6. UTILITIES, SERVICES AND FURNISHINGS

I will provide the following through the Association:

(a) Hot and cold water in reasonable quantities;

(b) Heat at reasonable hours during cold seasons of the year;

(c) Elevator service;

(d) Electricity in reasonable quantities; and

(e) Air conditioning during warm seasons of the year by through-the-window air conditioner.

The Unit includes a master television antenna and window shades. Either carpeting or hardwood flooring also will be furnished. I will not be required to provide utilities and services during any period when you are in default in payment of rent.

7. ABUSE OF UTILITIES AND SERVICES

You agree not to abuse the use of utilities and services provided by the Common Interest Community. If I or the Association believe you are abusing the utilities and/or services, then I may separately meter such utilities and services and charge you for excess use. The charge will be based on your excess use over the average consumed by all units in the Common Interest Community. The Association will compute any such charge.

8. YOUR RIGHT TO TERMINATE THIS LEASE IF TRANSFERRED OR DRAFTED

You may terminate this Lease if you are involuntarily activated into the armed forces or if your employer transfers you to a site more than 50 miles away. In order to terminate, you must do the following:

(a) Give me written notice of intent to terminate and of the date of termination, which will be not fewer than 2 months after the next rent payment is due following receipt of the notice;

(b) Give me written proof of transfer or involuntary activation; and

(c) Pay rent in full to the date of termination.

9. INSURANCE

If my cost for insurance coverage on the Unit, or the Association's coverage is increased as a result of your occupancy of the Unit and I receive an assessment for such increase, then I may do either of the following:

(a) I may terminate this lease by giving you 30 days' written notice; or

(b) I may charge my increased cost to you as additional rent.

You will pay such charge on demand.

You will be responsible for obtaining your own insurance coverage, including insurance against the risks described in Section 15.

10. BREACH OF THIS LEASE BY YOU

If you vacate the Unit or do not pay any installment of rent within 10 days after it is due, then I may take any of the following actions:

(a) I may sue you for damages; and/or

(b) I may terminate the lease immediately by giving you written notice of termination; and/or

(c) I may take any other action against you that I may legally take. Such action can include bringing a summary process lawsuit against you to have you evicted.

If you do not perform any other agreement in this Lease, then I may give you a written notice describing how you have breached the Lease and giving you 21 days from the date when you receive the notice during which you must cure the breach. If you do not cure the breach within 21 days, then I may take any of the following actions:

(a) I may sue you for damages; and/or

(b) If the notice so states, I may terminate this Lease 30 days after your receipt of the notice; and/or

(c) I may take any other action against you that I may legally take. Such action can include bringing a summary process lawsuit to have you evicted.

Nothing in this Section will limit my statutory remedies for breach of this Lease.

11. COMMON INTEREST COMMUNITY PROVISIONS

I assign to you my rights, and privileges associated with my ownership of a Unit. You assume, and agree to undertake, the duties and obligations of a Unit Owner. These are described in the Declaration Bylaws, Rules and associated documents for the Common Interest Community ("Common Interest Community Instruments").

However, I exclusively retain the right to vote, to affect my ownership interest, to hold office and receive insurance and other awards and proceeds.

You must communicate with the Association through me, and you must notify me whenever you receive any communication from the Association.

You will hold me harmless for any of your acts or omissions of any kind that adversely affect me under the Common Interest Community Instruments.

Default of any requirement under the Common Interest Community Instruments is a default of this Lease.

You acknowledge receipt of a copy of the Common Interest Community Instruments, which you have examined to the extent you desire—in particular, the Rules attached as an Exhibit to the Public Offering Statement. You also understand that the Association can take enforcement action directly against you for the breach of the Common Interest Community Instruments (as if it were the landlord) and that it may levy fines and other penalties.

12. COSTS; ATTORNEY'S FEES

You promise to pay all of my costs of correcting any breach of this Lease by you. If I sue you to enforce my rights under this Lease, then you will pay all of my costs of suit, including attorney's fees to the extent permitted by law.

Figure 4.11: Condominium Unit Apartment Lease, continued

13. OCCUPANCY

This Lease is contingent on the Unit being ready for occupancy by you on the starting date of the term. If it is not ready and I do not give you possession on that date, then the following will result:

(a) The starting date of the term of this Lease will be postponed until possession can be given; and

(b) I will not be liable for any damage incurred by you as a result of such delay; and

(c) The ending date of the term of this Lease will not be extended; and

(d) Your liability for rent will start on the date when I notify you that the Unit is ready for occupancy; and

(e) If occupancy is delayed more than 60 days, you will have the option to cancel this Lease by giving written notice to me.

If you do not take possession of the Unit when possession is offered, or if you vacate or abandon the Unit during the term of this Lease, then I may do the following:

(a) I may enter the Unit as your agent, without a court order and without liability to you;

(b) I may lease the Unit to another tenant, for any term, as your agent; and

(c) I may collect the rent and apply it to your rent and other sums due under this lease.

In such a case, you will be liable for any damages suffered by me. The Unit will be deemed abandoned when you vacate, regardless of whether keys are delivered to me.

14. COMMON ELEMENTS

The Common Elements are provided to accommodate you and the other occupants of the Common Interest Community. To the extent permitted by law, you use those areas solely at your risk. To the extent permitted by law, neither I nor the Association will be liable for any damage, injury or loss of property occurring in the Common Elements, unless caused by our gross negligence.

15. INJURY OR DAMAGE

To the extent permitted by law, neither I nor the Association will be liable for injury or damage to persons or property resulting from risks against which you can insure under an all-risk, extended coverage, comprehensive property insurance policy, including sprinkler leakage insurance.

To the extent permitted by law, neither I nor the Association will be liable for injury or damage resulting from falling plaster or from steam, gas, electricity, water, rain, ice or snow that may leak or flow from or into the Common Interest Community or Unit. To the extent permitted by law, neither I nor the Association will be liable for injury or damage resulting from breakage, leakage, obstruction, or other defects in the pipes, wiring, appliances, plumbing or lighting fixtures in the Common Interest Community, nor resulting from any other cause, unless due to our gross negligence.

You promise to give me and the Association prompt notice of any accident to or defects in the water pipes, gas pipes, heating apparatus, or other equipment or appliances in the Unit.

To the extent permitted by law, neither I nor the Association will be liable for any latent defect in the Common Interest Community, any package left with any of the Association's employees, or any loss by theft or otherwise. Neither I nor the Association will be liable for the acts of the other occupants or for the acts of our employees during the course of work contracted for by you with such employees.

16. RIGHT TO ENTER THE UNIT

I and the Association may enter the Unit without your consent in case of emergency.

We may enter the Unit with your consent at reasonable times after giving you reasonable oral or written notice. Such entries may be made to inspect the Unit, to make necessary or agreed-to repairs, alterations, or improvements, to supply necessary or agreed-to services. I may also enter to show the Unit to interested people. "Interested people" include prospective or actual purchasers, mortgage lenders, tenants, workmen or contractors. You will not unreasonably withhold your consent to such entries.

I and the Association will have all other rights to enter the Unit as may be provided by law.

We will not be responsible for any damage from such entries, except damage caused by our own negligence.

17. REDUCTION OR ABATEMENT OF RENT; INTERRUPTION OF SERVICES

You also will not be entitled to any reduction or abatement of rent or other compensation when services or utilities are interrupted by causes beyond my control or by repairs, alterations or improvements to the Common Interest Community. Such interruptions will not be considered constructive evictions.

18. DAMAGE CAUSED BY YOU

You are liable to me and the Association for any damage sustained by us, or the Unit Owners and caused by you or your guests, family, agents, or employees. I will charge such damage to you as additional rent, which will be due on demand.

19. TERMINATION OF LEASE

You will vacate and surrender the Unit promptly at the end of the term or on the earlier termination of this Lease. You will leave the Unit in good condition, broom clean, reasonable wear and tear excepted. You will repair any damages caused by you, restoring the Unit to its condition at the starting date of this Lease. You will clean, scrub, and polish all fixtures, appliances, and apartment surfaces prior to surrender. If you delay in surrendering the Unit, you will indemnify me against any damages resulting from such daily delay. Such damages may include claims by a succeeding tenant against me based on delay in delivering possession.

20. DAMAGE TO COMMON INTEREST COMMUNITY

If the Common Interest Community is damaged by fire or other cause, where applicable, the Association will repair the Common Elements, and that portion of the Unit that it must insure, to the extent of insurance, pursuant to the Common Interest Community Instruments. I will repair the damage on that portion of the Unit that I must insure as quickly as is reasonably possible after receipt of notice of the damage. You will notify both me and the Association of any such damage. The time for making repairs will be extended by any time lost due to adjustment of insurance claims, labor disputes, or causes beyond control.

If the damage is so extensive as to render the Unit untenantable, then you will not be required to pay rent from the time of the damage until the Unit has been restored to a tenantable condition.

If the Common Interest Community suffers substantially total destruction, or if the damage cannot be repaired within 90 days, or if the Association decides to remodel or reconstruct the Common Interest Community, then this Lease will terminate as of the date of the destruction. You will have no duty to pay rent after such destruction. Any rent paid for a period after the destruction will be refunded. In such event, you will promptly vacate the Unit. You will remain liable for any damage caused by you or by your family, guests, agents, or employees.

21. EMINENT DOMAIN

If any part of the Common Interest Community is taken by eminent domain, then I will have the option of terminating this Lease. In order to terminate, I must give you 10 days' written notice of termination. If I elect to terminate this Lease, you will be liable for rent up to the time of termination.

You will have no claim to any awards for or taking by eminent domain. You hereby assign all such awards to me.

22. ASSIGNMENT, SUBLET

You will not assign this Lease, sublet, or permit occupancy of any portion of the Unit by anyone other than you, without my prior written consent, which I may withhold in my absolute discretion.

23. RENT COLLECTION

If I accept a partial payment of rent, it will not constitute a waiver of my right to full payment. No endorsement on a check or letter accompanying a partial payment of rent will be a waiver of my right to full payment or will be an accord and satisfaction.

If rent is not paid or postmarked by the 5th day of the month, a late charge of $15.00 per month will be added. You will pay such late charge promptly, without my having to make a demand.

If this Lease is assigned or sublet, or if the Unit is occupied by anyone other than you, I may collect rent from such other occupant. Acceptance of rent will not be a waiver of your promise not to assign, sublet, or permit occupancy. Nor will acceptance of rent be acceptance of the other occupant as tenant. You will remain personally liable for all promises in this Lease, regardless of any assignment, sublease, or other occupancy.

24. TRANSFER BY LANDLORD

Whenever any third party succeeds to my rights under this Lease, I will be released from my obligations under this Lease. Your only remedy for any subsequent violation of my promises in this Lease will be against the third party. The terms of this Section will apply whether or not the third party has assumed my duties under this Lease.

25. SUBORDINATION

This Lease is subordinate to all existing mortgages, of the Unit and the Common Interest Community and to any mortgages of the Unit or the Common Interest Community in the future. You will not have to sign any documents to make this Lease subordinate to those mortgages. However, if any of my mortgage lenders so request, you will sign such a document. You hereby irrevocably appoint me your attorney-in-fact to sign and deliver any such documents.

26. CONTINUING POSSESSION

If you do not vacate the Unit when this Lease expires and if you remain in possession with my consent or acquiescence, then your occupancy will be a two-month-to-two-month tenancy under the terms of this Lease.

I may notify you at least 45 days before this Lease expires that I intend to extend this lease for an additional period of time equal to the original term of this Lease. Any such extension must be on the same terms as this Lease, except that I may increase the rent.

If you receive such a notice and *do not want* to extend this Lease under those terms, you may give me notice of your intent to leave. You must deliver that notice to me at least 30 days before the expiration of this Lease. You also must vacate the Unit by the time when the Lease expires. This Lease will be extended automatically if you do not give the required notice and vacate.

If you receive such a notice, and you *want* to stay in the Unit under those terms you do not have to take any action. This Lease will be extended automatically.

27. WAIVER

If either party does not insist on strict performance of the promises in this Lease, it is not a waiver. Either party may insist on strict performance if the Lease is breached in the same manner again.

Figure 4.11: Condominium Unit Apartment Lease, continued

---

28. MODIFICATIONS
Any modifications of this Lease must be in writing, signed by me and by you.

29. ENTIRE AGREEMENT
This Lease is the entire agreement between me and you. It supersedes all previous discussions or agreements, whether written or oral, execpt as described in Section 30.

30. LEASE APPLICATION
Your lease application is made a part of this Lease. If your application contains any material misrepresentations, it will be a breach of this Lease by you.

31. NOTICES
Notices must be in writing and must be mailed or hand delivered to me or to you at the addresses shown in Section 1 and to you at your Unit.

32. ALTERATIONS
You will make no alterations, additions or improvements to the Unit without my prior, written approval. If such alterations are those requiring approval, you must also receive that approval, which must be requested through me. If approved, you will use only contractors or mechanics acceptable to me. I and the Association must also approve the time and manner of performing the work. You will keep the Unit free of mechanics' liens resulting from the work. You will promptly remove any such liens that attach to the Unit.

Any alterations or improvements that are attached to the building or grounds so that they cannot be removed without injury to the building or grounds will be my property.

33. SEVERABILITY
If any portion of this Lease is found to be void, unenforceable, or against public policy, the remaining portions of this Lease will not be affected.

34. RULES
You will comply with the following rules and the rules of the Association. These rules may be modified or supplemented by me or the Association from time to time. Any new or modified rules will not substantially alter the terms of this Lease. You will be notified in writing of any changes in the rules.

   (a) You will not post any sign of any kind on the Unit.

   (b) No sign indicating commercial uses may be displayed outside a Unit.

   (c) You will not attach any awnings or other projections to the outside of the Unit. You will not install any blinds, shades, screens, or drapes, except drapes having a beige lining, without my prior written consent.

   (d) You will receive two keys to the Unit. Additional keys will be furnished at a charge of $2.00 each.

   (e) I, the Executive Board, and the Manager or its designated agent may retain a pass key to the Unit for immediate entry in emergency situations and entry for general repair purposes on 12 hour notice. No new locks may be installed and no locks may be altered without my consent. If consent is given, you will provide me, the Executive Board, and the Manager or its designated agent with all keys necessary to gain access to the Unit.

   (f) If you require the loan of a duplicate key from the Association, there may be a charge. The charge is payable to the employee giving you entrance.

   (g) No lessee will alter any lock or install a new lock on any door of any premises without immediately providing the Executive Board and the Manager or its agent, with a key therefor.

   (h) Employees of the Association will not be sent on errands off the property by a tenant, at any time, for any purpose.

   (i) Nothing will be allowed to fall from windows or doors. Nothing will be swept or thrown into the Common Elements, ventilators or other areas.

   (j) Nothing will be hung from windows or doors.

   (k) No air conditioning or appliance installation, telephone extension, or exterior radio or television antenna installation will be made without my prior, written consent. Any attachment to the outside of the building without the Association's consent may be removed by me or the Association. When consent is granted, you will pay the cost of installation.

   (l) You and your visitors, agents, employees, and family members may park only in the area, if any, assigned to your Unit. You will abide by the Parking Rules established by the Association.

   (m) Each Unit is restricted to residential use as a single-family residence including home professional pursuits not requiring regular visits from the public or unreasonable levels of mail, shipping, trash or storage requirements. A single-family residence is defined as a single housekeeping Unit, operating between its occupants on a nonprofit, noncommercial basis, cooking and eating with a common kitchen and dining area, with not more regular overnight occupants than two per bedroom as designated on the plans on file with the building official of [Town] or by local ordinance.

   (n) Roomers and boarders paying consideration for their tenancy are prohibited.

   (o) Rent will be paid at the address above, by mail or in person. Checks will be payable to me.

   (p) The garbage disposal will be used only for food waste.

   (q) Any changes in your family size or composition must be reported to me.

   (r) I will provide light bulbs at the start of the Lease. You will replace all light bulbs that burn out during the term of this Lease.

   (s) Any packages, keys, money, or other property left by you with any employee of the Association are left at your risk.

   (t) Nothing will be fastened to any part of the Unit or the Common Elements. No holes will be drilled or nails or screws inserted in any structure, and no interior surfaces will be decorated or covered, without my prior, written consent.

   (u) You will not run any exposed wires for electrical appliances or fixtures.

   (v) Toilets, sinks, faucets, and other water equipment will be used only for the purposes for which they are intended. No improper articles may be thrown into them. No faucets will be left open. Damage caused by the misuse of water equipment will be borne by you, if it is caused by you or occurs in the Unit.

   (w) Carpeting will be cared for in accordance with my instructions.

   (x) All noises, including music, television and radio, will be held to reasonable levels. During the time from 11:00 p.m. to 7:00 a.m., no noises will be audible outside of the Unit.

   (y) You must not place doormats or other obstructions at the Unit entrance.

   (z) All exterior Unit doors must be kept closed. Sliding windows and glass doors will be kept closed when the Unit is unoccupied.

   (aa) You must exercise diligence to conserve heat, air conditioning, electricity, and water.

   (bb) You must comply with all government laws and regulations, whether federal, state, or municipal, and the Association rules, that impose on you the duty of compliance. You will indemnify me against any damage or fines resulting from your violation of any such laws and regulations.

   (cc) Nothing may be done or kept in any Unit which will increase the rate of insurance of the buildings or the contents thereof beyond the rates applicable for residential apartments without prior written consent of the Executive Board. No Unit owner may permit anything to be done or kept in his Unit which will result in the cancellation of insurance on any of the buildings or the contents thereof or which would be in violation of any law. You will comply with the rules and regulations contained in any fire insurance policy, Association or landlord policy affecting the Unit.

   (dd) No electrical appliances may be used in the Unit except those that may be connected or disconnected by a standard floor or wall plug. No washers or dryers may be installed or used in the Unit, except where outlets and vents are located.

   (ee) No dogs, cats or other pets will be kept in the Unit without my prior, written consent, and the consent of the Association. Seeing eye dogs will be permitted for those persons holding certificates of blindness and necessity (20/200 in the better with correction).

   (ff) Pets may not be kept, bred or maintained for any commercial purposes.

   (gg) Any pet causing or creating a nuisance or unreasonable disturbance or noise will be permanently removed from the Property upon three (3) days' written Notice and Hearing from the Executive Board.

   (hh) No knockers may be installed on any doors.

   (ii) No noxious of offensive activities may be carried on in any Unit nor may anything be done therein either willfully or negligently which may be or become an annoyance or nuisance to the other Unit Owners or occupants or which interferes with the peaceful possession and proper use of the property by its residents. All valid laws, zoning ordinances and regulations of all governmental bodies having jurisdiction thereof will be observed. Each Lessee will be obligated to maintain his/her own Unit and keep it in good order and repair.

   (jj) Each Unit may have closets, safes or vaults not exceeding 50 cubic feet in capacity which may be locked and to which the Executive Board may not have access.

   (kk) No sprinkler head will be tampered with, painted, blocked, enclosed or otherwise interfered with so as to hinder its efficiency or purpose, nor may anything be hung from it.

   (ll) Weathertight integrity of windows and doors will be maintained by the Unit Owner and/or Lessee.

   (mm) Lessees will not cause or permit anything to be hung or displayed on the windows or placed on the outside walls of any of the buildings and no sign, awning, canopy, shutter or radio or television antenna will be affixed to or placed upon the exterior walls or roofs without the prior consent of the Executive Board, nor will they cause or permit anything to be hung or displayed on the inside of windows intended to be seen from the outside except for the standard blinds and draperies described below, as follows, including without limiting the foregoing, "For Sale" or "For Lease" signs and the like.

   (nn) A smoke detector must be installed, and operative, in every Unit.

   (oo) In the event any sales or service tax is imposed upon a Unit which is not owner-occupied or which is otherwise not imposed equally on all Unit Owners, the landlord or other Unit Owner will pay such tax through the Association as an additional Common Expense assessment. The Association may require certificates of status from Unit Owners in order to enforce and determine applicability of such impositions.

   (pp) The use of Common Elements is subject to the Bylaws and the Rules of the Association.

   (qq) Heat must be maintained in each Unit to at least _____°F at all times so as to maintain the integrity of the sprinkler system and to prevent freezing of lines or components.

Figure 4.11: Condominium Unit Apartment Lease, continued

(rr) Unit Owners or Lessees are advised to clean the air filters of their air conditioning and heat pump system at least 4 times per year to minimize operating costs and reduce risk of equipment failure.

(ss) No lease may be for a period of less than 60 days.

(tt) Utility charges through separate meters, community antenna T.V. and telephone charges will be paid directly by the Unit Owner and/or Lessee to the utility providing such service.

(uu) Washer hookups are provided in the Unit. Dryer connections and vents are provided; however, some dryer vent stacks may be long and require adequate fan pressure to get rid of the exhaust. Vents and stacks will have to be cleaned by the Lessee contributing to the lint build-up.

(vv) Trash removal is by dumpster at various locations in the premises. Each Lessee is responsible for removal of trash to the dumpster location. In the future, trash may have to be separated and segregated by type. This will be the occupant's responsibility.

(ww) Heat is by heat pump, with roof compressors maintained by the Unit Owner or Lessee and normal maintenance, major repairs or component replacement is at the cost of the appurtenant Unit Owner. Heat pumps are efficient down to air temperature in the twenties F°, at which point resistance heat is used to supplement the heat pump. Resistance heat is very expensive, and occupants should be judicious in maintaining high inside temperatures, open windows or other heat leaks or the cost may go up significantly. The Unit Owner is responsible for his or her own maintenance fees.

(xx) Except pursuant to Article _____ of the Declaration, nothing may be done to any Unit which will impair the structural integrity of the building or buildings or which will structurally change them. No Lessee may do any work which may jeopardize the soundness or safety of the property, reduce the value thereof or impair any easements, right of purchase or any interest constituting a Common Element.

35. SPECIAL TERMS
Special terms of this Lease, if any, are as follows:

_____
_____
_____
_____
_____

36. BINDING EFFECT
This Lease is binding on you and me and on our respective heirs, successors, executors, and administrators.

This Lease will be placed on file with the Association at its office or agent's office located _____

Dated, this _____ day of _____, 19_____.

WITNESS: LANDLORD:

_____

                                                               By: _____
                                                                   Its

_____

TENANT:

_____   _____

_____   _____

   I hereby acknowledge receipt of, and acceptance of compliance with, the Declaration, survey and plans recorded and filed pursuant to the provisions of the Common Interest Ownership Act, Bylaws, and Rules of the Common Interest Community, and to attorn to the Association as Landlord, granting it severally with the Unit Owner, the right following notice to the Unit Owner of a hearing and an opportunity to cure, to evict a tenant for violation of these documents in the name of, and as attorney-in-fact for the Unit Owner.

                                                               BY:

                                                               _____
                                                               Lessee

                                                               _____
                                                               Date

YOUR STATEMENT AS TO PHYSICAL CONDITION AND REPAIR

   You agree that you have examined the Unit and the Common Interest Community, and that you are satisfied with their condition. You agree that you have received them in good order and repair except as otherwise stated in this Lease. You agree that neither I nor the Association have made any representation as to condition or repair and no promise to decorate, alter, repair or improve the Unit except as otherwise stated in this Lease.

                                                               TENANT:

Date: _____   _____

                                                               _____

                                                               _____

Source: © Copyright 1988—Gurdon Buck, One Commercial Plaza, Hartford, CT 06103-3597; 203-275-8200.

Figure 4.12: Vehicle Information Form

Dear Resident:

Please complete the form below concerning your automobile. This information will allow us to update our records for the purpose of contacting you in the case of an emergency.

If you should change your home or business telephone number or purchase a different vehicle please remember to supply us with any new information.

I thank you in advance for this pertinent information that will enable us to become more efficient in managing this complex for the overall benefit of all our residents.

License Plate # _____ State _____

Make of Car _____ Color _____ Model _____

Owner's Name _____

Building Address _____ Apt. # _____

Home Telephone _____ Business _____

Garage Space # _____

License Plate # _____ State _____

Make of Car _____ Color _____ Model _____

Owner's Name _____

Building Address _____ Apt. # _____

Home Telephone _____ Business _____

Garage Space # _____

middle of a lease term. If tenants want to cancel their leases in mid-term, a different form can be used (Figure 4.16).

Prospective tenants may ask to have a transfer clause written into the lease that would suit the same purpose of breaking a lease term early, but it is better to use the cancellation rider instead because it clearly spells out the conditions and procedures a tenant must follow to invoke it, i.e., tenants must give 60 days' notice, must not be in default of the lease, must be current in their rent, and must pay a cancellation fee (the usual amount is one to two months' rent). The fee is payable in advance at the time the residents decide to exercise their right to cancel. As with all riders, a notation should be made on the original lease that a cancellation rider exists.

Figure 4.13: Lease Extension Agreement

This agreement made this day of 19____ by and

between (Lessor) _____

and (Lessee[s]). _____

Witnesseth _____

Whereas, Lessor and Lessee have entered into a certain lease agreement dated 19____ for the rental of a certain apartment, number _____ located at _____

Whereas, Lessor and Lessee desire to extend the duration of said Lease;

Now therefore, for value received, receipt of which is hereby acknowledged by Lessor, the parties agree as follows:

1. The termination date of said Lease is hereby extended from _____ to and
   including _____.
                                  Date   Date

2. The monthly rental amount during the aforesaid extension period will be $ _____.

3. Except as modified hereby, the terms and conditions of aforesaid Lease are hereby confirmed and ratified and made a part of this agreement and said Lease shall remain in full force and effect.

In witness whereof, this agreement has been duly executed by the parties hereto on the day and year first above written.

Lessor _____
                                                                           Date

Lessee _____
                                                                             Date

Furniture Rental Rider

If you rent your units as furnished apartments, you can attach a furniture rental rider (Figure 4.17) to your lease forms. This document spells out the terms and conditions under which a tenant accepts the apartment as a furnished unit.

Any additional rents and/or security deposit moneys should be indicated on the original lease in the space provided. On the rider, you would indicate the quantity of each item listed along with any additional items not printed on the form.

Before the tenant moves in, you, together with the tenant, should inspect the furnishings and create a written record of damaged items (a camera can be used to document the condition of your property). Repeat this process when the resident moves out, noting any new damage or missing pieces. The resident can be charged for any damages other than ordinary wear and tear, such as broken items, cuts or burns in upholstery, and so on. Pay particular attention to carpet stains if a pet will be in the unit.

Apartment lease forms, available at stationery or office supply stores, can be used for the same purpose.

Double Deposit Clause

This is not a separate rider, but a clause that is typed on the face of the lease document. The intent of this provision is to allow residents to build their credit with you.

If an otherwise desirable prospective resident has a salary that does not satisfy the minimum required to qualify for the apartment, or if the prospect is new to the area or has recently graduated college and has not yet established a credit history, you can elect to charge an additional security deposit.

Type the following clause in the special provisions section of the lease:

$_____ of security deposit may be used for (month year) rent provided all prior rents have been paid on the first of the month.

We suggest using the seventh month of the lease in the clause. The resident will demonstrate financial stability by paying rent on time for six months. You then apply the extra security deposit to pay the seventh months' rent.

The extra security deposit should also be listed on the top of the lease under "other required deposit."

Appliance Clause

If residents want to use their own appliances and you, as the landlord, allow it, you can type the following statement(s) on the front of the lease: "Lessee owns refrigerator," or "Lessee owns stove," or "Lessee owns air conditioner." Record the brand name and model number of the appliance(s) on a separate sheet of paper attached to the lease or in the tenant file. This procedure can be used for new or existing leases.

The resident should be required to pay for disconnecting, moving, storing and reconnecting your appliances.

Prorated or Free-Rent Programs

For a variety of reasons, tenants often do not, or cannot move in on the first day of the month. Your property may not allow moving in on the weekends, or the first day of the month may fall on a weekday and the tenant may not be able to take the day off to move. Lease start dates almost always begin on the first, and if tenants cannot move in that day, they may request a rent adjustment because of moving in late, or you may allow them to move in early.

For example, suppose you have a vacant apartment that was rented for October 1 and the tenants want to move in on September 27, four days before the lease actually begins. You could either waive the proration and allow them the four days for free, or you could charge the tenants for four days' rent.

On the other hand, if that same Saturday fell on October 4 or 5, and that day was the first opportunity the tenants had to move, you could rebate a couple of days' rent, if requested, or elect not to make an adjustment. If your rules prevented a tenant from moving in on the first, then you should probably prorate the rent for that month. If the tenant was in possession of the keys and could have moved on October 1 you would not allow a proration.

Rent also can be prorated for middle-of-the-month leases. For example, if tenants want to move in on the fifteenth, you can charge a half month's rent. A good idea is to require tenants to pay the half month plus the first full month before moving in. The lease date would begin on the fifteenth, but end on the last day of the month one year later.

If you are in a soft rental market with a potential vacancy coming up and have decided to offer free rent as a concession, the gratuity should be taken before the year's lease goes into effect. If a resident is going to move into an apartment on September 1, taking advantage of the free rent, you have two options. The first option is to give the resident a one-month lease at no rent for September and then a separate 12-month lease starting October 1. The second option is to start the lease on September 1 and end it on September 30 of the following year, indicating on the form that the rent begins October 1. This option has one disadvantage: The lease shows that there was a rent concession. You might want to avoid revealing this in case the building is offered for sale. In both cases, the residents occupy the apartment for 13 months but pay rent for only 12, and the residents have not been allowed to move into the building without signing a lease.

Security deposit moneys and the rent for October should be collected before turning over possession to the residents.

Delivering the Lease

Residents should not be permitted to move in until the lease is signed and all deposits are paid. Deposits should be paid with ample time to allow for checks to clear. While some owners may elect to allow partial payments or other special deals, this is not a good policy.

Figure 4.15: Lease Cancellation Rider

THIS RIDER is hereby made a part of and incorporated as part of a certain lease agreement dated _____ (i.e.: starting date of current lease), for an apartment ("the Premises") located at _____ in _____, Illinois, by and between _____ ("Lessor") and _____ ("Lessee").

> THE TERMS AND CONDITIONS OF THIS
> RIDER SHALL GOVERN OVER THE TERMS
> AND CONDITIONS OF THE ATTACHED
> LEASE AGREEMENT.

The Lessee shall have the right to terminate this Lease on the last day of any calendar month during the Lease term by giving the Lessor not less than sixty (60) days prior written notice of the Lessee's intention to terminate Lease.

The Lessee's right to terminate shall only be effective under the following conditions:

1. Not less than sixty (60) days prior written notice to the intended lease expiration.
2. Lessee is not in default of the Lease terms and conditions.
3. Lessee shall remit to Lessor the sum of $300.00 (three hundred dollars) as compensation for the cancellation.
4. Fee is to be paid at the time the written notice is given.
5. Cancellatior fee shall not be deducted from any security monies on deposit.
6. All rents and late charges are paid in full up to the time of the intended Lease expiration.

LESSOR:

BY: _____   _____
                                           LESSEE

DATE: _____   _____
                                           LESSEE

Preparing the Lease

When initiating a new lease, the letter N can be typed on the top left hand corner signifying that it is a new lease. For a renewal lease, type R$ (indicating a renewal) and the previous rental amount for example, R$350.

A replacement lease can be prepared whenever there is any change in the original lease; for example, if a resident takes a roommate or a resident moves from one apartment to another in the same building. The word "Replacement" can be typed in the top left-hand corner, and a note can be stapled to the front indicating the type of change.

Figure 4.16: Agreement to Cancel Lease

Agreement to Cancel Lease

FOR AND IN CONSIDERATION of _____, LESSOR, allowing the undersigned to cancel prior to its expiration, that certain Lease ("Lease") dated _____, 19 _____ between LESSOR and _____ for an apartment located at _____ in _____ Illinois, I hereby agree to the following:

1. To pay a sum equal to two months of Lease rent prior to moving from and vacating the apartment;
2. To promptly return the apartment keys to LESSOR prior to moving from and vacating the apartment;
3. To provide my forwarding address to LESSOR prior to moving from and vacating the apartment;
4. To leave the apartment in a clean condition and free of any and all damages;
5. To move from and vacate the apartment on or before _____, 19____ which shall be the cancellation date of the Lease.

It is further understood that my security deposit is fully refundable, provided that I have complied with the aforesaid and further provided that there are no unpaid charges of any kind on my account as of the date the Lease is cancelled.

In the event the undersigned is in default under the aforesaid Lease as determined by LESSOR then LESSOR shall have the right to keep and apply the aforesaid cancellation fee toward any damages arising as a result of such default.

The undersigned, as additional consideration for this Agreement, does hereby forever release any claim, cause, or causes of action which it may have or which shall arise in the future against LESSOR, its officers, directors, employees, or agents arising out of the aforesaid Lease.

This agreement shall be null and void if not strictly complied with.

Dated: _____

_____   _____
Resident Signature   LESSOR

_____
Resident Signature

For replacement leases, the starting date should be the date the change takes effect and the termination date should be the same as the termination date of the original lease. A replacement lease should not be used when an original resident vacates and someone else moves in.

Type the name(s) of the resident(s) under the lessee signature lines. You will then be able to see at a glance whether you are lacking signatures on move-in day. If there is a cosigner, both names should appear and the word cosigner should be typed after the name. Each copy of the lease and any lease riders should carry an original signature. Separate the copies for ease of signing.

Figure 4.17: Furniture Rental Rider

<u>FURNITURE RIDER</u>

This Rider is hereby made a part of and incorporated as part of a certain lease agreement ("Lease") dated_____, 19___, for an apartment located at_____ _____in_____ Illinois ("Premises"); by and between_____ ("Lessor") and_____

_____

_____("Lessee").

To the extent of any conflict in terms, the terms and conditions of this Rider shall govern over the terms and conditions of the aforesaid Lease.
In consideration of the furniture rental deposit of the sum of_____ ($_____) Dollars upon execution hereof and Lessee's covenant, hereby made, to pay to Lessor a monthly furniture rental fee in the sum of_____ ($_____) Dollars on the first day of each month commencing_____, 19___, the parties agree to the following:

1. Lessor shall permit Lessee to use the articles of personal property listed on Schedule I ("Furniture") solely in the Premises for the term of the Lease. For all purposes of the Lease not inconsistent with this Rider, the Furniture shall be considered part of the Premises, and the above rental fee shall be deemed rent under the Lease. Title to the Furniture shall at all times be in Lessor, and Lessee shall not remove from the Premises, dispose of nor cause any lien to be placed upon any of the Furniture.
2. Lessee has examined the Furniture before signing this Rider and is satisfied with its physical condition; and Lessee's execution of this Rider shall be conclusive evidence of Lessee's acknowledgement that the Furniture is in good condition and repair, except as may be indicated on this Rider and initialed by Lessor. Lessee shall at all times maintain the Furniture in good condition and repair, without alterations, and upon termination of the Lease for any reason, the Furniture shall be returned to Lessor in substantially the same condition as when received by Lessee. Lessee shall be liable to Lessor for any loss or destruction of, or damage to the furniture, from whatever cause, occurring during the term of the Lease, ordinary wear and tear excepted.
3. The Furniture is not subject to any express nor implied warranties from either the manufacturer thereof or Lessor. Specifically, but without limitation, THERE ARE NO IMPLIED WARRANTIES OF MERCHANTABILITY OR FITNESS FOR A PARTICULAR PURPOSE. Lessee shall indemnify and hold Lessor totally harmless from and against each and every claim for personal injury and/or property damage occurring in connection with any of the Furniture being on the Premises and/or its use by any person during the term hereof.
4. Lessee agrees that in the event of any violation of the terms and conditions of the Lease and/or of this Rider, in addition to all of its rights upon default under the Lease, Lessor shall have the right to make a demand for immediate possession of the Furniture. Any refusal by Lessee to comply with such demand shall entitle Lessor to retain the aforementioned deposit as well as to enforce any and all other remedies provided by law or equity. However, if Lessee returns the Furniture upon such demand, the deposit shall be returned less damages, if any, caused by violation hereof.

SCHEDULE I

Qty.	Item	Qty.	Item	Qty.	Item	Qty.	Item
	Chest Bed 1		3/3 Head Board		Chair		
	Dresser		4/6 Mattress		Ottoman		
	Mirror		4/6 Box Spring		Chair		
	Nite Table		3/3 Mattress		End Table		
	Lamp		3/3 Box Spring		Stick Lamp		
	Chest Bed 2		Frame		Cocktail Table		
	Dresser		Corner Unit		Table Lamp		
	Mirror		Corner Table		Dining Room Table		
	Nite Table		Sofa		Dining Room Chair		
	Lamp		Love Seat		Etagere		
	4/6 Head Board		Hida Bed		Bookcase		
	Bar		Bar Stool		TV		
	TV Stand		Res Desk		Res Desk Chair		
	Drapes		Picture				

IN WITNESS WHEREOF, the Lessor and Lessee have executed this document on the_____ day of_____, 19_____.

If any changes or corrections are made on the lease or lease riders after typing, each change must be initialed by both the lessor and lessee(s).

Signing the Lease

Documents in the lease package should be signed on, or preferably before, the actual day of move-in. When new residents arrive, ask them to take a few moments to read the lease package documents before signing them. If the residents seem reluctant to take the time, or are in a hurry, make sure they read at least the bold print at the top of the lease, the rules and regulations on the back of the lease, and the attached riders.

Explain that these documents detail such things as the charge for late payment of rent and the penalty for using a security deposit to pay rent, and that residents should be aware of these rules. If you have not already done so, explain the basic policies for residency now, so the residents cannot claim ignorance of these policies later on.

All occupants 18 years old or older should sign all copies of the lease, the security deposit rider, and all other riders and forms. The dates the lessee and lessor signed the lease should be noted under the signatures. If one of the occupants is not present at the time of move-in (and therefore cannot sign the lease documents), the move-in can and probably should be postponed to a later date.

Keys to the apartment should be given out only after the lease has been signed by all lessees.

The Lease Package

After the lease and other documents have been signed by both parties, the documents are ready to be sorted and placed in the lease package to be given to the resident.

Keep the originals, including all original copies of applicable riders. Staple the lease on top of all other papers. If a resident has paid any monies, for example, the first month's rent on a new lease or a security deposit upgrade on a renewal lease, a receipt, if issued, can be stapled in front of the lease. The second copy of the lease and all riders are placed in the lease package for the resident.

Unsigned or Undelivered Lease

If a previously agreed-to rental agreement that was signed by a resident is not countersigned by the owner and the owner turns over possession of the apartment and accepts rent, the rental agreement will, in most states, still be in effect, as if it had been signed by the owner and delivered to the resident. The same things hold true if an owner signs and delivers a previously agreed-upon lease to a tenant and the tenant does not countersign it. If the tenant takes possession of the apartment and pays rent, it will be as if the lease was actually signed.

Generally, if an unsigned or undelivered lease provided for a term longer than one year, it is effective only for one year under the Statute of Frauds in most states and, in effect, it becomes an oral lease. As an example, tenant Brown agrees to and signs a written lease covering a term of two years for a rental of $500 a month. Landlord Smith agrees to the terms of the lease but does not countersign nor deliver the document. Since it is oral, the lease term is effectively reduced to a period of one year.

Resident Files

It is important to maintain an active alphabetical file, using legal-size manila folders, containing vital information on each resident. Keep copies of the following items in the file for each resident: lease, application, lease riders, credit information, repair bills for the apartment, letters or other correspondence, rent receipts, and other receipts.

As a safeguard against possible discrimination claims, you should probably save all rejected applications for at least two years.

Moving New Tenants In

CHAPTER 5

David Audino owns and manages multiresidential income properties.

The Tax Reform Act stunned the real estate investor, it is more important than ever to take a hard look at what the government will and will not allow with regard to tax shelters.

In today's real estate environment, a concentrated effort must be made to play the game, especially with the type of sophisticated players out there. Remember, you must obtain a return on all three of the ingredients of a successful project: return for your time, a return for your skill, and a return for your money.

Move-in day is a critical event in the landlord-tenant relationship. It's important to make a detailed list of the apartment's condition prior to move-in. The list will be compared to a later list completed when the tenant moves out. Another important item is to make sure tenants have called the utility companies to have their services connected and the accounts placed in their names.

Coordinating moving a new tenant in with an old tenant moving out can be tricky. Once I had a tenant ready to move in on the first, but the old tenant had not yet moved out. Luckily for me, I had a special clause in the lease stating that the lease would not take effect until delivery of the apartment and actual occupancy. "Even so, this situation was a potential problem, but I solved it when the existing tenant vacated several days later. I prorated the rent for the new tenant and charged the old tenant $50.00 a day as hold-over rent (according to the lease). Fifty dollars per day is a financial disincentive to anyone thinking of staying on after the lease has expired. The money was deducted from the security deposit.

Make Moving Day Go Smoothly

The move-in process is important in setting the stage for the business relationship between you and the residents. Moving is an emotional and stressful experience, and if the new residents are dissatisfied with their move-in, this feeling will last for months, possibly even permeating their entire term of residency.

Some factors adversely affecting a move are out of your control. There can be problems with the movers, delays in leaving the old residence, and complications in unloading in the new apartment. If tenants are moving out of an elevator building on a busy day and cannot get an elevator reserved for their exclusive use, a relatively simple two-hour move could take all day.

You can't guarantee an easy move-in, but you can coordinate details to make the process as trouble-free and pleasurable as possible for the new residents. Make sure the keys are in order. If an elevator is involved, schedule it for their exclusive use. Check to see that the utilities have been turned on in the new tenants' names. Give instructions on where they can store extra items. Show them the laundry room facilities. Be on hand to handle any complaints.

This is a time to keep in close communication with the tenants, being ready to assist in any way possible to ease tensions and help expedite the moving process. If at all possible, you should be on the premises during the move-in. Your physical presence can serve to reassure tenants that you care about them and share their desire to make this difficult day go as smoothly as possible.

Preinspecting the Apartment

Inspecting the Apartment with the Residents

You should inspect the apartment with the new residents after they sign the lease. Items that are damaged, but not to an extent to warrant replacement (minor burns in carpeting, chips in a sink, scratches on the appliances), should be indicated on the preinspection forms (Figure 5.1 or 5.2). Wallpaper that is in good condition left by a previous resident and so on should be noted. If the damaged item, such as a missing closet roller or dripping faucet, is scheduled for repair, it should not be listed.

By signing this form, the residents indicate that the premises are in satisfactory physical condition at the time of move-in, and promise that the premises will be left in the same condition at the end of the tenancy.

Last-Minute Check

A few days before the residents arrive for move-in, inspect the apartment again. Fill out the property inspection form (Figure 5.3). Check for cleanliness and a good paint job; see that plumbing, lights, appliances, and utilities are operating properly. Make sure the doors and locks open and close easily. Ensure you have sufficient keys that properly work on all locks. This inspection should be done several days prior to move-in to allow sufficient time to make any necessary repairs. Then a follow-up inspection should be conducted when all deficiencies have been corrected.

Common Complaints at Move-In

Careful planning and scheduling and the physical inspections and hands-on testing of everything in the apartment should eliminate most potential problems. Even so, problems can arise. Here are some common complaints at move-in time, with suggested responses.

The apartment is dirty. Clean the apartment thoroughly before move-in. Hire professional cleaners, if necessary. On the day before move-in, vacuum or buff the floors, dust the windowsills and countertops, and so on. This should meet inspection of the most meticulous tenant.

The apartment is poorly painted. This complaint can be about the color of the paint, or poor quality of work. Always paint walls white or off-white, or allow the tenants to choose the colors. Hire professional painters and make sure they clean up paint spills and spatters on appliances, floors, countertops and hardware, or do it yourself. Check the paint job as part of your preinspection and correct any problems before the tenants move in.

The dishwasher (stove, refrigerator, or other appliance) doesn't work. Appliances should be checked at preinspection; even so, problems may arise. Arrange to have them fixed as soon as possible, and tell the tenants exactly when to expect service.

There are bugs in the apartment. If your building has an insect problem, arrange early on for an adequate extermination program. If, in spite of your best efforts, new tenants see a cockroach roaming around, act immediately to reassure the tenants that this is an isolated incident. Call your exterminator to make an emergency treatment of the apartment and schedule a follow-up call in a week or two.

Figure 5.1: Preinspection Form

DATE ISSUED TO RESIDENT _____ , 19 ___

RESIDENT MUST RETURN THIS FORM TO THE RENTAL OFFICE WITHIN 7 DAYS

Mid-America Management Corp.

PRE-INSPECTION

Bldg. _____ Unit _____

Resident _____ Bldg. _____ Apt. _____

Lease Date _____ No. of Occupants (Including Children) _____ Pets _____

KITCHEN	MGR'S INITIALS	RESIDENT COMMENTS	LIVING ROOM (cont'd)	MGR'S INITIALS	RESIDENT COMMENTS
Stove Top			Burns		
Clean			Intercom Working		
Burners			T.V. Antenna Plate In		
Light Works			Air Conditioner		
Hood			Clean		
Exhaust Fan			Working		
Light Works			Filter Inside		
Oven			HALLWAY		
Two Racks			Guest Closet		
Clean			Bi-fold Doors		
Broiler			Shelf & Rod In		
One Pan			Doors Clean		
One Grill			Handles On		
Clean			Linen Closet		
Refrigerator			Bi-fold Doors		
Freezer Clean			Clean		
Ice Trays			Shelves In		
Door Shelf Bars			Handles On		
Refrig. Clean			BATHROOM		
Shelves			Toilet		
Crisper Glass			Clean		
Crisper Drawer			Working		
Light Works			Sink		
Egg Bin			Clean		
Disposal			Faucets Okay		
Working			Medicine Cabinet/Vanity		
Removed			Clean		
Lights			Mirrors Intact		
Over Sink			Knobs on Mirrors		
Ceiling			Bathtub/Tile		
Dining Area			Clean		
Door			Faucet		
Deadbolt Lock			Shower Works		
No Deadbolt			Shower Rod In		
Chain Lock			Towel Racks		
Floor			Exhaust Fan Works		
Clean			Light Bulbs In		
Damage			BEDROOMS		
Cabinets Interior			Tile/Carpet Intact		
Shelves Intact			Color		
Clean			Type		
Cabinets Exterior			Doors Clean		
Clean			Closet Rod & Shelf In		
Damage			GENERAL		
LIVING ROOM			Bulbs In		
Sliding Door			Windows Clean		
Clean			Screens In		
Lock Bar			Screen Damage		
Lock Works			Air Conditioner		
Door			MISCELLANEOUS		
Deadbolt Lock					
No Deadbolt					
Chain Lock					
Carpet/Tile					
Color					
Clean					
Type					
Stains					

I have examined the said premises and am satisfied with the physical condition thereof. The said premises are in good order and repair except as otherwise specified hereon. I understand that I must leave the premises clean and undamaged, as stated in the Security Deposit Agreement.

Manager/Rental Agent _____   Lessee _____ Home Phone _____

Date _____   Lessee _____ Home Phone _____

Keys Issued _____ Deadbolt _____ Door _____ Chain _____ Mail _____ Other _____

4402 Rev. 8/91

CORPORATE OFFICE

Figure 5.2: Move-In/Move-Out Report

ELMWOOD VILLAGE APARTMENTS
472 NORTH SPRUCE AVENUE
ATLANTA, GEORGIA 30324
(404) 351-2070

MOVE-IN/MOVE-OUT REPORT

RESIDENT

UNIT NO.	PROPERTY
MOVE-IN DATE	MOVE-OUT DATE

The premises are being delivered in clean, sanitary, and good operating condition, with no spots, stains, marks or damages, unless otherwise noted below in the "Move In Exceptions" box.

ITEM	MOVE-IN EXCEPTIONS	MOVE-OUT CONDITION	ITEMIZED CHARGES IF APPLICABLE
LIVING ROOM, DINING & HALLS			
Walls/Ceiling			
Floor/Carpet			
Closets/Doors/Locks			
Lights/Mirrors			
Drapes/Rods/Blinds			
Windows/Tracks/Screens			
Fireplace			
KITCHEN			
Walls/Ceiling/Floor			
Counter Tops/Tile			
Cabinets/Closets			
Oven/Stove			
Hood/Fan/Lights			
Refrigerator			
Dishwasher			
Sink/Faucet/Disposal			
Windows/Doors/Screens			
BEDROOMS	Specify Bedroom #1, #2, or #3	Specify Bedroom #1, #2, or #3	
Walls/Ceiling			
Floor/Carpet			
Lights/Mirrors			
Drapes/Rods/Blinds			
Windows/Tracks/Screens			
Closets/Doors/Shelves			
BATHROOMS	Specify Bathroom #1, #2, or #3	Specify Bathroom #1, #2, or #3	
Walls/Ceiling			
Floor			
Cabinets/Mirrors			
Sink			
Tub/Shower			
Tile/Grout			
Lights/Vent Fan			
Toilets			
Windows/Doors			
Towel Bars/Accessories			
WASHER/DRYER			
HEAT/AIR CONDITIONING			
BALCONY/DECK/PATIO			
STORAGE/PARKING AREA			
GARDEN/PLANTS/GRASS			
SMOKE DETECTOR			
NUMBER OF KEYS	Unit ___ Entry ___ Mailbox ___ Other ___	Unit ___ Entry ___ Mailbox ___ Other ___	

MOVE-IN COMMENTS	MOVE-OUT COMMENTS

Resident has inspected the above premises prior to occupancy and accepts it with the conditions and/or exceptions noted above. Resident agrees to deliver the premises in like condition upon termination of tenancy, normal wear and tear excepted.

Resident_____ Date_____

Management_____ Date_____

Inspection is hereby completed:

Resident_____

Date_____

Management_____

Date_____

ITEMIZED CHARGES

KEYS/LOCKS: Unit $_____, Entry $_____, Mailbox $_____, Other $_____, TOTAL:_____

CLEANING: General $_____, Carpet $_____, Drapes $_____, Other $_____, $_____, TOTAL:_____

PAINTING: $_____, REPAIRS $_____, REPLACEMENTS $_____, DEBRIS REMOVAL $_____, TOTAL:_____

UNPAID RENT: Dates from _____ to _____ $_____, Late fee(s) $_____, TOTAL:_____

OTHER: _____

TOTAL CHARGES: $_____

CREDITS/SUMMARY	FORWARDING ADDRESS
Security Deposit .... $_____	
Prepaid Rent: from _____ to _____ $_____	
Other: _____ $_____	
TOTAL CREDITS: .... $_____	
Less TOTAL CHARGES: .... $_____	New Telephone # _____
☐ Balance Due from Resident: Rec'd on _____ $_____	
☐ Refund to Resident: Issued on _____ $_____	PREPARED BY _____ DATE _____

Source: Peachtree Business Products. Used with permission. (To order this form or a catalog, call 800-241-4623.)

Figure 5.3: Property Inspection Form

Property Inspection

Property Name _____   Building Address _____
Inspected By _____   Date _____

Area	Condition			Maintenance Required
	Good	Fair	Poor	
Exterior				
Signs				
Grounds				
Landscaping				
Parking Areas				
Sidewalks				
Trash Area				
Light Fixtures				
Entrance/Foyer				
Door				
Windows				
Mailboxes/Nameplates				
Light Fixtures				
Floors				
Walls				
Hallways				
Doors				
Floors				
Walls				

Figure 5.3: Property Inspection Form, continued

Area	Condition			Maintenance Required
	Good	Fair	Poor	
Hallways, cont.				
Light Fixtures				
Stairwells				
Ashtrays				
Laundry Rooms				
Floors				
Walls				
Machines				
Light Fixtures				
Miscellaneous				
Elevators				
Storage Area				
Trash Chutes				
Boiler Room				

Exterior Light Timer Setting: On _____ Off _____

Comments: _____
_____
_____

The plumbing leaks. This should have been checked; however, like appliances, plumbing has a way of acting up on move-in day. Ascertain if it is a minor problem (dripping faucet) that can be fixed in a few days, or a major disaster (overflowing toilet) that needs immediate action, and act accordingly.

You gave us the wrong keys. If the locks and keys are checked during inspection this problem can be avoided. Have an extra set of keys on hand in case of inadvertent mixups.

Turning Over Possession

After all papers are signed and the rent and security deposit funds received (and any former tenants have vacated the apartment), the tenants are then entitled to take possession of their new leased space. From a general legal standpoint, an owner has to give possession of habitable premises to the resident in compliance with the rental agreement; habitable means that the apartment is clean and all equipment, appliances, plumbing, and hardware are in good working condition.

Turning over possession includes providing the new residents with the keys that are necessary to enter the space, including the common area lobbies and parking facility if parking is provided in the lease.

If old tenants do not vacate an apartment at the end of their lease, or have prohibited possession in some other manner, you will have to take legal action to rectify the situation. Either an owner or a resident may file a lawsuit to gain possession and recover damages as provided by law. An owner may bring such action on behalf of the new residents even though the residents are the ones entitled to possession.

Giving Tenants Instructions (Lease Package and Move-In Kit)

To help facilitate the move-in process and make the new residents feel at home in their new apartment, you can provide information about the building and surrounding community. The *National Apartment Association* (703-518-6141) in collaboration with *Ryder Truck Rental Services* (800-GO-RYDER), has a free apartment moving planning guide available for distribution to new residents. The booklet contains helpful hints on the moving process, providing checklists to use for things like packing, utility hookups, etc.

Your move-in packet might include some or all of the following documents:

- Copies of the lease, security deposit agreement, applicable riders and an "as is" letter when processing a relet
- Completed utility and telephone service hook-up forms. The electric and gas companies may require completed forms prior to move-in. If tenants pay for utilities, these services will have to be put in their names. Tenants should make arrangements as soon as they sign the lease to have their services connected on or before move-in day.
- A set of keys or access cards to the apartment, mailbox, and building entrance, plus common areas such as laundry rooms, storage rooms, and so on. Always keep a set of spare apartment keys in your possession.
- Change-of-address cards
- Maps of the area
- A list of often-called telephone numbers: police, fire, hospitals, schools, stores, restaurants, cab companies, chamber of commerce
- Operating instructions for appliances, laundry equipment, and so on

These materials can be placed in one folder or envelope marked with the new residents' names, apartment number, new address, and move-in date.

Some Final Details

Moving day is made up of many details, large and small. You will have to coordinate your new tenants' move-in schedule with the former tenants' move-out schedule. Other details to consider are elevator problems, mailbox and doorbell name tags, utility hookups, disposal of packing debris, and perhaps a welcome gift for the new tenants.

Reserving Elevators

Some buildings, including most high-rises, require tenants to schedule their move-in/move-out with the management office in order to reserve the elevator. Quite often, elevator buildings will not allow a move-in or move-out on weekends because most residents are home then and the elevators are busier.

Condominium associations normally require tenants to schedule a move with the management office and will sometimes ask for a deposit or charge a fee for use of the elevator. The deposit is returned after an inspection of the elevator and common areas shows no damages. A one-time fee is not returned.

Name Tags

New tenants must have their names on the mailbox and doorbell. To maintain neat and uniform appearance of doorbells and mailboxes, it is better for you to order or make the name tags rather than have tenants make their own. Some owners charge a fee for this, and larger buildings usually have the management office handle this function, but unless the property is a high-rise, a name tag fee is not a common practice.

Key Control

New tenants will usually want their locks changed as a safeguard against old tenants and their friends still having keys. When locks are changed, be sure to get spare keys. If you own more than one unit, keep spare keys to all the apartments and buildings in a locked key cabinet. This serves two purposes: First, you can keep the keys organized and tagged, thus making it easier to locate keys in an emergency. Second, a locked key cabinet is better than a peg board in keeping the keys safe from possible theft, thus helping maintain security at your properties.

Utilities

Make sure your new tenants notify the utility companies to put the utilities in their names. If they do not, you may end up paying some of their electric or gas bills. Some owners contact these services themselves to ensure that the meters are put in tenants' names. The electric or gas service will have to be reactivated if previous tenants had them disconnected. Pilot lights must be relit. If your tenants are from out of town you may want to make these arrangements for them.

Empty Packing Cartons

New tenants usually have dozens of empty boxes and lots of waste paper to dispose of. Make sure you tell them how to dispose of this type of bulk rubbish. Otherwise your corridors or common areas may be filled with debris.

Welcome Gifts

As a gesture of good will, some owners give new tenants a welcome gift such as a plant, flowers, or a basket of fruit. These items are relatively inexpensive and can help maintain a positive feeling during this stressful time. Residents will appreciate your thoughtfulness and will remember gestures of this nature throughout their lease term.

Renewing Leases (or Not)

CHAPTER 6

Katherine Martinez holds undergraduate degrees in commercial interior design and business administration. She works as a regional sales manager for a large health insurance firm and, on a part-time/freelance basis, pursues her interests in interior design and residential real estate.

My experience in real estate over the past six years has been as an investor in residential properties. During this period, I owned three condominiums on the near north side of the city, and three three-flat buildings on the southwest and north sides.

As sole owner and manager of these properties, I collect rents, coordinate day-to-day maintenance, arrange for property improvements to comply with building codes, coordinate needed renovations for resale, and assume all building maintenance and improvement costs.

Even though my primary objective is to rent the property, improve it, and sell quickly at a profit, there are times when I have to retain ownership for several years. Because of this, once I develop good relationships with tenants who consistently pay their rent on time, I strongly encourage them to renew their leases.

I value having someone renew even if it means not getting as much rent as I could from a new tenant. The costs of redecorating far outweigh the additional rent increase.

I contact the tenant by phone 90 days before the lease expires. I want to know his or her intentions on renewing and at that time I state what the new rent will be. Most of the time, I will try to get a ten percent increase; if they are desirable tenants, I will negotiate this amount down to five percent.

Financial Benefits of Lease Renewals

Obtaining lease renewals can be one of your most productive activities. Resident turnover, which is estimated by the Institute of Real Estate Management (800-837-0706) to be 55.1 percent nationwide, carries many hidden costs. The common areas of your property may be damaged during the move. The apartment will need cleaning and may need a new carpet or other redecorating. Time, energy, and money must be spent on finding a new tenant and showing the apartment. You may not find a suitable tenant right away and the apartment may stand empty for a month or more. Even without lost income, it can easily cost three to four hundred dollars each time a tenant moves out and a new tenant moves in.

Renewing a lease, on the other hand, can afford a substantial savings. Advertising costs are lessened. Maintenance, decorating, and administrative expenses are substantially reduced. The risk of damaging the halls, stairwells, doors, and elevators is eliminated. Thus, it is important that every effort be made to renew leases of desirable residents.

Of course, not all residents are good candidates for renewal. Do not renew residents who are slow rent-payers, who have many late charges, who have unauthorized pets, or who have created noise or nuisance problems. Procedures for not renewing a tenant are listed at the end of the chapter.

Current market conditions will influence how strictly you will adhere to the general policies and procedures discussed in this chapter. If the market is soft and you have a large number of vacancies, you might decide to renew a resident who has been slow in paying rent, but has otherwise been a good resident.

Start on Day One

The process of renewing a lease begins the day a resident moves in. The possibility of obtaining a lease renewal is tested daily by your attitude, your professionalism, and your approach to dealing with residents. There is no substitute for dealing fairly with all residents.

Conscientious owners work on renewals all year long through positive interactions with residents. These landlords know their residents well enough to identify three and four months ahead of time individuals who should and should not be renewed.

Reinspecting the Apartment

All apartments should be reinspected approximately 90 days before the expiration of the current lease. Use the renewal inspection notice letter

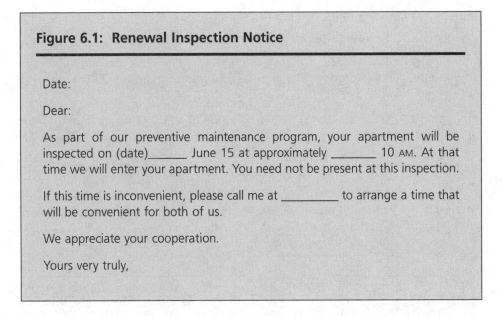

Figure 6.1: Renewal Inspection Notice

Date:

Dear:

As part of our preventive maintenance program, your apartment will be inspected on (date)_____ June 15 at approximately _____ 10 AM. At that time we will enter your apartment. You need not be present at this inspection.

If this time is inconvenient, please call me at _____ to arrange a time that will be convenient for both of us.

We appreciate your cooperation.

Yours very truly,

(Figure 6.1) to notify the residents in writing of the forthcoming inspection. Give them at least 48 hours' notice prior to the scheduled date. The details of the inspection are recorded on the renewal inspection form (Figure 6.2).

A renewal inspection serves three purposes: First, it allows you to make an annual assessment of the physical condition of your apartments, enabling you to observe unreported problems such as dripping faucets, damaged bathroom wall tiles, broken windows and screens, drywall damage, and so on.

Second, it gives you the opportunity to make sure the resident is not in violation of the lease. (Check for evidence of a pet with no pet rider, overoccupancy, poor housekeeping, and so on.)

And third, it allows residents to point out any defects or deficiencies they want corrected in the apartment.

Residents whose apartments are found in an unsanitary or damaged condition should not be renewed until a follow-up inspection indicates that the problems have been corrected and the resident has paid in full for the work performed.

Redecorating

Lease-renewal time is a pivotal point in the landlord-tenant relationship. This is when tenants request redecorating, carpet cleaning, new appliances, and other improvements.

During the first and second years, renewals will probably not warrant any improvements, but it is a good policy to repaint the apartment and clean the carpet every two or three years. This is not just to please the

Figure 6.2: Renewal Inspection Form

Renewal Inspection

Name _____ Unit Code _____

Address _____ Lease Exp. Date _____

Phone _____

Number of Occupants _____

Pets: ❏ No   ❏ Yes   Type: Cat/Dog/Other _____

Carpet: ❏ No   ❏ Yes   Color _____ Condition _____

Appliance Colors: Stove _____ Refrigerator _____ Dishwasher _____

Comments: _____

_____

_____

I. Entry Area _____
   A. Front Door _____
      1.) Locks Mastered _____ Keys _____
   B. Flooring _____ Condition _____
   C. Entry Closet Doors _____

II. Living Room _____
   A. Walls _____
   B. Floor Covering _____
   C. Windows/Screens _____
   D. Heating System _____

III. Kitchen _____
   A. Stove _____
      1.) Operation _____
      2.) Burners _____
      3.) Oven _____
      4.) Broiler _____
      5.) Handles _____
   B. Refrigerator _____
      1.) Operation _____
   C. Exhaust Fan _____
   D. Dishwasher _____
   E. Cabinets/Drawers _____
      1.) Counter Top _____
      2.) Caulk _____
   F. Floor/Condition _____
   G. Sink _____
      1.) Faucet _____
      2.) Spout _____

IV. Bathrooms _____
   A. Vanity _____
   B. Sink _____

Figure 6.2: Renewal Inspection Form, continued

C. Plumbing _____
D. Toilet _____
   1.) Seat _____
   2.) Base _____
E. Shower _____
   1.) Tile Grout/Caulk _____
   2.) Plumbing _____

V. Bedrooms _____
A. Floor/Covering _____
B. Door _____
C. Closet _____

VI. General _____
A. Door Stops _____
B. Air Conditioner _____
   1.) Filter _____
   2.) Caulk _____
   3.) Tip _____
C. Heating Unit _____
D. Balcony _____
   1.) Railings _____
   2.) Caulk _____
   3.) Doors _____

tenants, but also to prevent any serious maintenance problems through general neglect.

If the apartment is well maintained by the resident and does not need decorating or carpet cleaning, you might give the resident a rent rebate in an amount slightly less than what it would cost you for these expenses. This gesture on your part can also act as an incentive for the resident to renew.

If you agree to replace or repair an item as a condition of a resident agreeing to renew a lease, it is a good policy to honor that commitment as soon as possible.

Raising the Rent

It does not make much sense to own and operate rental property if you cannot generate a positive return on your investment. Investment properties can show a negative cash flow occasionally, and for short periods, but if such a situation continues you will have to sell the property or see it placed in default.

Operating rental property is like any other business; to improve cash flow you must either reduce expenses or increase income. Chapter 10 presents ideas and suggestions that can work toward expense reductions. Increasing income is sometimes easier to accomplish, but unless the residents are on month-to-month leases, the only times you can increase rents is when year-long leases terminate, assuming the market will permit an increase.

Some areas of the country allow utility and/or sales tax cost increases to be passed on to residents, if the provision is indicated in the original lease that the tenant signed.

Even professionals find it difficult to decide what percent increase to charge renewal tenants. Rent increases in the 4 to 6 percent range are somewhat common, but it is not unusual to see hikes as low as 2 percent or as high as 10 percent.

The problem is complicated by several considerations. If you raise the rent too much, the resident may not renew—leaving you with a potential vacancy and decorating costs. If you increase the rent too little, the resident may stay, but you might not have enough additional income to offset inflationary increases in operating expenses.

Some professionals use the 20 percent resistance theory: After a renewal increase has been selected and the tenants notified, if more than 20 percent of the tenants resist, the increase was too high. If fewer than 20 percent resist, the increase was too low. This theory can be applied only to properties with multiple units and even then, it acts only as a factor to consider the next time an increase is due.

Determining an Increase

In the long run, the renewal rent is a result of successful negotiations between you and the resident. In order to begin the negotiation process, you need a starting point.

Know Market Rent

The first step in determining a renewal increase is to ascertain the current market rent for vacant comparable apartments in your area. This can be accomplished by looking at the classified ads in your local newspaper or by checking with other owners and managers in your community.

Find out what similar properties are instituting as an increase. Local newspapers periodically print articles on projected rent increases for their region. Try to acquire this information before you determine your own increases.

Figure Tenants' Moving Expenses

Another consideration, in addition to how much it will cost you, is how much it may cost your tenants to move and redecorate a new apartment. Total moving expenses, including new utility service hookup charges, can be more than $1,000 depending on how much furniture they own and whether or not they use professional movers. Additionally a move often means a new phone number, a new cable service, and new schools. You might set a rent increase that is slightly less than what it would cost the tenants to move. If tenants object to the rent increase, remind them of how much it would cost them to move.

Criteria for a Successful Rent Increase

Weigh all the facts you have gathered from your investigations to select a rental increase that meets the following criteria:

- The increase should offset increases in expenses, including the fixed expenses that have increased due to inflation, and capital or decorating improvements.
- The increase, expressed on an annual basis, should not be much more than the cost of moving expenses for the tenant, unless you own properties that are in the high-rent district with rents in the over $1,000-a-month range.
- The increase should not be substantially higher than what comparable properties are charging. A comparable property would closely resemble your apartments in size, age, location, and amenities.
- The increased rent should be slightly higher than what vacant comparable apartments are commanding. You may be able to get an existing tenant to pay $10 to $20 more a month on a renewal than what a vacant apartment would cost in the same building, but you may also run the risk of creating a bad relationship with this tenant who might resent being taken advantage of.

Having decided on an increase, your task now is to convince the tenants to accept it and renew their lease. This is normally the time tenants start their negotiations and you should be prepared to justify the rent hike.

Expect Some Turnover

Despite your best efforts, some tenants will choose to move anyway. The national average for small investors is 45 percent retention, so if you have 10 apartments and five residents renew, you are doing slightly better than average.

Often tenants will leave because they have an opportunity to rent an apartment in a new building. Professional managers in large urban communities that have constant new construction consider a 60 percent retention of tenants to be exceptionally good. This means that even professional managers have to cope with over a third of their residents moving out each year.

The Renewal Process

As indicated earlier, the renewal process begins on the day the tenant moves in, but the actual procedure of administratively obtaining a renewal should be initiated approximately four months before the expiration of the lease.

At least one lease (Arizona Multi-Housing Association Apartment Rental Agreement) contains an automatic renewal clause stating that *unless* the resident gives management a 30-day notice to vacate, the lease will be renewed on a month-to-month basis under the same terms and conditions. (A resident is not considered renewed until all the lease documents are signed and delivered by the appropriate parties.) Management reserves the sole option not to renew.

When the renewal process is completed, update all resident files and security deposit records.

Form Letters

You may use a series of form letters to assist in obtaining renewals, but letters and notices are not substitutes for information-gathering through personal contact.

90 Days Before the Lease Ends

If, in your judgment, an individual is a desirable resident, send the 90-day notice (first renewal letter) (Figure 6.3). Enclose the proposed renewal agreement (Figure 6.4) and/or lease and security deposit agreement. This packet should be sent 90 days prior to the date the current lease expires. As an added incentive to reply promptly, you can offer a one month-time rebate of $25–$30 for signing the renewal lease 60 or more days before the lease ends.

If a resident has accrued unpaid late charges or other fees and you have still decided to seek renewal, send copies of the documents with a letter requesting that these charges be brought up-to-date. Advise residents that they cannot be renewed until their account balances are paid in full.

Figure 6.3: 90-Day Notice (First Renewal Letter)

Date:

Dear:

I am writing to offer to renew your lease, which is due to expire soon.

I am enclosing your proposed lease renewal agreement. You will note that there is an increase in rent. This increase is necessary because of increases in taxes, utilities, labor, and overhead, and other operational expenses.

We have kept the rent increase to a minimum, and, in fact, this rental rate is available only if you sign your renewal ninety days prior to expiration of your present lease. If you sign later, the rent will be more per month, to allow for further increases in costs.

I also have enclosed your security deposit agreement. Since your security deposit must equal your monthly rental, you are asked to increase your deposit by an amount equal to cover the increase in rent.

Please sign and return the lease renewal agreement and security deposit agreement, along with your payment of $_____ (to cover additional security deposit) before _____. After that date, if you want to renew, I will issue another renewal lease, at the higher rate.

Please feel free to call me if you have any questions.

Very truly yours,

enc: (2): Lease Agreement
Security Deposit Agreement

Approximately one week after sending out the renewal packet, call the residents to make certain the materials were received and to encourage prompt responses.

60 Days Before the Lease Ends

If you have not received a reply from the residents within 30 days of sending the packet, send a follow-up, the 60-day notice letter (Figure 6.5).

45 Days Before the Lease Ends

If the resident has not returned the lease documents 45 days prior to the lease expiration date, send a second follow-up, the 45-day notice letter

Figure 6.4: Renewal Form

ASHFORD PROPERTY MANAGEMENT
3420 BRIAR VISTA ROAD
TEMPLETON, ARIZONA 85365
(602) 321-4842

The lease on your apartment will expire on:

_____

We hope that you will want to continue occupancy, so we request that you sign all copies of the lease renewal and return them to us.

—Thank You.

To:

_____
_____
_____
_____

RENEWAL OF APARTMENT LEASE

THIS RENEWAL AGREEMENT dated _____ 19_____

is a rider to and forms a part of the original lease (the "Lease") dated _____ 19_____

between _____ ,Lessor,

and _____ ,Lessee,

for the apartment located at _____
                    APARTMENT NO.   BLDG.

_____
     STREET ADDRESS   CITY & STATE

known as_____
                  NAME OF APARTMENT

The Lease is hereby extended for an additional term of_____months

commencing _____ 19_____ and ending _____ 19_____

and the RENTAL RATE during this period shall be_____

_____ Dollars ($_____) per month.

All other covenants and conditions of the Lease shall remain in effect, and no covenant or condition of the Lease shall be deemed waived by any action or non-action in the past.

_____   _____
Lessor or Agent   Lessee

                                     _____
                                     Lessee

Source: Peachtree Business Products. Used with permission. (To order this form or a catalog, call 800-241-4623.)

(Figure 6.6). This letter informs the residents that they must contact you within 24 hours if they choose to renew. Otherwise, the apartment will be considered available for showing to prospective residents.

30 Days Before the Lease Ends

For residents who have not responded or have indicated in writing that they will not be renewing, send a "Notice to Vacate" letter (Figure 6.7) specifying the condition in which the apartment is to be left when vacated. This letter is sent 30 days prior to the lease expiration date.

Not Renewing a Tenant

Occasionally you will not want to renew a tenant. Your decision not to renew might be based on any number of reasons: collection problems, poor housekeeping, overoccupancy, tenants who continually disturb other residents and so on. Give such a resident a 30-day notice (Figure 6.8) as a courtesy.

In some states you may be obligated to tell the tenants why you are not renewing the lease. You currently are not required to renew a lease; however, pending legislation in at least one state proposes just that.

As always, stay current on landlord-tenant legislation and keep in touch with your attorney.

Figure 6.5: 60-Day Notice (Second Renewal Letter)

Date:

Dear:

According to our records your current lease expires on _____ and you have not yet signed and delivered the renewal lease we sent you on _____.

We need to know as soon as possible whether or not you intend to stay in the apartment, so we can begin showing it for rerental.

Note also that _____ is the last date that the renewal rent of $_____ is valid. After that date, the renewal rent will be $_____.

We would appreciate your prompt attention to this matter. Please contact us if you have any questions.

Very truly yours,

Figure 6.6: 45-Day Notice (Third Renewal Letter)

Date:

Dear:

We have not yet received your signed lease document for the coming term. Since your lease expires on _____ it is extremely important that you contact us within 24 hours to let us know your plans.

If we do not hear from you by _____ we will start showing the apartment to prospective residents on _____.

If you are not planning to renew your lease, please complete the bottom part of this letter, detach and return to us immediately.

Thank you for your cooperation,

Date:

We will vacate our apartment on _____ (date)

New address:

Signature: _____

Figure 6.8: 30-Day Notice

Date:

Dear:

This letter will serve as notification that we have decided not to renew your lease. Please turn in your keys at our office no later than _____. Also supply us with your forwarding address and new telephone number at that time.

Your security deposit is fully refundable provided your apartment is left in a clean, orderly, and undamaged condition as detailed in the enclosed notice to vacate. Also refer to the preinspection form, which details the condition of the apartment when you moved in.

If you have any questions regarding this matter, please feel free to contact me.

Very truly yours,

enc: "Notice to Vacate" preinspection form

Figure 6.7: Notice to Vacate

Mid-America Management

Reply To:

Date:_____

Dear Resident:

This letter will acknowledge receipt of your notice of intention to vacate your apartment on or before _____, 19_____. We thank you for your residency and trust your stay with us has been a pleasant one.

In order to insure the maximum return of your security deposit, please refer to the reverse side of your current lease form to be sure that all requirements regarding the move-out condition of your apartment are met. It is also suggested that you contact your site office and schedule an appointment for a final inspection walk-through of your apartment.

Should you be unable to vacate your apartment on or before the above specified date, please be advised that you will be considered a "holdover" resident and we will be strictly enforcing paragraph 31(c) of your lease which states:

> "The Lessee's continued occupancy shall be for a month to month term at a monthly rental which shall equal the monthly rental reserved herein plus a 20% increase in said amount."

As you can see, it is of utmost importance that you vacate your apartment on or before the above specified date. Failure to do so will leave you liable for an amount of _____, which represents a sum equal to 120% of your monthly rent. Please remember you are responsible for your apartment until all keys are returned to the site office.

Should you have any questions regarding your move, please contact your site office at _____.

Sincerely,
MID-AMERICA MANAGEMENT

Site Manager

Form 4505 / 9-92

Mid-America Management Corp.
2901 Butterfield Road, Oak Brook, Illinois 60521 (708) 574-2400

When Tenants Move Out

Gerry Lynch is the production director of a major publishing company. Ten years ago, she purchased a town house with a garden apartment that she rents to a tenant. Five years ago, she also invested in a small building in a nearby suburb.

I learned the hard way not to rent to friends or to become too friendly with my tenants. I once rented to friends who, when they moved out, left behind a roach-infested apartment. I learned about the roaches while showing the unit to a prospective tenant. The whole building had to be thoroughly exterminated, costing hundreds of dollars. Fortunately I was able to deduct the expense from the security deposit.

Renting has taught me two things: inspect the apartment periodically while the tenant is living there, and inspect the vacant apartment thoroughly before showing it to a prospective tenant.

On another occasion, the tenants asked me if they could vacate the apartment and stop paying rent before the lease ended. When I said no, they became almost hostile and threatened to damage the apartment. Ultimately they moved out, changing the locks in the process to prevent me from protecting the apartment. I had to hire an attorney and a locksmith; I eventually recovered the expenses because I had a valid, enforceable signed lease.

Ending a Lease on Time

It would be nice if all good tenants stayed in their apartments year after year, paying the rent on time and never creating any problems. But of course there comes a time when tenants move out.

If they are leaving simply because the lease has expired and they want to move on, the event should not be too stressful. But if the tenants are being evicted, or you decided not to renew the lease, or the tenants want to terminate the lease early, there could be a good deal of tension until the moving day is at hand and the tenants have physically vacated the unit.

If tenants inform you that they will move out at the end of the lease, there are several steps to follow.

Notice to Vacate

Send the tenants a "Notice to Vacate" form (Figure 6.7) at least 30 days before the end of the lease. This notice reminds the tenants that you will inspect the apartment before returning the security deposit, and lists the particular areas of the apartment that will be checked for cleaning and damage.

The notice also states the date the apartment must be vacated, asks for a forwarding address, and tells the tenants where to return keys.

Move-Out Inspection

The move-out inspection can be conducted on the day the tenants vacate the apartment, or a few days before. The purpose of this inspection is to document the condition of the apartment and to ascertain what needs fixing or replacing. Based on this inspection, you will compute the amount of security deposit to return to the tenants.

To conduct the inspection, use a copy of the preinspection form (Figure 5.1) that was completed when the tenants moved in. Review this form along with any completed apartment work orders to verify deficiencies accepted by the residents and defects corrected through work orders.

Refer also to the notice to vacate form, which requires the tenants to leave the apartment clean and free of debris.

If possible, conduct the move-out inspection together with the tenants to avoid disputes about the condition of the apartment and appropriate charges for repairs and cleaning. If time permits, you might allow the residents to correct minor deficiencies such as paint touch-ups, oven cleaning, and so on.

Regain Possession

Ascertain the exact day the tenants will be leaving and be on hand to receive the keys and regain possession of the apartment.

Ending a Lease Early

When tenants want to move out before the lease is over, you have several options. If you want to enforce the lease, you have a legal right to hold tenants to the signed agreement to pay for a complete year. A lease is a contract; both parties mutually agreed to uphold their obligations in compliance with the stated terms and conditions. However, it may not always be wise to take such a hard line.

There are ways in which each party can mutually agree to terminate a lease early. You can elect to cancel the lease completely. Or you might allow the tenants to sublet the apartment or assign (relet) the lease to substitute tenants.

If you let your tenants know that you are willing to negotiate an early termination of the lease, they will be less likely to move out without giving notice. In the latter case, the landlord can initiate a legal suit, but it is a good idea to avoid such costly and stressful legal battles.

Subletting

Subletting occurs when a tenant enters into a separate agreement with a third party (subtenant) to use the apartment on a temporary or permanent basis. The two parties are responsible to each other for performing whatever obligations they have agreed on. You should be involved with the transaction, and not let the tenants do this on their own.

As an example of a temporary sublet, tenant Smith gets a business assignment out of town for three months and decides to sublet his apartment to a friend for the period he will be gone. The friend, subtenant Jones, agrees to pay Smith an amount of rent for use of the premises. Smith, in turn, continues to pay rent to you and when the three months have expired, Smith returns and Jones moves out. If everything went well, you might not even know about the transaction.

Smith also could decide to permanently move out of his apartment before the lease expired, and to sublet the apartment for the balance of the lease. He would collect rent from the subtenant, and pay rent to you, the landlord and would remain obligated to you until the old lease expired. The sublet tenant usually accepts the apartment in an "as is" condition and does not benefit from any redecorating until the lease expires.

In this case you are more likely to be a party to the sublet because the new tenant would probably want to enter into a new lease with you when the sublet expired, where permitted by law. It is a common practice to charge a small fee to allow a sublet, to cover administrative expenses.

Assignment (Reletting)

When tenants must terminate their lease early you may choose to assign the lease (or relet) to new tenants who will finish the remainder of the term. If it takes several months to locate a suitable replacement, the original tenants are still liable and must pay rent, even though they may not be occupying the unit.

Assignment differs from subletting in that once new tenants have signed the lease, the original tenants are fully released from any additional obligation. In some cases, landlords will ask the replacement tenants to sign a brand new one-year lease instead of completing the obligation under the old lease. Landlords usually charge a higher fee to accommodate an assignment.

Assignment is, in effect, a termination of one lease and the creation of a new one. Thus, when the old tenants move out you should inspect the apartment for damages and deduct the cost of repairs and redecorating from the security deposit. The original tenants' security deposit is refunded and a new one is taken from the replacement tenants.

Assignment Is Preferable to Subletting

The reasons for this are clear when you think how involved and complicated the situation would be if subtenants had to first contact the original tenants to get repairs and service for the apartment. And if landlords had to enforce the rules and regulations of occupancy with a sublet, they would have to contact the original tenants who may have moved to another state.

With an assignment, you have what amounts to a new lease with new tenants and your dealings with the former tenants are at an end.

Sublet/Assignment Clauses in Standard Leases

Many lease and rental agreement forms address the issue of subleasing and assignments in a similar fashion. State laws generally allow rental agreements to require tenants to obtain the owner's prior consent in order to sublet or assign an apartment. Written permission may be necessary if the lease is in writing.

Owners should not unreasonably withhold permission, and sublease/assignment clauses in form leases normally do not contain any language that would constitute an unreasonable withholding of permission.

The following provisions are fairly common and are considered generally acceptable by both landlords and tenants:

- Residents may be prohibited from transferring their lease interest to a trustee in bankruptcy or for the benefit of the residents' creditors or any other act of bankruptcy or insolvency.
- Owners may reserve the right to rent other vacancies in the premises before consenting to reletting the dwelling unit. [This clause could be considered antagonistic and you can waive the right if the tenants are responsible for finding their own sublessee.]
- Prospective residents may be required to meet the criteria customarily used to evaluate the acceptability of residents for similar dwelling units in the premises.
- Sublet/assignment may be restricted during the last 90 days of the lease term. During this period of time a landlord could require prospective sublessees to sign new, full-term leases.

Obligations and Liabilities

Current tenants usually remain liable for responsibilities under the lease until a new lease is signed. You may require financial assurance from the old tenants or the prospective lessees, including advance payment for rent and expenses of reletting. Such expenses might include decorating, repairs, replacements, advertising, commissions, and reasonable administrative fees for performing the details involved in this type of transaction.

Unless agreed, you generally do not have a responsibility to advertise or incur expenses on behalf of the residents or yourself in conjunction with reletting an apartment. A resident who subleases is normally liable to his sublessee for the performance of the owner's obligations under the rental agreement.

A landlord is not directly liable to a sublessee in regards to obligations under the rental agreement and the sublessee is not directly liable to the owner with respect to the resident's obligations, unless otherwise agreed.

Obey State and Local Laws

While some states have given residents a right to sublet or relet, most states honor the rental agreement if subletting or reletting is specifically prohibited. If you are in doubt about your rights in this regard, it is best to check with your local municipality or REALTOR® association on the issue of subletting and assigning leases. Unless your city has a landlord/tenant law, the lease document and specific subletting policies that have been agreed to by the tenant will prevail.

The Relet Agreement

If you agree to relet, execute a relet agreement (Figure 7.1) that spells out the terms and conditions of a relet.

The relet agreement gives the tenants the responsibility for finding suitable new tenants for the apartment. Suitable tenants are ones who meet your usual financial and other requirements, and who are willing to assume the balance of the lease term. You have the right to reject the prospective sublessees on the basis of a credit check.

The form spells out exactly when the old tenants' responsibilities end. Only upon the new residents' paying a full security deposit, signing a lease, paying the first month's rent, and accepting the keys, are the old tenants given their security deposits back and released from the lease.

The agreement lists the amount of reletting fee (if any) and states the exact day the apartment will be vacated.

It also provides new tenants with two options:

The first is to accept the apartment in "as is" condition, at the same rent, and without redecorating or cleaning. In this case you should have the new tenants sign an "as is" letter (Figure 7.2), which indicates in writing that the new residents accept the unit in its existing condition.

The second option is to sign a new one-year lease at a higher rent. This option provides for redecorating and cleaning the apartment, as with any new lease. In this case, the old tenants agree to leave the apartment a few days before the reletting residents' move-in date, to allow the landlord to prepare for the new tenants.

In either case, you should send the old residents a "Notice to Vacate" form and inspect the apartment for damage. This inspection should be done in the presence of both old and new tenants, if possible.

The relet agreement also deals with details about return of security deposits, payment of outstanding bookkeeping charges, providing forwarding addresses, and return of keys.

Both you and the old residents should sign the relet agreement and a copy of the form should be kept in your permanent files.

Cancellation

When tenants must terminate a lease early they may choose to cancel the obligation rather than take the time to find a suitable subtenant. In such a case, you may agree to cancel the lease.

In a lease cancellation, residents buy out their lease by agreeing to a set of conditions. In return for a fee you take on the responsibility of finding a new tenant and fully release the tenant from any further obligation as of the effective date.

Figure 7.1: Relet Agreement

UNIVERSITY PRINTING COMPANY
CHICAGO. ILL 60637

FORM NO19
RELETTING AGREEMENT
Designed to be used with CREB Form 15

©CHICAGO REAL ESTATE BOARD
COPYRIGHT 1976
ALL RIGHTS RESERVED

DATE OF LEASE	TERM OF LEASE		MONTHLY RENT	SECURITY DEPOSIT*
	BEGINNING	ENDING		

TENANT   LESSOR

TENANT   •   •

APARTMENT •   •

BUILDING   •   •

CITY   •   •

A. Owner/Agent and Tenant have heretofore entered into the above described Apartment Lease.

B. Tenant desires to terminate the Apartment Lease and Owner/Agent and Tenant desire to enter into this Reletting Agreement.

NOW, THEREFORE, in consideration of the foregoing and the mutual covenants and agreements hereinafter set forth, Owner/Agent and Tenant agree as follows:

1. Owner/Agent agrees to review the application of any prospective new tenant for the Apartment tendered by Tenant. Each such application shall be made in the form of the application customarily used by Owner/Agent for new tenants and shall include all such information as Owner/Agent customarily requires in considering applications of new tenants. Owner/Agent may reject any prospective new tenant for failure, based on information and data made available to Owner/Agent or which Owner/Agent may otherwise gather, of such prospective new tenant to meet the criteria customarily employed by Owner/Agent to evaluate the acceptability of prospective tenants for similar apartments in the Building. During the last three (3) months of the Term Owner/Agent shall be obliged to accept an otherwise qualified prospective new tenant only if such prospective new tenant enters into a lease for a term for which leases are customarily offered for similar apartments in the Building.

2. Tenant agrees to pay to Owner/Agent an administrative fee of $_____. This administrative fee shall be paid in all events for Owner/Agent services in the reletting and shall not be refunded, even if this agreement is terminated before a new tenant is found.

3. When an acceptable lease has been executed by a suitable new tenant, Owner/Agent and Tenant agree to cancel Tenant's Apartment Lease effective as of the day before the new tenant's lease begins, provided that:

(a) Tenant pays all amounts due under this Agreement and all amounts due under the Apartment Lease, including repairs and replacements which Tenant would have been obligated to pay under the Apartment Lease and any deficiency if the aggregate rent to be paid by the new tenant for the balance of the Term of the Apartment Lease is less than the aggregate rent remaining to be paid by Tenant under the Apartment Lease.

(b) Tenant agrees to pay a portion of the decorating cost required for the new tenant, the amount to be determined by the following formula: Decorating cost X $\frac{\text{Remaining months of Term}}{\text{Total Months of Term}}$. In the alternative, if Owner/Agent so agrees, Tenant may pay the portion of the decorating cost of the Apartment at the *commencement* of the Term determined by the same formula.

(c) Tenant surrenders Tenant's copy of the Apartment Lease and makes arrangements satisfactory to Owner/Agent and the new tenant for delivery of possession to the new tenant.

4. Owner/Agent has no duty to procure prospective new tenants for Tenant or otherwise mitigate damages. Owner/Agent's attempt to procure prospective new tenants shall in no event constitute a new agreement by Owner/Agent to assume such duty. Owner/Agent may lease other vacancies in the Building first before reletting or attempting to relet the Apartment.

5. It is expressly agreed and understood by all parties to this Agreement that during the period from the execution of this Agreement until the effective date of the cancellation of TENANT'S Apartment Lease, TENANT shall be fully responsible for all obligations under said lease and that his obligations and Owner/Agent rights and remedies under said lease are in no way modified by the execution of this agreement.

_____   _____

Owner/Agent   **Tenant**

FOR OFFICE USE ONLY:

FORWARDING ADDRESS:

NAME_____

ADDRESS_____

CITY_____STATE_____ZIP_____

PHONE (HOME)_____

PHONE (OFFICE)_____

☐ $_____ADMINISTRATIVE FEE PAID

☐ COPY OF TENANT'S LEASE RECEIVED

$_____SECURITY DEPOSIT AMOUNT

RETURNED_____
                          Date

PROCESSING OFFICE_____

BY_____

Source: Chicago Association of REALTORS®. Used with permission.

> **Figure 7.2: "As Is" Letter**
>
> _____
>
> Date:
>
> Dear:
>
> We are glad to welcome you as a new resident in apartment _____.
>
> This letter is to verify that you are accepting the apartment "as is" and will not request further cleaning or redecorating for the duration of the lease.
>
> Also, you agree that upon termination of your lease, you will leave the apartment in the same condition to comply with the provisions of your security deposit agreement.
>
> Very truly yours,
>
>
> Accepted by: _____
>   (tenant)   (date)

To cancel a lease, execute an Agreement to Cancel Lease form (Figure 4.16). If the tenants requested a cancellation rider when they signed the lease, this form can be used in conjunction with that rider.

Terms and conditions of this agreement require tenants to pay a fee equal to two months' rent. This fee can vary; it is intended to cover your costs of reletting the apartment, including cleaning and redecorating, and to cover the risk of possibly losing a month's rent if you can't find suitable tenants right away.

The form specifies the day the apartment will be vacated, which is also the cancellation date of the lease, and deals with details of returning keys and providing forwarding addresses.

As in any move-out, tenants must leave the apartment in good condition. Send a Notice to Vacate form and inspect the unit for damages before returning the security deposit.

Return of Possession

However the lease is ended, your goal is the same: You want to regain possession of the apartment in good condition and on time.

Tenants' Rights to Possession

When tenants rent an apartment, they are given and retain possession of the unit throughout the lease term. During the lease term, if tenants are in compliance with the terms of the lease, you may not take any action to regain possession except in the case of an abandonment or as otherwise permitted by law.

Even if the tenants are not in total compliance with the lease, you cannot take possession of the apartment unit by locking the tenants out, removing part of the dwelling unit (for example, the front door), or withholding services (utilities, water, garbage removal).

Turning Over Possession

When a lease is terminated, tenants must relinquish possession immediately. The tenants do this by removing all personal belongings from the apartment and delivering all keys to the owner.

Usually turning over possession is a routine businesslike procedure. You and the tenants agree to terminate the lease or to sublet the apartment; the old tenants move out on the agreed-upon day; and the new tenants move in without a hitch.

However, sometimes things do not go smoothly.

Forcible Detainer

Tenants may fail to return possession by not vacating the unit or not returning the keys. This normally constitutes a forcible detainer, meaning that you the owner (or new tenants, if there are any) may initiate eviction proceedings (see Chapter 8) and request actual and punitive damages.

Abandonment

Occasionally tenants will abandon an apartment without notice. Sometimes this happens when you are in the process of filing an Owner's Five-Day Notice for nonpayment of rent (Figure 8.3) or a Termination Notice for breach of contract (see Figure 2.3). If you check the apartment and find it is or appears to be vacant and not occupied for a period of at least seven days, an Abandonment Notice (Figure 7.3) should be prepared. (Comply with state and local laws governing the posting of notices.) A copy of the form must be posted on the apartment door for 10 days. The original is kept in your files.

When the 10-day period has elapsed, you regain full dominion and control over the premises and property and can begin preparing the apartment for rerental.

Abandoned Personal Property

Occasionally tenants will move out and return the keys, but leave behind some personal property, which must be disposed of properly.

Figure 7.3: Abandonment Notice

Notice and Declaration of Abandonment

_____
Date

To:

Please be advised that as of this date, your rent has been outstanding and unpaid for ten (10) days, and you have been absent from the premises without notice to the Management/Owner for seven (7) days and there is no reasonable evidence that you are occupying the premises, or your rent has been outstanding and unpaid for five (5) days and you have been absent from the premises for five (5) days and none of your personal property remains in the premises.

Consequently, you are advised that the premises have been deemed abandoned in accordance with A.R.S.§ 33–1370 and unless you contact the Manager/Owner within five (5) days of the listing and mailing of this Notice, the Manager/Owner will take the following action:

1. Enter the premises and take possession of the premises;
2. Make reasonable efforts to rent your apartment at the fair rental value;
3. Your refundable security deposit will be forfeited and applied to damages, if any, accrued and unpaid rent, and any other costs incurred by the Manager/Owner as a result of your abandonment of the apartment;
4. Your personal property in the premises (if applicable) will be removed and you will be notified of its location; and
5. Your personal property will be stored for a period of ten (10) days after the completion of the abandonment and if you fail to claim and remove your personal property, it will be subject to being sold with the proceeds of the sale being applied to any outstanding rent, taxes, late charges, damages and any other reasonable costs incurred by the Manager/Owner.

Should you prefer to avoid these actions, please contact the Manager/Owner and make arrangements for the payment of all outstanding rent and other charges immediately.

Sincerely,

By _____
Manager

Time and date personally delivered/mailed
by certified mail:

_____

Generally, personal property left in an apartment is considered abandoned if the residents appear to have moved out (except in the case of eviction), and the apartment no longer contains food or clothing.

Abandonment is a term that has technical meaning in the law and some states have specific statues defining it.

Your lease form may contain language governing abandoned property and your rights to dispose of same. The general procedure to follow for disposing of the property is as follows:

- Try to contact the residents by telephone through their new number or through the emergency or employment telephone numbers provided on the lease application. If you reach the residents, request that the property be removed from the apartment during the next seven days.
- If the resident fails to claim personal property at the end of the time period, you should make an inventory of the property, noting any damaged items.
- If you reasonably believe that the abandoned property is valueless or of such little value that the cost of storage would exceed the amount that would be realized from sale, or if the property is subject to spoilage, dispose of it immediately.
- If the property is of value greater than the cost of storage, store the property for a reasonable time, not exceeding 60 days. Take reasonable care against loss or damage. You should not feel responsible to the residents for any loss not caused by your negligence. The residents may claim the property during the term of storage by paying for the transfer and storage costs. Property not claimed during the term of storage may be disposed of in any reasonable manner without liability to you.

Rent Collection

CHAPTER 8

Jim Bastl and his wife Debbie own and manage a six-flat building. The Bastls work about two hours a week on their property. They give one of the tenants a rent discount in exchange for maintaining the common areas of the building.

I realized at an early age that I would not become wealthy by working for a living. At the same time, I have always known that I can make money as long as someone else is willing to lend it to me. As a computer programmer, I used my analytical ability to search for an investment vehicle that would build wealth without requiring substantial amounts of my own money. After considering all the investment options available today, I found only one where this is not a problem: real estate. Banks will loan up to 80 percent of a property's value.

Collection of rent has not been too much of a problem, since I am careful in screening my tenants. I buy professional forms and envelopes from an office supply store and I send a rent invoice with a return envelope in enough time for the tenant to pay. Although a few of my tenants have had to pay late charges, I usually call to see if we can work out the problem.

The Most Important Management Task

Many of your property management activities occur once a year (renewal of leases, inspection of apartments, and so on), and others, such as maintaining positive resident relations are a continuing responsibility. Collecting the rent, however, is a regular, once-a-month task, and in many ways this function is the owner's most important management activity. The rent is your income from the property. Without it you won't be able to operate and maintain your property.

You need to set a policy of when and how the rent should be paid each month, and then consistently enforce this policy. Try to anticipate problems that might arise, i.e., tenants who habitually pay the rent late, the possible need to evict a tenant—and decide ahead of time how you will deal with these eventualities. A lot of stress can be avoided if you plan ahead and deal with these matters in a businesslike way.

Payment Policies

The strictest policy is to demand that rent be paid in full on or before the first of the month. A more lenient policy is to allow a five-day grace period, which allows tenants to pay the rent any time between the first and the fifth of the month, inclusive, without penalty. Either of these policies might include a provision for a late fee. Whatever policy you establish, the key to enforcing it is to be consistent and not waver from one month to the next or from one tenant to the next.

Where to Collect

There are several ways to go about collecting the rent. One is to ask the tenants to bring it to you in person, but residents may object to this unless you live or have an office on the property. Another way is to go to the tenants' apartments on the first of each month. Some owners prefer this method, but it may not always be convenient. The most common procedure is to have tenants mail the rent. To make it easy, you may provide tenants with 12 preaddressed envelopes.

When to Collect

Rent is due at the beginning of any term of one month or less, otherwise rent is payable in equal monthly installments at the beginning of each month. Unless otherwise agreed, rent is normally uniformly apportioned from day-to-day using a 30-day month.

Most leases clearly state that rent is due and payable in full on or before the first day of each month. It is very important to note that if your rental agreement does not address this issue or if you do not have a written lease agreement that provides that rent is payable in advance on the first of the month, then the rent is generally payable at the end of the rental period, that is, at the end of the month.

Methods of Payment

The rent is considered paid if it is made by any means or in any manner customarily used in the ordinary course of business. This includes cash, money orders, certified and cashier's checks, etc. It does not include farm animals, produce, food stamps, products or goods, or other personal property.

Payment by check is conditional. If a tenant gives you a check on the first of the month and it is subsequently returned for insufficient funds, it is as if that tenant never paid. The owner may require a bad check replaced by cash and all future payments made in cash.

Second-party checks, including payroll checks and/or government checks, should not be accepted. Be sure the residents are told to whom to make out the rent payment checks.

Give a Receipt

A receipt book, which can be purchased in most stationery stores, can be used to receipt all money, including application fees, initial security deposits, rents, credit check fees, partial payments, relet fees, lock-out fees, and cancellation fees. You may or may not want to keep copies of receipts placed in the residents' files.

Delinquencies and Late Charges

The lease will indicate when the rent is to be paid, and at what point it becomes delinquent. If the rent is due on the first of the month, it is considered delinquent on the second (or the fifth, if you allow a grace period). At this point you could choose to immediately file a five-day notice and proceed with an eviction. However, unless you want to get rid of the tenants because of other lease violations, you may want to consider taking a less extreme action.

Reminder Letter

If the rent is late, you may want to send the tenants a rent reminder letter (Figure 8.1). If it is your policy to charge a late fee as soon as rent becomes delinquent, indicate this on the letter. Otherwise, send a late charge notice (Figure 8.2) on the day the late charge goes into effect.

Figure 8.1: Rent Reminder Letter

Date _____

Dear _____:

Our records indicate that your rent is not yet paid. To avoid late fees, please remit your past due rent immediately.

Sincerely,

Figure 8.2: Late Charge Notice

Date _____

_____

_____

_____

Dear _____:

Our records indicate that your rent is still not paid. A $10.00-per-day late charge is now in effect. I am sure you will want to take care of this matter immediately.

If I can be of any help to you in this matter, please feel free to contact me at _____.
(Phone Number)

Sincerely,

Late Charges

Some form leases have a built-in late charge and most leases at least have a provision allowing it. Depending on the specific lease, the late charge is usually assessed between the sixth and tenth day of the month, but it can be assessed as early as the second day. Certain leases specify the exact amount to be charged; for instance, a charge of $5 on rent paid after the fifth and $10 after the tenth. Without a written provision being stated somewhere in the lease, a late charge cannot be demanded.

The charge should be high enough to discourage habitual lateness, but not so high as to be unreasonable. An exorbitant late charge, say over $50, could possibly be challenged as unreasonable.

There is a valid argument against charging late fees. Although they are intended to encourage tenants to pay rent on time, late fees indirectly give tenants permission to pay the rent late. Tenants may think that it is acceptable to pay late as long as they agree to pay the late charge.

You must decide what is more important to you: getting the rent on time, or getting an additional income from the late fee. If you have enough funds in reserve to make the mortgage payment before receiving the rent, a late charge, if rigidly enforced, can provide additional income.

You can choose to waive the late fee, but by doing so you are excusing the lateness and encouraging it to happen again. If you habitually allow late payments, you cannot suddenly change your attitude and begin eviction proceedings when the tenants are late again. If you want to return to the strict terms of the lease, you must first notify the tenants of your intention. This is yet another area to consider Fair Housing Laws. If you waive late fees for some residents, but inconsistently not waive them for others, you may be making yourself vulnerable to a discrimination suit. Whatever policy you establish, you must make every effort to uniformly enforce it with every resident.

Whether or not you charge a late fee, you should attempt to make personal contact with residents whose rent is outstanding and find out why it is late. Get the residents to set a firm date when the rent will be paid. Remind the residents to include fees for late payment. Start eviction procedures if the residents do not pay on the promised date.

Collecting Late Rent

Most tenants will pay their rent on time or within a reasonable grace period. Some will not. If sending reminder letters or making personal contacts is not effective, you will have to take further action. Typically, you will serve a five-day notice, send a follow-up letter, and then begin eviction proceedings.

The Five-Day Notice

In most states, a five-day notice (Figure 8.3) is the first step in processing rent-delinquent residents through the court system. It is usually served on the tenth of the month, but you can issue it as early as the second. Do not put off sending a five-day notice just because the residents have promised to pay. Issue the notice anyway; if and when the residents pay, you can tear up the notice.

Be aware that, in effect, this is a six-day notice. If you serve the notice on the tenth of the month, you cannot file any further papers in court until the sixteenth.

At the same time that you issue the five-day notice, you can include an explanatory cover letter (Figure 8.4).

Filling Out the Notice

Office supply stores that sell legal forms can supply you with five-day notice form. Use Figure 8.3.

The top part of the five-day notice is filled out before being delivered to the resident. States vary in their requirements of posting and delivering notices. Check with your attorney to make sure the method described below is correct in your area.

The amount indicated as due must be rent only; it should not include late charges, security deposit, repair charges, etc. Write in the amount of one normal month's rent as shown on the resident's lease or extension. If a partial payment has been made, fill in the actual amount of rent still owed.

The rent is considered due for the full month, even if the resident has already paid a partial amount. A month's rent is not considered paid until the full amount is received. The beginning and ending dates of that month must be recorded on the notice.

Other information to record on the top part of the form is the complete name and address of the tenant; and a complete description of the property, including location (city and county), street address, and apartment number.

The bottom part of the five-day notice (Affidavit of Service) is completed after the resident has been served with the notice. Upon delivery, the original copy is filled out according to the sample.

The first line of the bottom section ("Served by") is for the name of the person who actually serves the five-day notice. This individual should be the owner or agent.

The person who served the notice signs the form at the bottom in the presence of a notary public any time prior to the time of filing for court eviction.

Delivering the Notice

The form offers four possible modes of delivery.

The preferred mode of delivery is for the owner to personally serve the notice to the principal adult resident. The notice also can be served to an occupant above 13 years of age or to an individual in charge, such as a babysitter.

Figure 8.3: Owner's Five-Day Notice

OWNER'S FIVE DAY NOTICE

FORM 16R COPYRIGHT 1990
CHICAGO BOARD OF REALTORS®

RECOMMENDED BY THE CHICAGO BOARD OF REALTORS® FOR USE WITH CBOR® APARTMENT LEASES 15, 15C, 15C-TH

You are hereby notified that there is now due the owner the sum of $_____

(1) Rent per month $_____, (2) Rent Due from_____to_____

being rent for the premises situated in_____, County of_____

and State of Illinois, and known and described as follows, to wit: _____

_____together with all

buildings, storage areas, recreational facilities, parking spaces and garages used in connection with said premises.

And you are further notified that payment of said sum so due has been and is hereby demanded of you, and that unless payment thereof is made on or before the expiration of five days after service of this notice, your right of possession under the lease of said premises will be terminated.

ONLY FULL PAYMENT of the rent demanded in this notice will waive the landlord's right to terminate the lease under this notice, unless the landlord agrees in writing to continue the lease in exchange for receiving partial payment.

To_____

is authorized to receive said rent, so due.

_____
                                          OWNER

By_____
                           AGENT OR ATTORNEY

Dated this_____day of_____ 19_____

FORM 16-R UNIVERSITY PRINTING CO., CHICAGO 60613

— FOLD —

STATE OF ILLINOIS   } SS.
COUNTY OF_____ }

AFFIDAVIT OF SERVICE

_____, being duly sworn, on oath deposes and says

(Served by)

that on the_____day of_____, 19_____he served the above notice on the tenant named above, as follows:*

☐ (1) by delivering a copy thereof to the above named tenant, _____ .

☐ (2) by delivering a copy thereof to _____, a person above the age of twelve years, residing on or in charge of the above described premises.

☐ (3) by sending a copy thereof to said tenant by certified or registered mail, return receipt requested, postage prepaid, at the address for tenant at the beginning of tenant's lease or such other address as tenant may previously have designated by written notice.

☐ (4) (in the event of apparent abandonment only) by posting a copy thereof on the main door of the above described premises, no one being in actual possession thereof.

Subscribed and sworn to before me this_____day of

_____, 19 _____.

_____ Notary Public

x_____

*Identify the method of service used by placing a check in the proper box. Sign on line marked X.

Source: Chicago Association of REALTORS®. Used with permission.

Delivery by certified mail is not recommended because the eviction cannot be filed until the proof of receipt has been returned.

It used to be permissible to post the notice on the apartment door, but this practice is no longer acceptable in most states.

Partial Payments

Residents may attempt to pay part of the overdue rent during the period covered by the five-day notice. You do not have to accept a partial

Mid-America Management

_____

_____

_____

Dear Resident:

Enclosed, please find a copy of a five-day notice for your unpaid rent. This five-day notice is a legal notice that you have five days in which to pay your rent. This is a demand for payment! Do not construe this as a release from your responsibilities for the apartment which you now occupy. Should you not pay your rent in the prescribed time, legal action in the form of forcible eviction will be entered against you. Should you move out and not pay your rent, a five-day notice is not a release. As stated earlier, this is a demand for payment.

Under the law, you will be responsible for the apartment for the remaining term of the lease, whether you are occupying the apartment or not, until the apartment is re-rented. Therefore, it is important that you understand that merely vacating the apartment does not release you from the responsibility of the lease. To avoid any further charges, such as late charges and legal fees, which the lease states you are required to pay, please pay your rent within the prescribed five-day period. Please be advised that, to assist you with your debt, we do accept VISA and MASTERCARD for rent payments. Should you vacate without paying, a judgment will be entered against you which will appear on your credit record. You would also be liable for wage garnishments against your earnings or any savings or checking accounts you may have in effect.

Should you have any further questions concerning this matter, please contact your site manager.

Regards,

Darren A. Jordan

Darren A. Jordan
Collection Manager

4704/11-92

Mid-America Management Corporation
2901 Butterfield Road, Oak Brook, Illinois 60521 (708) 574-2400

payment. You are only obligated to accept the full amount indicated on the five-day notice.

If you want to keep the tenants, it might be a good idea to accept a partial payment; but if you want to evict the tenants, insist on full payment. Accepting partial payments may only delay the inevitable.

If you accept a partial payment, you must serve another five-day notice indicating the balance due. Whatever you do, be consistent in the treatment of all residents. Do not make exceptions for some, and not for others.

Follow-Up Action

In most cases a five-day notice will motivate tenants to pay. If not, you will have to take further action. On the sixth day following service of the five-day notice, if the tenants have not given you the rent, a legal action notice letter (Figure 8.5) can be issued.

This form lets the tenant know that you are serious about an eviction and it might motivate them to pay. Otherwise if you seriously want to evict the tenant, proceed directly to filing eviction papers.

Eviction

It is a good idea to retain a lawyer to represent you for your first eviction; after that you can probably carry out evictions yourself. The following five steps describe the usual process:

1. On the seventh day after filing the five-day notice, file eviction papers in county circuit court and obtain a court date, usually in two or three weeks. The court (or possibly you or your lawyer) will serve the eviction papers to the tenants.
2. Show up for court on the court date. If the tenants do not show up, the judge will order an eviction. If the tenants do show up, a lenient judge may grant an automatic two-week stay to allow the tenants more time to come up with the rent. If the tenants claim hardship (illness, unemployment, small children involved, difficulty finding other housing) the delay may be a month or more.
3. If the tenants do not pay within the court-decreed stay, you appear in court again, and the judge will enter a judgment against the tenants (monetary award) and order the eviction. Another stay is possible for hardship.
4. You take the eviction order to the Sheriff's department to set up an eviction date, usually in two or three weeks. Again, these papers are served to the tenants.

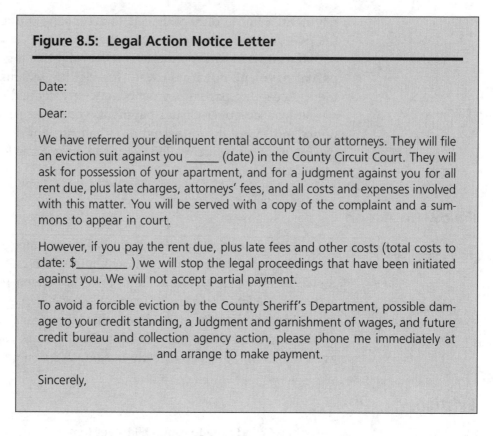

Figure 8.5: Legal Action Notice Letter

Date:

Dear:

We have referred your delinquent rental account to our attorneys. They will file an eviction suit against you _____ (date) in the County Circuit Court. They will ask for possession of your apartment, and for a judgment against you for all rent due, plus late charges, attorneys' fees, and all costs and expenses involved with this matter. You will be served with a copy of the complaint and a summons to appear in court.

However, if you pay the rent due, plus late fees and other costs (total costs to date: $_____) we will stop the legal proceedings that have been initiated against you. We will not accept partial payment.

To avoid a forcible eviction by the County Sheriff's Department, possible damage to your credit standing, a Judgment and garnishment of wages, and future credit bureau and collection agency action, please phone me immediately at _____ and arrange to make payment.

Sincerely,

5. Usually the tenants will move out before actual physical eviction; if not, a moving company hired by the Sheriff (and paid for by you) will come and move the tenants out. At this time you regain possession of the apartment.

Clearly this is a long, time-consuming process. A number of filing fees must be paid, even if you do not retain an attorney. If the tenants have decided not to pay, you will lose a month or more of rent during the eviction process.

Attorney fees to process an eviction vary; these fees may be awarded to you by the court.

Collecting a Judgment

Partial Payments

If the resident attempts to pay part of the overdue rent during the period covered by the five-day notice you do not have to accept it. You are only obligated to accept the full amount indicated on the five-day notice.

In general, accept partial payments from tenants you want to keep; and do not accept partial payments from tenants you want to evict.

After a resident makes a partial payment, you will have to serve another five-day notice indicating the balance due.

After delinquent tenants move out you can begin activities to recover the amount due. Winning in court does not mean that you will automatically be paid. The court may award you a judgment, but you must enforce it. You will probably have to take additional action to collect the funds.

Using a Collection Agency or Attorney

When residents have moved out without notice, or have been evicted, or have damaged the apartment in excess of the security deposit, or moved owing you back rent, the debt can be turned over to a collection agency or attorney.

Depending on the circumstances, it might be better to use a collection agency rather than an attorney. Collection agencies are usually licensed by the state and licenses can be revoked in the event a collection law is violated. Collection attorneys operate on their own and are controlled only by their peers in the bar association.

In either case, it is vital to select a reputable and talented attorney or agency. Collecting bad debts requires special skills and experience and is usually best handled by professionals.

Collection agencies normally work on a contingency basis. They generally charge a percentage of the amount collected as their fee.

Even with the help of a professional collection specialist, you may not always be successful in collecting bad debts from tenants. Thus, you should initiate legal proceedings promptly to minimize potential loss.

A collection agency will need as much information as possible to track down the former residents. You can use the transmittal form (Figure 8.6) to forward information to the collections manager.

If possible, obtain the residents' forwarding address before they leave the apartment, for the purpose of forwarding mail or returning the security deposit. It is important to obtain their current places of employment in case it is necessary to garnish wages, if permissible by law.

Other approaches that might prove successful in obtaining a forwarding address include recording the license plate number on the residents' car and contacting the Secretary of State, contacting the moving company, calling the old telephone number to see if calls are being referred to a new number, and contacting the person listed on the application for notification in case of emergency.

Figure 8.6: Transmittal Form

Date: _____

_____

_____

_____

Gentlemen:

Enclosed are the necessary documents relating to the EVICTION, POSSESSION, FORCIBLE DETAINER and/or COLLECTION of Accounts Receivable for apartment: _____ at

_____

Names of Residents: _____/_____

Monthly Rent:	$_____ times _____ months		=	$ _____
Months Included:				
Other Charges:	$_____ for _____		=	$ _____
SUBTOTAL:			=	$ _____
Attorney's Fees:			=	$ _____
Court Costs:			=	$ _____
TOTAL DUE:			=	$ _____

Please send COLLECTION letter first before beginning suit.   _____

Please begin suit immediately.   _____

Please do not sue—COLLECTION ONLY.   _____

Please send letter demanding tenant take remedial action to cure default as listed.

Comments: _____

_____

Please notify us of any actions taken by tenant as a result of your efforts. We will notify you immediately of any action or receipt of any funds on behalf of the tenant.

Insurance

CHAPTER 9

Cathie Moscato owns a business services company and is married to a school teacher. Two years ago, before getting married, Cathie bought a small six-flat apartment building in the suburbs.

I've always believed real estate to be the best investment around. Fortunately, my husband and I live on the property and are able to service the tenants immediately. My business hours are somewhat flexible, which allows me time to maintain a well-kept property.

A couple of months after I bought the building, there was a fire in one of the top floor units. The fire was discovered at around 2 AM by one of the tenants. Although the fire was contained in that one apartment, by the time the fire department extinguished it, there was considerable smoke and water damage throughout the building.

The fire department's official report listed the cause of the fire as the tenant's careless smoking.

What could have been a financial disaster turned out to be a minor incident thanks to my independent insurance agent, who counseled me in purchasing the correct insurance for the property.

Not only did my insurance cover the cost of repairs, but it also covered my loss of rental income during the repair period. My premium payments did not increase because my insurance company won the lawsuit against the tenant's insurance company, who ultimately paid the claim.

The Language of Insurance

The following definitions, explanations, and examples are provided so you may better understand this chapter.

All-risk: There is coverage for all perils except those excluded. Be sure to read the exclusions portion of your policy.

Bailee: Whenever property is delivered into the custody of a person other than the rightful owner, the person in control of the property becomes the bailee, and assumes certain responsibilities for the safety of property in his or her care.

Care, custody, and control: Damage to personal property of others which is in the care, custody, or control of the insured is excluded under all standard liability forms. You should purchase a bailee endorsement or policy to cover this exposure.

As a bailee you may store an article for another, accept packages for your tenants to pick up from you, and/or borrow a piece of equipment. Discuss with your agent your possible bailee exposure.

Certificates of insurance: You should require contractors who do work for you to supply a certificate of insurance in order to limit your liability in case of mishaps. Certificates should show liability coverage for bodily injury and property damage and for workers' compensation/employers' liability. Figure 9.1 shows how one sample of a certificate of insurance form looks when completed.

If a suit arises and you cannot provide proof that the contractor had insurance, your policy may pay on your behalf when you are sued. However, your insurance company may then require you to pay a premium for this additional exposure, or may cancel your coverage as a result of this discovery.

Coinsurance: Coinsurance indicates a sharing of the insurance by the insurance company and the insured. The word coinsurance has a more limited and restricted meaning within the insurance business.

The mandatory and minimum amount of coinsurance is usually 80 percent. Illustrating the coinsurance clause by example best explains its meaning and application. For example, a property with an actual cash value of $100,000 must be insured for at least 80 percent of the value of the property, or $80,000.

In this case $80,000 would be the minimum coverage required to avoid penalty in the event of a loss. If the same building is insured for $60,000 in lieu of the required $80,000, it would be insured for only three-fourths of the minimum coverage demanded by the coinsurance requirements. In this instance, a penalty would be imposed should a loss occur.

In the event of a $1,000 loss, exclusive of all deductibles, the insured would receive not $1,000, but three-fourths of the loss, or $750. In the event of a total loss, however, the insured would collect the full face value of the policy, or $60,000. Since the property was valued at $100,000 before the loss, the insured is still penalized for not having insured sufficiently, a $40,000 penalty.

The coinsurance clause is taken very seriously in the insurance business and an insured who does not adhere to its requirements can expect to receive less than full value when faced with a loss.

Deductibles: The use of a deductible means the insured pays the first dollar amount for a loss, as specified in the policy. Unless changed by endorsement, a standard $100 deductible may apply separately to each building (and its contents), subject to a $1,000 aggregate per occurrence.

Premium dollars can be saved by increasing the deductible. A larger deductible will mean a larger financial outlay in the event of a loss and may mean total responsibility for smaller losses, but it will also result in an immediate savings on the premium.

Deductibles are applied in three different ways:

1. *Occurrence*: One fire or other insured loss equals one occurrence and one deductible applies.
2. *Per claim*: This applies to every claim filed regardless of number of occurrences. One fire may produce six or more claims and six or more deductibles will apply.
3. *Aggregate* (either occurrence or annual): With a $25,000 annual aggregate deductible, the insured retains a maximum of $25,000 of losses in a given year and the insurer is responsible for any additional loss payments in that year.

Physical hazard: This is a characteristic that increases the chance of loss. Some hazards arise from a repairable defect in the property (for example, a broken step); others are inherent characteristics of the property (for example, a building is of frame construction).

Premium: This is money that the insured pays the insurer for coverage of a defined nature. This exchange must take place prior to or at the inception date of coverage. You may be surprised to find you are not insured if a loss occurs prior to premium payment. A large premium can be financed with monthly or quarterly payments by a premium finance company at interest rates close to bank prime rates.

Property values: Insured values reflect not market value but the construction cost; that is, the cost to rebuild at the time of loss.

Unless specifically endorsed or stated in the coverage form, all property will be valued at actual cash value (ACV) at the time of loss. ACV is defined as the cost to repair or replace the damaged property less an amount for physical depreciation. This basis of adjustment may be modified, however, by the attachment of a replacement cost endorsement.

Punitive or exemplary damage awards: Most companies will exclude responsibility for payment of any award for punitive or exemplary damage. Responding to and complying with insurance company recommendations will add to your noticeable effort to provide a safe environment for your tenants and will be beneficial in the defense of suits that may arise.

Self-insured retention (SIR): That portion of a loss that you pay.

Vacancy: There are no furnishings or other personal property in the building. Some insurers consider property vacant when there are no full-time occupants. Most policies contain a clause that suspends coverage when a building is vacant beyond a stated period of time, normally 30 days. Vacancy policies are available, but are very expensive.

Property Insurance

As the owner of an income property, carrying insurance to protect your investment and its income against catastrophe is a good practice. The following summary is provided for general information purposes only and is subject to the terms and conditions of your individual policies, which may vary.

Because no two properties are alike, there is no all-purpose insurance policy that will cover all buildings. Instead, the insurance agent will issue a multiperil package (sometimes called a business-owners' package). This package consists of property and liability insurance, along with a number of endorsements and/or riders. The purpose of this coverage is to protect you from loss from damage to your property.

There are two types of property to be considered:

1. Real property
2. Business personal property

Virtually all real property, except foundations and underground improvements, is included in the definition of a building under a policy. Most policies define a building as: buildings, structures, additions, fixtures, appliances, permanent equipment, and machinery used for the maintenance and service of a building. Some companies include fences and TV antennas, most do not. Piers, wharves, docks, pools, and valuable landscaping must be separately insured. Be sure to check what is included in the definition of real property on your policy.

Business personal property includes rental office contents on premises, lobby and recreational room contents, model apartment contents, and furnished unit contents.

Limitations or Exclusions

Types of property that might have limited coverage or be excluded from this package of coverage include tenant improvements and betterments, boiler and machinery, leased equipment, money and securities, valuable papers, private collections, landscaping, and mobile equipment such as trucks, automobiles, watercraft, and aircraft.

Endorsement Options

Endorsements are separate documents attached to policies that modify the policy's original terms. There are ten common endorsements:

1. Agreed-amount endorsement
2. Inflation-guard endorsement
3. Replacement-cost endorsement
4. Demolition and increased cost of construction endorsement
5. Difference-in-conditions (DIC) endorsement
6. Earthquake endorsement
7. Fine arts schedule
8. Glass endorsement
9. Loss of rents endorsement
10. Flood

Agreed-Amount Endorsement

It is practical to establish a fixed value on your real insurable property to which the insurance underwriter will agree in advance. This agreement serves to eliminate coinsurance. For superior property, an agreed-amount clause is a means of protecting against the consequence of inadvertent under-insurance in an inflationary environment.

Through this endorsement, a coinsurance clause is superseded and a specified amount of insurance takes the place of a specified percentage of actual cash value (ACV) or replacement cost. Partial losses are paid in full, after the application of the deductible. Total losses are paid to the policy limit after the deductible.

Inflation-Guard Endorsement

Under this type of endorsement, the property coverage is automatically increased by a specific percentage each month (or quarter) to help meet rising construction and replacement costs.

Ask your agent to include this feature in your policy to prevent future coinsurance penalties or underinsurance.

Replacement-Cost Endorsement

This endorsement eliminates the deduction for depreciation in property valuation at the time of a loss. It is used in lieu of Actual Cash Value (ACV) or depreciated value.

Coverage is limited to either the cost of restoring the property to its original (nondepreciated) condition or the actual cost of repairing or replacing the property, whichever is less.

Policies will pay on a replacement cost basis only if the damaged property is repaired or replaced at the same premises within a reasonable time after the loss.

Where replacement may take a significant amount of time, you may elect to settle on an ACV basis initially and, after the property has been restored, settle the balance due on a replacement cost basis.

Demolition and Increased Cost of Construction/Contingent Liability Endorsement

The ordinance or law exclusion in most property policies excludes loss from operation resulting from the enforcement of building codes that require demolition of partially damaged structures and mandate superior construction in new or replacement buildings. Demolition coverage, which may be included by endorsement to the standard fire or all-risk policies, provides coverage for the cost of demolition and the loss from that remaining undamaged portion of the building that must be demolished when required by local ordinance.

The demolition endorsement is often combined with an increased cost of construction endorsement that affords coverage for the difference in costs between the original damaged construction and the new upgraded construction required by current building codes. Ordinances mandating superior construction are common in many cities where fire or earthquake codes have been changed over the years. Check your local ordinance.

Difference-in-Conditions (DIC) Endorsement

This endorsement can add back coverage for some of the normal exclusions found in most policies. Backup of sewers and drains, wind-driven rain, off-premises power failure, and off-premises water damage (example: a break in a city water main resulting in damage to premises) are normal exclusions under the basic fire policy.

Earthquake Endorsement

Coverage for damage from earthquake, and resulting aftershocks within 72 hours, may be provided by endorsements to the standard fire or all-risk policy or by special all-risk forms and DIC policies. Coverage includes damage to excavations, foundations, and pilings, which are excluded under the standard fire policy.

Deductibles are generally quite high and rates are determined primarily by location and building construction.

Fine Arts Schedule

Any sculptures, antiques, and other art work must be scheduled by endorsements on the policy. Be sure to advise your agent of the existence of these objects if you wish to insure them.

Glass Endorsement

Most apartment package policies limit glass coverage. If there is a large percentage of glass in the makeup of the building structure, additional coverage should be purchased. This may be accomplished by endorsing the apartment package policy or by purchasing a separate policy.

Discuss with the insurance agent any unique types of glass such as stained glass, neon and fluorescent signs, and structural glass and lettering or ornamentation thereon. Coverage includes the repair or replacement of frames when necessary.

Loss of Rents Endorsement

This clause provides for reimbursement of rents lost, less any discontinued expense, when the loss is caused by an insured peril under the policy. Try to purchase this coverage on the basis of actual loss sustained within a 12-month period or 100 percent of annual value whenever possible.

Flood

The Federal Flood Program will provide up to $250,000 per building for flood damage when the building is located in a designated flood zone.

Your local zoning or building code office will be able to tell you if your property is located in such a zone. This is a separate policy, not an endorsement. Apply for coverage through your insurance agent. The coverage is not effective until 30 days after a completed application and payment of premium is received by the Federal Flood Program Agency.

Additional coverage may be purchased through a DIC (difference in conditions) policy. You may use the National Flood Program as coverage for the large deductible required under the DIC policy.

Liability Insurance

The purpose of liability insurance is to protect you against a lawsuit arising from some accidental or unintended occurrence. General liability protects against claims arising from premises, products, incidental contracts, libel, false arrest, etc.

The liability portion of a policy generally is written on a comprehensive basis for any occurrence arising out of the ownership, maintenance or use of the premises and for operations that are necessary or incidental to the property such as lawsuits arising out of slips and falls, and certain liabilities assumed under contracts or agreements. The limits are usually combined single limits for bodily injury and property damage liability and range from $300,000 to $1,000,000. Coverage of employee injuries is not included and must be purchased under a workers' compensation/ employers' liability policy.

An annual aggregate limit restricts the total amount that will be paid for liability coverage in any one policy year. Most policies include a limit for all occurrences within a policy year as well as the per occurrence limit. Be sure to check which limit you have purchased because of this annual aggregate limitation. An umbrella or excess policy purchase will be important to your protection.

Liability Policies

Liability policies are of two types:

1. Claims-made
2. Occurrence-based

Claims-made differs from an occurrence policy primarily in the manner in which coverage is triggered.

Occurrence-based policies cover events that occur during the policy period, and the insurance company is obligated to defend and pay for claims that arise from such covered occurrences at any time in the future, even years later. On the other hand, claims-made policies obligate the insurance company to defend and pay only for those claims reported while the policy is in force, and for incidents that occurred on or after the retroactive date (usually the policy effective date). In other words, in a claims-made policy the company will pay claims for any occurrences on or after the retroactive date, and only up until the policy expires.

If your coverage is the claims-made type, yet you want coverage to last for a certain period of time after the policy expiration or cancellation, one option is to purchase an extended reporting period (sometimes called tail coverage) for your policy. This extends coverage to protect against claims that may be made after a policy is no longer in force.

Umbrella or Excess Liability

It is prudent to protect your assets with an umbrella or excess limits liability policy. The policy adds at least $1,000,000 of protection to primary liability policy limits of commercial, auto, and employers' liability, and insures many uncovered liability exposures for $1,000,000 or more over a self-insured retention, normally $10,000 or $25,000.

Pollution Liability Exclusion

The *commercial liability* policy excludes all pollution coverage. The exclusion is built into the policy itself and cannot be removed by endorsement. You should research your property to determine whether or not you have an exposure to pollution liability. If an exposure exists and coverage is desired, a special application and survey must be completed.

There is a growing need for property owners to protect themselves against financial liability associated with environmental damage. Environmental impairment insurance is available.

Broad Form Commercial General Liability (CGL)

Broad form commercial includes: contractual, personal injury that includes libel, slander, and false arrest (discrimination or humiliation coverage is included but limited), advertising, premises medical, host liquor, fire legal, incidental medical malpractice, nonowned watercraft, limited worldwide coverage, employees as additional insureds, automatic coverage for newly acquired entities, and broad form property damage that adds back coverage for property in your care, custody, and control. Some of these are discussed below; others were defined earlier in this chapter. Your agent can explain how these options apply to your property.

Contractual (Independent Contractors)

You may have occasion to enter into contracts employing others, such as painters, roofers, and so on. When the contractor enters your premises or does work on your behalf, she or he may incur or cause injury claims for which you may be held liable. Some of the claims asserted against you by people injured by the contractor are covered by your own policy under the commercial general liability section if your agent has included independent contractors on an "if any" basis.

In some states, if a contractor cannot respond to a workers' compensation claim, the person for whom the injured employee is working (you) may have to respond. Therefore, you should request evidence that the contractor carries liability and workers' compensation insurance, prior to beginning the job. This evidence is normally provided in the form of a certificate of insurance and is obtained from the contractor's insurance broker (Figure 9.1).

Medical Payments

Coverage is automatically provided in the amounts of $1,000 or more per person and $10,000 or $25,000 for all persons requiring medical attention as a result of a single accident arising from owned or rented premises. Some policies exclude payments on behalf of tenants or residents. Liability need not be proven.

Personal Injury

You face risks for claims other than bodily injury or property damage. If you libel or slander someone, invade a person's privacy, commit a trespass or mistakenly accuse someone of a crime, he or she can sue you.

Indemnity for certain personal injuries is in the insuring agreement of the commercial liability section of the policy.

Host Liquor

If a host serves liquor (without charge) to guests who subsequently, while intoxicated, cause bodily injury or property damage to others, the host may be held liable.

Making Claims

One of the conditions of an insurance policy is that you give prompt notice to the insurer of any accident or occurrence and of any claim or suit brought against you. An occurrence is an incident such as someone falling

Figure 9.1: Certificate of Insurance Form

SET TAB STOPS AT ARROWS

CERTIFICATE OF INSURANCE

ISSUE DATE (MM/DD/YY): Must be completed

PRODUCER

Name & Address of
Contractor's Insurance Representative

THIS CERTIFICATE IS ISSUED AS A MATTER OF INFORMATION ONLY AND CONFERS NO RIGHTS UPON THE CERTIFICATE HOLDER. THIS CERTIFICATE DOES NOT AMEND, EXTEND OR ALTER THE COVERAGE AFFORDED BY THE POLICIES BELOW.

COMPANIES AFFORDING COVERAGE

COMPANY LETTER **A**	Name of Insuring Company
COMPANY LETTER **B**	Name of Insuring Company
COMPANY LETTER **C**	Name of Insuring Company
COMPANY LETTER **D**	Name of Insuring Company
COMPANY LETTER **E**	Name of Insuring Company

INSURED

Name & Address of
Contractor hired

COVERAGES

THIS IS TO CERTIFY THAT POLICIES OF INSURANCE LISTED BELOW HAVE BEEN ISSUED TO THE INSURED NAMED ABOVE FOR THE POLICY PERIOD INDICATED. NOTWITHSTANDING ANY REQUIREMENT, TERM OR CONDITION OF ANY CONTRACT OR OTHER DOCUMENT WITH RESPECT TO WHICH THIS CERTIFICATE MAY BE ISSUED OR MAY PERTAIN, THE INSURANCE AFFORDED BY THE POLICIES DESCRIBED HEREIN IS SUBJECT TO ALL THE TERMS, EXCLUSIONS, AND CONDITIONS OF SUCH POLICIES.

These Sections Must Be Completed

CO LTR	TYPE OF INSURANCE	POLICY NUMBER	POLICY EFFECTIVE DATE (MM/DD/YY)	POLICY EXPIRATION DATE (MM/DD/YY)	LIABILITY LIMITS IN THOUSANDS	EACH OCCURRENCE	AGGREGATE
	GENERAL LIABILITY [X] COMPREHENSIVE FORM [X] PREMISES/OPERATIONS [ ] UNDERGROUND EXPLOSION & COLLAPSE HAZARD [X] PRODUCTS/COMPLETED OPERATIONS [X] CONTRACTUAL [X] INDEPENDENT CONTRACTORS [X] BROAD FORM PROPERTY DAMAGE [ ] PERSONAL INJURY	These sections must be completed	This date should reflect a date prior to commencement of job.	This date should reflect a date past completion of job.	BODILY INJURY	$	$
					PROPERTY DAMAGE	$	$
					BI & PD COMBINED	$ 500	$500 *2
					PERSONAL INJURY		$
	AUTOMOBILE LIABILITY [ ] ANY AUTO [ ] ALL OWNED AUTOS (PRIV. PASS.) [ ] ALL OWNED AUTOS (OTHER THAN PRIV. PASS.) [*1] HIRED AUTOS [*1] NON-OWNED AUTOS [ ] GARAGE LIABILITY	*1 Minimum requirement if vehicles are not required for the job			BODILY INJURY (PER PERSON)	$	
					BODILY INJURY (PER ACCIDENT)	$	
					PROPERTY DAMAGE	$	
					BI & PD COMBINED	$ 500	
	EXCESS LIABILITY [X] UMBRELLA FORM [ ] OTHER THAN UMBRELLA FORM				BI & PD COMBINED	$1,000	$1,000
	WORKERS' COMPENSATION AND EMPLOYERS' LIABILITY				STATUTORY		
						$ 100 (EACH ACCIDENT)	
						$ 100 (DISEASE-POLICY LIMIT)	
						$ 100 (DISEASE-EACH EMPLOYEE)	
	OTHER				*2 All limits shown are suggested minimums		

DESCRIPTION OF OPERATIONS/LOCATIONS/VEHICLES/SPECIAL ITEMS as relates to job contracted

Your name and trust in which your property is titled should appear here as additional named insured for job described herewith.

CERTIFICATE HOLDER

Your Name
& Address

CANCELLATION

SHOULD ANY OF THE ABOVE DESCRIBED POLICIES BE CANCELLED BEFORE THE EXPIRATION DATE THEREOF, THE ISSUING COMPANY WILL ~~ENDEAVOR TO~~ MAIL 30 DAYS WRITTEN NOTICE TO THE CERTIFICATE HOLDER NAMED TO THE
* ~~LEFT, BUT FAILURE TO MAIL SUCH NOTICE SHALL IMPOSE NO OBLIGATION OR LIABILITY OF ANY KIND UPON THE COMPANY, ITS AGENTS OR REPRESENTATIVES.~~

AUTHORIZED REPRESENTATIVE

This section must be signed

* Have this wording crossed out

on your premises, or an error that causes loss or injury to a person, or any unplanned event that could give cause to a lawsuit.

If you fail to give reasonable notice, you may be shocked to find that the insurance company's obligations to defend you and pay any claims have been waived. Try to report any notice of a lawsuit the same day it is received.

Notice is normally given by contacting the agent or broker who sold you the policy. To protect yourself, it is wise to give notice in writing and to get written confirmation from the agent acknowledging that your notice has been received and forwarded to the insurer.

Do not attempt to judge whether or not insurance will apply. The report should be made regardless of coverage. If there is a serious question in your mind whether the policy covers the claim, consult your attorney for assistance in giving notice to the insurer. A poorly drafted notice may prompt the insurer to deny coverage rather than to investigate and pay the claim.

Property Claims

Property damage claims should be made promptly. To report property claims, use the property loss form provided by your insurance carrier. A sample is included as Figure 9.2.

Photos should be taken when damage to your property occurs and you need to make immediate repairs to prevent further loss. It is not necessary to wait for the claims adjuster before you do whatever emergency repairs are necessary to prevent further loss. Be sure to retain any damaged, replaced materials or objects for the adjuster to view upon arrival. Most property policies cover your insured property if you move it to a safer place to avoid loss or further damage.

Liability Claims

To report liability claims use the liability loss report form and the incident report form provided by your carrier to assist you in providing necessary information to the insurance company's claim adjuster. Samples are included as Figures 9.2, 9.3, and 9.4.

The incident report is beneficial in tenant-landlord communications. Using this form to extract information from the tenant or visitor at the time of complaint assures the complainant that proper attention is being given to the incident. The report is then forwarded to the insurance carrier, who

Figure 9.2: Property Loss Report

Property Loss Report

Reported By: _____ Date: _____

Complex: _____

Date of Loss: _____

Contact Person: _____ Phone Number: _____

Location of Loss: _____

Kind of Loss (Fire, Wind, Explosion, etc.): _____

Description of Loss and Damage: _____

_____

_____

_____

_____

Estimated Amount of Loss: _____

Police or Fire Department Reported to: _____

Claimants Name, Address, and Phone Number: _____

_____

_____

_____

Additional Comments: _____

_____

_____

_____

_____

_____

responds to the complaint. Some important notes to remember regarding liability incidents are:

- Make no statement admitting liability or authorizing medical treatment.
- Take photos of the area when an accident occurs, prior to proceeding with any necessary immediate repairs. If any machine or object may have been responsible for the accident, preserve it, as is, in a safe place until it can be examined by experts.
- Advise any employees not to discuss the case with anyone until instructed by your claims adjuster or attorney.

Other Types of Insurance

FAIR Plan

In the past, if you were unable to buy insurance for property because it was in a riot-prone or environmentally hazardous urban area, coverage was made available through the Federal Riot Reinsurance Program under the FAIR (Fair Access to Insurance Requirements) Plan. While this program is no longer federally active, in many states it has become a statewide program.

A building must be otherwise insurable except for its location in a blighted or deteriorated eligible urban area.

You must submit an application for eligibility and may be accepted, conditionally accepted, or unconditionally declined. You cannot be declined for reason of environmental hazards in urban areas.

Coverage is generally limited to fire, extended coverage, vandalism, and malicious mischief. Maximum limits are $500,000 at any one location.

Tenants' Insurance

As a landlord, encourage your tenants to carry adequate personal property and liability insurance.

The landlord has limited liability for injury or damage occurring within the rental portion of the premises. Both landlord and tenant have a duty to take reasonable care in the portion of the premises under their control. For example, if tenant Jones on an upper floor allows his bathtub to overflow and the water drips through the ceiling and ruins rugs in tenant Smith's apartment below, the landlord is not liable, since Smith is in exclusive possession of his apartment. However, the landlord, on being advised, must attempt where possible to aid the tenant suffering the loss by turning off the water.

Figure 9.3: Incident Report

Incident Report

Date: _____   Time: _____   Name of Reporting Person: _____

Date of Incident: _____   Time of Incident: _____   Property: _____

Specific Location of Incident: _____
                              (Floor, apt., room, area, address, etc.)

Type of Incident: Accident _____   Crime _____   Fire _____   Ambulance _____   Vandalism _____
                  Mechanical _____   Theft _____   Loss _____   Other _____

What Happened? _____
_____
_____
_____
_____

List Injuries   _____
or Damages   _____
                    _____

List People   _____
Involved   _____
                    _____

Prevalent Conditions at Time of Incident: _____
(weather, lighting, environment, etc.)
_____
_____

- -

For Management Use Only

Insurance Notified: _____   By Phone: _____   By Mail: _____
                   (date)

Name of Insurance Agent: _____

Board Notified: _____   Name of Board Member: _____

Police Notified: _____   Report Number: _____   Name of Officer: _____

Follow-up Action Required: _____
_____
_____

Figure 9.4: Liability Loss Report

Liability Loss Report

Reported by: _____ Date: _____

Complex: _____

Date of Loss: _____

Contact Person: _____ Phone Number: _____

Injured Party or Damage to Personal Property of Tenants, Etc.

Name: _____

Address: _____

Phone Number: _____ Work Number: _____

Age: _____ Sex: _____ Date of Injury: _____

Where Injury Sustained (Address): _____

How Injury Sustained: _____

_____

_____

_____

_____

(If additional space is required, please use reverse side.)

Type of Injury: _____

_____

_____

Treating Hospital: _____

Was Police Department Called? If So, Please Indicate: _____

Additional Comments: _____

_____

_____

_____

_____

If a tenant causes a fire, damages are paid by the apartment building owner's insurance company, who could then seek recovery from the tenant's liability policy, thus protecting the good claims record of the building owner. A high and frequent claims record usually means higher premiums for the building owner, as well as the risk of nonrenewal or cancellation of your policy.

Boiler and Machinery Insurance

Boiler and machinery insurance can be endorsed into many packages or written on a separate policy. Protection includes property damage and legal liability for damage to the property of others in your care, custody, and control, and associated defense costs. A large component of the boiler and machinery premium is for engineering and inspection services.

Boiler coverage. Almost all apartment building policies exclude damage to the insured property resulting from internally caused explosion of boilers or other pressure vessels. Consequently, boiler coverage is needed if the property contains any heating or process boiler or steam generator that operates under pressure. Boilers include hot water boilers, steam boilers, and steam piping.

Boiler explosions are rare. However, even one such explosion can be a catastrophic event in terms of potential destruction and injury. A far more common occurrence is the less destructive but still costly cracking, burning, bulging, or collapse of boilers and pressure vessels.

One of the most common failures of boilers is the failure of the low-water cutoff, the control that shuts off the burner when the water level is low. Such failure generally results in damage from overheating, and in the case of cast iron boilers, cracked sections. Some apartment building insurance policies do not include coverage for damage caused to the building as a result of a boiler problem (consequential damage). In this case, if your insurance policy includes a boiler inspection service, this can be as valuable as the coverage itself.

Machinery coverage. Machinery coverage provides insurance against damage and loss resulting from the breakdown of machinery on the premises. Machinery includes objects such as air compressors, fans, air conditioners, blowers, pump units, engines, turbines, and miscellaneous electrical equipment such as switchboards and other apparatus used for power distribution. This coverage also extends to surrounding property that is excluded under the apartment building package policy.

It is wise to insure only those machines that are extraordinarily expensive and time-consuming to repair or whose function is critical to the entire operation. Again, the insurance company's machinery inspection service can be a valuable component of the insurance policy.

Coverage options in boiler and machinery insurance. Some options to consider when choosing how to allocate insurance dollars are:

- Repairs and replacement: essentially an elimination of depreciation
- Extra expenses for the period of restoration
- Joint loss agreement (loss adjustment endorsement) should be obtained when you have different insurers for building and boiler and machinery. This means the boiler carrier will settle the loss and subrogate against the property insurer if necessary.
- Business interruption (loss of rents): on a valued daily or weekly indemnity basis. There are two coverage options:
  1. *Actual loss sustained*: The loss of net profit plus specified fixed charges and expenses that continue despite the accident. This loss must be proven. If coverage is on a coinsurance basis, you should obtain a waiver of coinsurance, if possible. Care must be taken in establishing the valuations.
  2. *Valued form*: A daily indemnity is specified which is the amount of recovery for each day during which rents are totally suspended. In the case of a partial suspension, a portion is paid based on reduction of current business.

Workers' Compensation

Each state has its own workers' compensation law, whereby all workers suffering injury or illness related to the job are reimbursed for medical costs, lost earnings, and rehabilitation costs. Where death occurs, an employee's heirs are entitled to death benefits provided by statute.

If you hire employees such as rental agents, cleaners, or maintenance personnel, you must purchase workers' compensation/employers' liability insurance.

Even if you have no direct employees, you still should have voluntary workers' compensation/employers' liability insurance for those situations where a subcontractor is uninsured or an independent contractor can show employee status. State workers' compensation courts do not always recognize independent contractor arrangements.

The objective of workers' compensation is to indemnify the employee for loss of earnings and expenses. The employer is obligated to pay for the reasonable cost of medical, surgical, hospital, and nursing services as required. The injured employee also is entitled to weekly compensation payment for the length of the disability and rehabilitation services. Workers' compensation statutes in all states now include disease.

Every worker injury involving medical treatment or lost time must be reported on the form used in your state. Each state has its own form; copies are available from your local adjuster or agent. For samples of the Illinois, Indiana, Arizona, and Wisconsin forms see Figures 9.5 through 9.8.

Employers' Liability

A further exposure facing an employer is an action instituted by a third party. This could arise where an injured employee sues and recovers from a legally responsible third party such as the manufacturer of machinery. This third party manufacturer may in turn seek recovery from the employer, contending, for example, that the employer is liable for having negligently maintained the machine or having inadequately trained the employee.

A few work-related injuries do not fall under workers' compensation law. If that is the case, the claim is one of employers' liability, which is part of the workers' compensation policy.

Employers' liability coverage, in contrast to workers' compensation coverage, is subject to a specified limit of liability. This is customarily written at a limit of $100,000 but can be increased to $500,000. It is advisable to have this coverage scheduled on the umbrella or excess liability policy to assure that the higher umbrella limits apply. Some umbrella insurers have refused to insure employers' liability incurred by employee disease; therefore, you should request a higher employers' liability on the workers' compensation/employers' liability policy.

Dealing with Insurance Companies

Begin shopping for insurance coverage at least 60 days prior to the expiration of your current coverage to allow sufficient time to find the best coverage for the lowest premium.

New agents will typically request three years of past claims history. This information should be requested annually from your insurance company and retained with your records.

Be sure to provide accurate information about construction and square footage of your building. The premium you pay is partially based on this information. Tell your agent about any improvements or updates, such as new roofing, heating, plumbing, and electrical wiring that have been done within the past ten years. This information can reduce your premium as much as 50 percent in some cases.

Coverages are essentially the same throughout the United States, but local variations will apply. Your insurance agent can assist you in choosing your insurance format and assembling an appropriate insurance program.

Figure 9.5: Workers' Compensation Claim Form—Illinois

FORM 45: **Employers First Report of Injury or Illness**   PLEASE TYPE OR PRINT

Filing of this report does not affect your liability under the Workers' Compensation Act and is not incriminatory in any sense.

A	*45	ILLINOIS UNEMPLOYMENT COMPENSATION NUMBER		DATE OF REPORT — MONTH DAY YEAR	CASE OR FILE NUMBER
B	EMPLOYER'S NAME				Is this a lost workday case? ☐Yes ☐No
C	DOING BUSINESS UNDER THE NAME OF			CITY, STATE	ZIP CODE
D	MAIL ADDRESS			CITY, STATE	ZIP CODE
E	EMPLOYER LOCATION IF DIFFERENT FROM MAIL ADDRESS				
F	NATURE OF BUSINESS OR SERVICE	SIC CODE	TOTAL NUMBER OF EMPLOYEES AT THE LOCATION WHERE ILLNESS OR INJURY OCCURRED		
G	NAME OF WORKERS' COMP. INSURANCE CARRIER	POLICY NUMBER	SELF INSURED YES ☐ ☐NO	COUNTY WHERE INJURY OCCURRED	
H	EMPLOYEE'S NAME (LAST, FIRST, MIDDLE)		SOCIAL SECURITY NUMBER		
I	HOME ADDRESS			CITY, STATE	ZIP CODE
J	MALE ☐ FEMALE ☐ MARRIED ☐ SINGLE ☐ WIDOW(ER) ☐ DIVORCED ☐	BIRTH DATE — MONTH DAY YEAR	NUMBER OF DEPENDENT CHILDREN UNDER 18 AT TIME OF INJURY OR ILLNESS		
K	DATE AND TIME OF THE INJURY OR EXPOSURE — MONTH DAY YEAR a.m. p.m.	EMPLOYEE'S AVERAGE WEEKLY EARNINGS $	LAST DAY EMPLOYEE WORKED — MONTH DAY YEAR		
L	JOB TITLE OR OCCUPATION	DEPARTMENT NORMALLY ASSIGNED			
M	ADDRESS OF LOCATION WHERE INJURY OR EXPOSURE OCCURRED			CITY, STATE	ZIP CODE
N	DID EMPLOYEE DIE AS A RESULT OF THE INJURY OR ILLNESS? YES ☐ NO ☐	IF EMPLOYEE DIED AS A RESULT OF THE INJURY OR ILLNESS, GIVE DATE OF DEATH — MONTH DAY YEAR			
O	WAS THE INJURY OR EXPOSURE ON THE EMPLOYER'S PREMISES? ☐YES ☐NO	DID THIS INCIDENT RESULT IN: ☐ OCCUPATIONAL INJURY ☐ OCCUPATIONAL DISEASE		Was Employee given Industrial Commission Handbook? YES ☐ NO ☐	
P	NATURE OF THE INJURY				
Q	PART OF THE BODY AFFECTED (BE SPECIFIC)				
R	WHAT TASK WAS EMPLOYEE PERFORMING WHEN ILLNESS OR INJURY OCCURRED?				
S	OBJECT OR SUBSTANCE RESPONSIBLE FOR INJURY OR ILLNESS (SOURCE)				
T	HOW DID ACCIDENT OR ILLNESS OCCUR (TYPE)?				
U	WHAT HAZARDOUS CONDITIONS, METHODS OR LACK OF PROTECTIVE DEVICES CONTRIBUTED?				
V	WHAT UNSAFE ACT BY A PERSON CAUSED OR CONTRIBUTED TO THE INJURY OR ILLNESS?				
W	HAVE MEDICAL SERVICES BEEN RENDERED TO THE EMPLOYEE? YES ☐ NO ☐	IS OR HAS THE EMPLOYEE BEEN HOSPITALIZED? YES ☐ NO ☐			
X	NAME AND ADDRESS OF PHYSICIAN			CITY, STATE	ZIP CODE
Y	NAME AND ADDRESS OF HOSPITAL			CITY, STATE	ZIP CODE
Z	REPORT PREPARED BY: (NAME—PRINT OR TYPE)	SIGNATURE	TITLE AND TELEPHONE NUMBER		

REPORT ALL ACCIDENTS IMMEDIATELY AND SEND ORIGINAL AND 2 COPIES TO:

NOTE: DISCLOSURE OF THIS INFORMATION TO THE INDUSTRIAL COMMISSION IS MANDATORY UNDER IL. REV. STAT. CH. 48, § 138.6. FAILURE TO PROVIDE ANY INFORMATION COULD RESULT IN PROSECUTION. APPROVED BY FORMS MANAGEMENT.

Figure 9.6: Workers' Compensation Claim Form—Indiana

State Form 34401

STATE OF INDIANA

Industrial Board Division

FORM No. 24

Employer's Report to Industrial Board of Injury to Employee

Revised March, 1976

State's Number For:

File: _____
Carrier: _____
Employer: _____

Carrier's File No. _____

(The spaces above not to be filled in by Employer)

EMPLOYER

(1) Name: _____ (2) I.D.#: _____ (FOR STATE USE ONLY)

(3) Mail Address: Street: _____ (4) City: _____

(5) County: _____ (6) State: _____ (7) Zip: _____

Actual location: (8) Street: _____ (9) City: _____
(IF DIFFERENT FROM MAILING ADDRESS)

(10) County: _____ (11) State: _____ (12) Zip: _____

(13) Nature of business: _____

EMPLOYEE

(14) Name: _____

Address: (15) Street: _____ (16) City: _____

(17) County: _____ (18) State: _____ (19) Zip: _____ (20) Tel. No.: _____

(21) Age: _____ (22) Date of Birth: _____ (23) Social Security No.: _____

(24) Sex: _____ (25) Marital Status: _____ (26) Names, ages of all dependents: _____

(27) If a minor, is an employment certificate or permit on file: _____ (28) Length of employment: _____

(29) Regular department: _____ (30) Regular occupation _____

(31) Occupation when injured/exposed: _____ (32) No. of hours worked per day: _____

(33) Days per week: _____ (34) Piece or time work: _____ (35) Wages per hour: _____

(36) Wages per day: _____ (37) Any other compensation: _____ (38) Average weekly earnings: _____

TIME and PLACE

(39) Date: _____ (40) Time: _____ AM/PM (41) Exact address of incident: _____

(42) Was this employer's premises: _____ (43) Department: _____

(44) If in a mine, did it occur on surface, underground, shaft, drift or mill: _____

(45) When and to whom was first report of incident reported: _____

CAUSE OF INJURY

(46) Machine, tool or substance causing injury/illness: (Be specific. If he was using tools or equipment or handling material, name them and tell what he was doing with them.) _____

(47) Kind of power: _____ (48) Part of machine on which accident occurred: _____

(49) Was safety appliance or regulation provided: _____ (50) Was it in use at time: _____

(51) Was incident caused by employee's failure to use or observe safety appliance or regulation: _____

(52) Describe fully how accident/exposure occurred: (Tell what happened and how it happened. Name any objects or substances involved and tell how they were involved. Give full details on all factors which led or contributed to the accident. Use separate sheet for additional space.) _____

(53) State what employee was doing when injured/exposed: _____

(54) Name and addresses of witnesses: _____

NATURE OF INJURY

(55) Date and time disability began: _____ AM/PM (56) Was employee paid in full for this day: _____

(57) Lost Workdays: _____ (58) Has employee returned to work: _____ (59) If yes, what date and time: _____ AM/PM

(60) What wage: _____ (61) What occupation: _____ (62) If no, probable length of disability: _____

(63) Nature and location of injury/illness (describe fully exact location of amputations, fractures and part of body affected): _____

(64) Has employee died: _____ (65) Date: _____

(66) Name and address of physician: _____

(67) Name and address of hospital: _____

(68) Is this an IOSHA Recordable Injury: Yes _____ No _____ IOSHA Case or File #: _____

(69) Employer has compensation insurance with: _____

(70) Date of this report: _____ (71) Firm Name: _____

Signed by: _____ Title: _____

Telephone _____ (TO BE FILED IN TRIPLICATE)

Figure 9.7: Workers' Compensation Claim Form—Arizona

EMPLOYER'S REPORT OF INDUSTRIAL INJURY

COMPLETE AND MAIL THIS REPORT WITHIN 10 DAYS FROM NOTICE OF ACCIDENT
FATALITIES MUST BE REPORTED WITHIN 24 HOURS

Employer must on this form notify his insurance carrier of every injury or disease suffered by an employee, fatal or otherwise which is claimed to arise out of and in the course of employment.
ARIZONA REVISED STATUTES 23-908 & 23-1061

INDUSTRIAL COMMISSION OF ARIZONA
P.O. BOX 19070
PHOENIX, ARIZONA 85005

MAIL TO: (CARRIER NAME & ADDRESS)

FOR CARRIER USE ONLY

FOR OSHA PURPOSES ONLY
OSHA Case No. _____
RECORDABLE INJURY _____
NON-RECORDABLE INJURY _____

EMPLOYEE

| 1. LAST NAME | FIRST | M.I. | 2. SOCIAL SECURITY NUMBER | 3. BIRTH DATE |

4. HOME ADDRESS (NUMBER & STREET) — CITY — STATE — ZIP CODE — 5. TELEPHONE

6. SEX ☐ MALE ☐ FEMALE
7. MARITAL STATUS ☐ SINGLE ☐ MARRIED ☐ DIVORCED ☐ WIDOWED

EMPLOYER

8. EMPLOYER'S NAME — 9. POLICY NO. — 10. NATURE OF BUSINESS (MANUFACTURING, ETC.)

11. OFFICE ADDRESS (NUMBER & STREET) — CITY — STATE — ZIP CODE — 12. TELEPHONE

ACCIDENT

13. DATE OF INJURY — 14. HOUR OF INJURY ☐ a.m. ☐ p.m. — 15. DATE EMPLOYER NOTIFIED OF INJURY / / — 16. LAST DAY OF WORK AFTER INJURY / / — 17. DATE OF RETURN TO WORK / /

18. EMPLOYEE'S OCCUPATION (JOB TITLE) WHEN INJURED — 19. CLASS CODE ON PAYROLL REPORT — 20. EMPLOYEE'S ASSIGNED DEPARTMENT — 21. DEPARTMENT NUMBER

22. ADDRESS OR LOCATION OF ACCIDENT — CITY — COUNTY — STATE — ZIP CODE

23. ON EMPLOYER PREMISES? YES NO — 24. NATURE OF INJURY (SCRATCH, CUT, BRUISE, ETC.) FATAL? YES NO — 25. PART OF BODY INJURED

26. ATTENDING PHYSICIAN (NAME) — ADDRESS (STREET, CITY, STATE & ZIP CODE)

27. IF HOSPITALIZED, HOSPITAL NAME — ADDRESS (STREET, CITY, STATE & ZIP CODE)

28. IF VALIDITY OF CLAIM IS DOUBTED, STATE REASON

CAUSE OF ACCIDENT

29. HOW DID ACCIDENT HAPPEN (STATE ALL DETAILS: USE OTHER SIDE IF NEEDED)

30. SPECIFY MACHINE, TOOL, SUBSTANCE OR OBJECT MOST CLOSELY CONNECTED WITH ACCIDENT

31. WHAT WAS EMPLOYEE DOING WHEN ACCIDENT OCCURED (LOADING TRUCK, WALKING DOWN STAIRS, ETC.)?

32. IF ANOTHER PERSON NOT IN COMPANY EMPLOY CAUSED ACCIDENT, GIVE NAME AND ADDRESS

EMPLOYEE'S WAGE DATA

33. WAS WORKER IN YOUR EMPLOY WHEN INJURED YES ☐ NO ☐
34. HOURS PER DAY EMPLOYEE WORKED FROM A.M. P.M. ☐ ☐ THRU A.M. P.M. ☐ ☐
35. WAS EMPLOYEE ON OVERTIME WHEN INJURED YES ☐ NO ☐
36. NUMBER OF DAYS PER WEEK EMPLOYEE USUALLY WORKED COMPANY USUALLY WORKS

IMPORTANT IF WORK LOSS IS EXPECTED TO EXCEED SEVEN CALENDAR DAYS, COMPLETE ITEMS 37 THRU 44
37. DATE OF LAST HIRE
38. WAS WORKER PAID FOR DAY OF INJURY YES ☐ NO ☐ IF YES $ _____ AMOUNT
39. WAS EMPLOYEE HIRED FOR PERMANENT EMPLOYMENT YES ☐ NO ☐

40. NUMBER OF MONTHS EMPLOYMENT AVAILABLE DURING THE YEAR _____ MONTHS
41. GIVE EMPLOYEE'S WAGE STATUS AS APPLICABLE $ _____ PER HOUR ☐ DAY ☐ WEEK ☐ MONTH ☐
42. IS EMPLOYEE FURNISHED ☐ LODGING ☐ BOARD ☐ BOTH $ _____ VALUE

43. ACTUAL GROSS EARNINGS OF EMPLOYEE FOR THE 30 CALENDAR DAYS PRECEEDING INJURY (EXAMPLE: IF INJURED APRIL 8, GIVE EARNINGS FROM MARCH 9 THRU APRIL 7) $ _____
44. DOES EMPLOYEE CLAIM DEPENDENTS YES ☐ NO ☐

IMPORTANT IF EMPLOYEE IS PAID OTHER THAN FIXED WEEKLY OR MONTHLY SALARY, COMPLETE ITEMS 45 THRU 52
45. IF EMPLOYEE EARNS EXTRA PAY FOR OVERTIME, WHAT IS BASIS OF PAYMENT? _____ PER HOUR
46. NUMBER OF HOURS OVERTIME CONSIDERED NORMAL PER WEEK

47. GROSS WAGES OF EMPLOYEE DURING 12 MONTHS PRECEEDING INJURY FROM _____ THRU _____ $ _____
48. IF EMPLOYEE WORKED LESS THAN 12 MONTHS, SHOW GROSS WAGES FROM DATE OF HIRE THROUGH DAY PRIOR TO INJURY FROM _____ THRU _____ $ _____

49. DATE OF LAST WAGE INCREASE IF WITHIN 12 MONTHS PRIOR TO INJURY
50. WAGE BEFORE INCREASE $ _____
51. WAGE AFTER INCREASE
52. GROSS EARNINGS FROM DATE OF INCREASE THRU DAY PRIOR TO INJURY $ _____

AUTHORIZED SIGNATURE

| DATE | AUTHORIZED SIGNATURE | TITLE |

NOTE TO EMPLOYER: 1. Mail one copy to the Industrial Commission within 10 days
2. Mail one copy to your insurance carrier within 10 days
3. Keep one copy, for not less than 5 years, as your supplementary record of injuries required by the Federal Occupational Safety and Health Act of 1970.

ICA 04-0101 (Rev. 88)

(THIS FORM APPROVED BY THE INDUSTRIAL COMMISSION OF ARIZONA FOR CARRIER USE)

Figure 9.8: Workers' Compensation Claim Form—Wisconsin

TO REPORT WORKERS' COMPENSATION INJURIES
CALL 1-800-832-7839

THINGS TO REMEMBER WHEN COMPLETING THE INFORMATION BELOW:

Call The Travelers Telephone Reporting Center toll-free to quickly and easily report all Workers' Compensation injuries.

We will be asking you the following questions, so please have the information handy. The Travelers will produce and submit the necessary state forms.

DO NOT DELAY IN CALLING IF YOU DO NOT HAVE ANSWERS TO ALL OF THE QUESTIONS.

ACCOUNT INFORMATION

CALLER'S PHONE NUMBER / EXTENSION ( )	CALLER'S NAME (FIRST, MI, LAST)	CALLER'S TITLE	BENEFIT STATE
EMPLOYER'S NAME	EMPLOYER'S ADDRESS (STREET, CITY, STATE & ZIP)	EMPLOYER'S MAILING ADDRESS (STREET, CITY, STATE & ZIP) □ SAME	
PARENT COMPANY / INSURED'S NAME	LOCATION CODE / NATURE OF BUSINESS	POLICY FORM	POLICY NUMBER

EMPLOYEE INFORMATION

EMPLOYEE'S NAME (FIRST, MI, LAST)	GENDER □ MALE □ FEMALE	SOCIAL SECURITY NUMBER
EMPLOYEE'S MAILING ADDRESS (STREET, CITY, STATE & ZIP)	IS EMPLOYEE'S HOME ADDRESS THE SAME? IF NO, STREET, CITY, STATE & ZIP □ YES □ NO	

MARITAL STATUS	EMPLOYMENT STATUS CODE □ FULL-TIME □ PART-TIME	NO. OF DEPENDENTS	CLASS CODE	DATE OF BIRTH	WAGE PERIOD	HOME PHONE NUMBER ( )

ACCIDENT INFORMATION

DATE OF INJURY	TIME OF INJURY : A.M. P.M.	DATE CLAIM REPORTED TO EMPLOYER	WAS THE ACCIDENT ON THE EMPLOYER'S PREMISES? □ YES □ NO
LOCATION OF ACCIDENT ADDRESS (STREET, CITY, STATE & ZIP)			COUNTY

DID EMPLOYEE LOSE ANY TIME FROM WORK? □ YES □ NO	IS THE EMPLOYEE BACK AT WORK? IF YES, DATE RETURNED □ YES □ NO	DATE EMPLOYEE LAST WORKED	WAS EMPLOYEE PAID FOR DATE OF INJURY? □ YES □ NO
DATE EMPLOYEE LAST PAID	DATE DISABILITY BEGAN	DATE DISABILITY ENDED	IS / WAS EMPLOYEE'S SALARY CONTINUED? □ YES □ NO
WAS EMPLOYEE'S INJURY RELATED TO A COMPANY-SPONSORED EVENT? □ YES □ NO		WAS ACCIDENT FATAL? IF YES, DATE OF DEATH □ YES □ NO	

FULL DESCRIPTION OF ACCIDENT

CAUSE OF ACCIDENT (E.G., SLIP/FALL, LIFTING, CHEMICAL)	IF MOTOR VEHICLE ACCIDENT, DRIVER'S LICENSE NUMBER	STATE WHERE ISSUED
CONTRIBUTING FACTORS	EQUIPMENT, MATERIAL OR SUBSTANCE INVOLVED	

IF OTHER PARTIES WERE INVOLVED NAME (FIRST, MI, LAST)	ADDRESS	PHONE NUMBER

WERE SAFEGUARDS PROVIDED? □ YES □ NO	DESCRIPTION OF SAFEGUARDS	WERE SAFEGUARDS IN USE? □ YES □ NO
WITNESS INFORMATION NAME (FIRST, MI, LAST)	ADDRESS	PHONE NUMBER

INJURY INFORMATION

PART OF BODY INJURED (E.G., HEAD, NECK, ARM, LEG)	NATURE OF INJURY (E.G., FRACTURE, SPRAIN, LACERATION)	PREVIOUS RELATED CONDITION? □ YES □ NO	PRE-EXISTING MEDICAL CONDITION(S)
CUMULATIVE INJURY? IF YES, LENGTH OF EXPOSURE □ YES □ NO	NATURE OF DUTIES	LENGTH OF TIME DOING ACTIVITY	

TREATMENT ("X" ALL THAT APPLY)

□ FIRST AID –	NAME (FIRST, MI, LAST)	WHAT TYPE OF FIRST AID WAS ADMINISTERED?		1ST DAY OF TREATMENT
□ HOSPITAL / CLINIC –	NAME AND ADDRESS (STREET, CITY, STATE & ZIP)	TREATMENT	LENGTH OF STAY	1ST DAY OF TREATMENT
□ PHYSICIAN –	NAME AND ADDRESS (STREET, CITY, STATE & ZIP)	PHONE NUMBER ( )	TREATMENT	SPECIALTY	1ST DAY OF TREATMENT

C22148W-WI   *CONTINUED ON REVERSE SIDE*   WISCONSIN (5/92)

Figure 9.8: Workers' Compensation Claim Form—Wisconsin, continued

EMPLOYEE JOB INFORMATION

OCCUPATION WHEN INJURED	REGULAR OCCUPATION	DATE OF HIRE

SCHEDULE
REGULAR WORK HOURS: | HOURS PER DAY: | DAYS PER WEEK:

WAGE
HOURLY: | ANNUAL: | AVERAGE WEEKLY: | OVERTIME: | PER | ADDITIONAL BENEFITS: | PER:

SUPERVISOR'S NAME (FIRST, MI, LAST) | PHONE NUMBER / EXTENSION ( ) | SCHEDULED WORK HOURS

STATE OF WISCONSIN SPECIFIC INFORMATION

FEDERAL EMPLOYER ID #:

TYPE OF BUSINESS (INDIVIDUAL/PARTNERSHIP/CORPORATION:)

IF EMPLOYEE HAS NOT RETURNED TO WORK, ESTIMATE DATE OF RETURN:

IF EMPLOYEE IS UNDER 18, WAS PERMIT FILED?   ☐ YES   ☐ NO

DID INJURY OCCUR BECAUSE OF: ("X" ALL THAT APPLY)

   ☐ INTOXICATION   ☐ FAILURE TO USE SAFETY DEVICES   ☐ FAILURE TO OBEY RULES

DID INJURY OCCUR IN THE COURSE OF WORKER'S EMPLOYMENT?   ☐ YES   ☐ NO

IN ADDITION TO WAGES, DID EMPLOYEE RECEIVE: ("X" ALL THAT APPLY)

   ☐ BOARD   ☐ ROOM   ☐ TIPS | TOTAL AVERAGE AMOUNT WEEKLY: $

IF FATAL, PROVIDE NAME, RELATIONSHIP AND ADDRESS OF CLOSEST DEPENDENT OF DECEASED:

FOR THE QUARTER IN WHICH INJURY OCCURRED AND THE 3 PRECEEDING QUARTERS, REPORT THE NUMBER OF WEEKS WORKED IN THE

SAME KIND OF WORK, AND THE TOTAL WAGES, SALARY, COMMISSION AND BONUS OR PREMIUM EARNED FOR SUCH WEEKS.

NUMBER OF WEEKS: GROSS AMOUNT: $

IF PIECE WORK, NO. OF HOURS:

FULL-TIME EMPLOYMENT INFORMATION - EMPLOYEE'S SCHEDULED WORK WEEK:

START TIME: :   M. | HOURS PER DAY: | HOURS PER WEEK: | DAYS PER WEEK:

IF PART-TIME EMPLOYMENT INFORMATION -

ARE THERE OTHER PART-TIME WORKERS DOING THE SAME WORK WITH THE SAME HOURS?   ☐ YES   ☐ NO   IF YES, HOW MANY?

NUMBER OF FULL-TIME EMPLOYEES DOING THE SAME TYPE OF WORK:

COMMENTS AND ADDITIONAL INFORMATION

COMMENTS

CARRIER NAME AND ADDRESS (STREET, CITY, STATE & ZIP)

Rating of Insurance Companies

Insurance companies are rated on their financial condition and operating performance. These are called Best ratings (named after the company that does them). Your mortgage may require that you obtain coverage from a company with a Best rating of A (superior) or A+ (excellent). This is a good idea, as companies may experience financial or service difficulties from time to time. A good Best rating gives you some assurance that you are obtaining your insurance from a financially strong company. Your insurance agent can provide this information.

Insurance Agents

There are two types of insurance agents: independent and direct writers. An independent agent may represent many different insurance companies, such as Hanover, Kemper, Cigna, Chubb, Fireman's Fund, Travelers, Continental, USF&G, and Reliance to name a few. A direct writer normally represents one company, such as Allstate, State Farm, or Farmers.

You may wish to obtain quotes from both the direct writer and the independent agent. This will allow you to obtain the most competitive coverage.

Your agent should be insured for errors and omissions, and you should require proof of this coverage. This can be produced in the form of a certificate of insurance. You may have recourse under this coverage if your agent mistakenly fails to provide coverage for which you paid.

Inspections

The insurance company may inspect your property before or after the inception of your policy. If they find conditions and/or physical hazards that will encourage or contribute to a loss on your premises they will issue a notice of recommendations for eliminating or reducing these exposures.

Inspectors from fire, liability, boiler and machinery, and workers' compensation insurance companies should be given every cooperation.

Boiler and machinery inspectors (but no others) have the authority to shut down any object that they feel poses an imminent danger.

Respond to an inspector's notice of recommendations by informing your insurer in writing of your intentions to comply with the recommendations, and supply an estimate of the time needed to comply.

Recommendations with which you agree should be carried out. For those on which there is any question, your objections should be put in writing to the insurance agent. It is a good idea to comply, whenever reasonable, because eliminating or minimizing losses results in direct savings in the long run.

If you do not respond and a reinspection reveals the same hazardous conditions, the insurer may cancel your coverage within the first 60 days of inception. Coverage will then be more difficult to obtain elsewhere.

The insurer may cancel for reasons of increased hazard by giving the named insured and the mortgagee at least 30 days advance notice in writing. If possible, negotiate a 60-day or 90-day notice to allow ample time to shop for your next insurance company.

Maintenance

*A*ndy Chychula is an emergency medical technician with the fire department. His 24-hour work shift every three days allowed him time to earn extra income repairing and fixing neighborhood homes. He eventually purchased a three-flat and a five-flat apartment building. Two of his friends involved in real estate finance and brokerage persuaded him to combine his talents and assets with them and buy a larger apartment building. They formed a partnership and purchased a 49-unit apartment building valued at more than a million dollars.

Apartment property maintenance is the process of allocating human resources, supplies, and services to continue the physical operation of a multitenant property. Property maintenance is often confused with property management. Property management focuses on operations of a property as a business concern, while maintenance focuses on the operation of a property as a physical asset.

The key element of property maintenance is foresight. Trying to save money by avoiding preventative maintenance usually leads to financial loss. Property maintenance should be active, not reactive. An astute property maintenance program will continuously plan ahead and anticipate problems before they occur.

After all, it is cheaper to repair or replace a bad pipe before it bursts. After it bursts, it is too late. Not only do you have to fix it, but other damages may have occurred to carpeting, plaster, and furniture. Worst of all, such disasters cause very bad tenant relations.

Preserving the Asset

One of the primary responsibilities of owning rental property is the preservation of tangible assets. You must safeguard your property from physical damage and loss of income. Beyond keeping the property in good physical condition, a good maintenance program that includes regular upgrades or cosmetic improvements can actually increase the value of your investment.

Owning and operating rental property requires ongoing physical maintenance. Vacant apartments must be cleaned and decorated to make them more appealing and rentable. Broken or worn-out items need to be repaired or replaced. You can either hire a contractor to maintain your property or do it yourself.

Routine maintenance expenses should run about five percent of gross income. As an example, if the gross annual income from your property is $10,000, maintenance expenses may total around $500. By setting aside $45 a month, you will have enough in reserve for normal anticipated repairs. Having the money handy when you need to get a job done will be less stressful than having to delay a repair until the funds are available.

Good preparation and planning will help keep maintenance problems under control. Preparation includes keeping spare parts, tools, and service telephone numbers on the property or in some other convenient location. Preparation also means developing the skills and acquiring the equipment necessary to do the work yourself or developing relationships with good electricians, plumbers, cleaning and decorating contractors, and so on.

Repair and Deduct Laws

A comprehensive cleaning and maintenance program will help you fulfill your responsibility to provide habitable living accommodations to your tenants.

In many states, maintaining habitable premises is mandated by law, and the rules are getting tougher all the time. New state and local ordinances being introduced contain a provision called repair and deduct. This ordinance already exists in the landlord-tenant acts of many states and municipalities. The intent is to force landlords to keep their properties in good condition.

The old general rule was that tenants and landlords could negotiate the landlord's basic obligation to make repairs through mutual agreement. For example, a landlord could require a tenant to maintain everything inside an apartment while the landlord maintained the outer shell of the building and common areas. If a landlord agreed to make repairs and failed to do so, the tenant did not have much recourse.

Under a repair and deduct ordinance, tenants are allowed to have repairs made and deduct the expenses from the rent, regardless of any preexisting agreement with the landlord. If a landlord does not maintain the property in habitable condition, the tenant can take action by calling professional contractors to perform the work and deducting the bill from the rent. The only requirement generally is that the tenant give the landlord sufficient notice, usually 10 to 14 days.

Even if a municipality has a repair and deduct ordinance, an owner and tenant may still agree in writing that the tenant is to perform specific repairs, maintenance tasks, or minor remodeling. The four conditions for such an agreement to be enforceable are:

1. The agreement is entered into in good faith and is not for the purpose of evading the obligations of the owner.
2. The agreement does not diminish the obligations of the owner to other residents.
3. The terms and conditions of the agreement are clearly and prominently disclosed.
4. The consideration for such agreement is specifically stated.

Renting "As Is"

Some landlords rent apartments "as is," and require tenants to decorate and upgrade. In this way, the landlords save money and tenants can decorate the apartments to their specific tastes. But most tenants do not want to invest their own money and time improving someone else's property. Also, you may get a tenant who wants purple walls with a dragon mural. If you allow tenants to do their own decorating, limit colors of paint and wallpaper patterns.

There is another drawback to renting an apartment "as is." Few prospective renters can visualize how a shabby-looking apartment can be transformed with new carpeting, freshly decorated walls, and a thorough cleaning job. Thus, good tenants will be reluctant to rent an apartment "as is" and you may have to allow a big deduction on the rent.

Upgrading

From time to time you will have to spend money to upgrade an apartment. Upgrading includes replacing aging appliances, worn-out carpets, and outdated lighting fixtures. You may have to remodel a kitchen or bathroom. Upgrading should be planned for and done on a regular schedule. It is better to replace a refrigerator before it breaks down on a hot Sunday in July.

Sometimes you will upgrade an apartment for an existing tenant, at or before lease renewal time. Other times you will make these improvements in order to make the apartment attractive for a prospective tenant.

The decision of whether to repair or replace is based on economics, and some upgrading can be put off. However, a malfunction in an essential appliance such as furnace, air conditioner, stove, or refrigerator requires immediate action.

How do you make the decision to upgrade?

- Consider the market for rental units in your location. If the demand is strong you may not have to do any upgrades. However, if the market is weak, you may need to invest in some improvements to remain competitive and attract renters.
- Look realistically at the overall condition and physical appearance of the unit. Check for worn-out shades, draperies, or blinds; torn or stained carpeting and flooring; broken, deteriorated, or severely outdated appliances, light fixtures, or plumbing fixtures. Perhaps the apartment needs a total rehab. Good tenants will expect and demand the apartment be in like-new condition before they move in. Existing tenants also deserve an attractive, well-maintained unit.

Decide how much money can be invested in upgrades compared to how much the rent can be increased to amortize these expenses. Suppose you put $2,000 of improvements into an apartment that is currently renting for $400 a month. If rents are increased 6 percent a year for the next three years, the additional income would be only $915. To amortize a $2,000 expense over three years, rent would have to be increased 13 percent per year. At a 6 percent rent increase, it would take almost seven years to pay off the cost of improvements.

The easiest practical way to determine how much can be spent on improvements is to work backwards from the projected rent increases. If the $400 apartment has a 10 percent rent increase per year for the next five years, the additional income would amount to $2,928. Deducting a conservative figure for inflationary operating expenses of 2 percent per year, approximately $2,432 would be available for necessary improvements for the five-year period.

Doing Your Own Maintenance

If you want to perform your own routine maintenance tasks you will need tools and equipment. Following is a list of what the pros feel is necessary.

Cleaning supplies.

- Canvas trash bag with shoulder strap
- Steel wool
- Furniture polish
- Straw broom
- Scouring powder
- Whisk broom
- All-purpose cleaner (powder and/or liquid)
- Dustpan
- Plastic trash bags
- Spray deodorizer
- Mop and mop wringer
- Spray wall-tile cleaner
- Sponge mop
- Sponges
- Wooden pick-up stick with pointed end
- Five gallon paint bucket
- Scrub brush
- Wide floor broom
- Spray bottles
- Shovel
- Razor blade scraper
- Rags
- Spray window cleaner
- Buckets
- Liquid floor wax and applicator
- 6" and 12" squeegees
- Wax stripper
- Handy box carrier
- Metal polish
- Three-foot stepladder
- Toilet-bowl cleaner (liquid or crystal)
- Toilet brush
- Floor cleaner and wax for hard-wood floors
- Spray oven cleaner
- Drop cloths

Basic tools.

- Claw hammer
- Needle-nose pliers
- Phillips screwdriver
- Wire strippers
- Metal files or rasps
- Putty knives
- Channel-lock pliers
- Razor knife
- Black electrical tape
- Paint roller
- Electric continuity tester
- Razor blade scraper
- Flat-head screwdriver
- Flashlight (plastic cover to avoid electrical contact)
- Awl or punch (ice pick)
- Regular pliers
- Pipe wrenches
- Vise-Grip pliers
- Wood saw and hacksaw
- Wire cutters
- Spirit level
- 20-foot tape measure
- Crescent wrenches
- Paint brushes
- Electric drill

Preparing a Vacant Apartment for Rental

Vacant apartments must be in good rentable condition when they are shown to prospective residents. The preparation process for vacant apartments consists of possible upgrading, surface cleaning, painting, and thorough cleaning and repair. Use the Apartment Make-Ready Checklist (Figure 10.1) as a guide to prevent overlooking or forgetting an item.

Figure 10.1: Apartment Make-Ready Checklist

Property _____	Unit _____
Unit Size _____	Date to be Occupied _____
Inspected by _____	Date _____

Checklist	Instructions (C) clean (P) paint (R) repair (RPL) replace
Check all plumbing (toilets, faucets, pipes). Check for leaks, pressure, etc.	
Check all appliances for proper operation, bulbs, etc.	
Check all hardware (doorknobs, hooks, rods, locks, catches, etc.)	
Check all windows and screens (tracks, locks, operation, cracks, tears, etc.)	
Check all walls, ceilings, baseboard (holes, cuts, nail pops, seams, woodwork trim).	
Check all floors (cleaned and waxed, carpet rips, shampoo, vacuum).	
Check bathrooms (cleaned tubs, toilets, walls, vanities, mirrors, medicine cabinets, sinks, towel bars, toilet paper holders, soap dishes polished).	
Check all closets (shelves, lights, floor, doors).	
Check all thresholds for cracks, dirt, loose screws.	
Check all other doors (warping, rubbing, cracks, squeaks, etc.).	
Check all vents, registers (dirt, operation).	
Check heating and air-conditioning for proper operation (filters, thermostats, etc.).	
Check all kitchen cabinets (doors work, cleaning, peeling, etc.).	
Check all lighting (new bulbs, switches, cleanliness, hanging properly).	
Check for chips or cracks in sinks, countertops, appliances.	
Replace These Missing Items	
Cleaning Date	
Painting Date	
Maintenance Date	
Follow-Up Inspection Date	
New Carpeting Date	

Surface Cleaning

Vacant apartments should be cleaned as soon as possible after the old tenants move out. This initial cleaning includes removing all the trash, wiping down the appliances and countertops, sweeping and vacuuming the floors, and cleaning the windows. Once the vacant apartment is clean, you can show it to prospective tenants, even if it still needs painting and repairs.

Minor Repairs

Inspect vacant apartments, using the preinspection checklist (Figure 5.1). You will usually see a number of things that need repair or replacement. Some common maintenance items are:

- Broken or loose doorknobs on cabinets and closet doors
- Loose closet shelving or rods
- Loose shower rods, towel bars, and hooks
- Leaky faucets or toilets
- Clogged faucet aerators
- Clogged drains
- Burned-out light bulbs
- Broken electrical switches or outlets
- Blown electrical fuses
- Torn window screens, shades, and blinds
- Broken windowpanes
- Torn or missing wall or floor tiles in kitchens and baths
- Doors that stick (entrance, bedroom, or bathroom)
- Dirty heating and air-conditioning filters

Most items listed above can be repaired with the tools suggested earlier. Replacement parts can be purchased in most hardware stores. Inspect the apartment personally to determine if you can restore the broken items yourself before calling in professionals.

Painting

The next step in getting a vacant apartment ready is painting. Although you may decide to hire a professional painter, you should know the basic process of painting an apartment. The task is divided into three steps: preparation, painting, and cleanup.

Preparation

Remove all nails, screws, anchors, and so on and fill all holes with matching plaster. Patch holes five inches in diameter and smaller following directions on the package. Holes larger than five inches will need a section of drywall or plaster lath inserted before patching.

Remove electric switch plates and outlet plates. If walls are very dirty, scrub them. Do not try to paint over dirt. Seal water marks, grease marks, crayon marks, and so on with a product designed for this purpose. Scrape loose paint.

Painting

Paint the entire apartment with one coat of flat white latex paint, including ceilings, walls, closets, doors, frames, windows and trim, if applicable. Use semigloss paint in kitchens and bathrooms. (Some people prefer to use semigloss paint for trim as well.) Use brushes for trim and rollers for walls and ceilings. Extension poles make ceiling painting easier. Use drop cloths to facilitate cleanup.

Cleanup

Replace the switch plates and outlet plates. Remove all paint splatters on countertops, cabinets, appliances, floors, and woodwork. Scrape paint smears off windows. Clean paint out of bathtubs and sinks. Sweep up paint chips on the floors.

Final Cleanup

When the apartment is painted and all repairs have been completed, it can now undergo a final cleaning. Follow these procedures for a comprehensive cleaning program:

Kitchen. To clean the oven: Take out any removable oven parts and put them in the sink to soak. Spray the oven with oven cleaner (if it is not self-cleaning). Follow directions on the package; oven cleaners are corrosive. Some oven cleaners take a few minutes to work, others must be left overnight.

Using an all-purpose cleaner, wash the outside of the range: top, front, sides, and doors. Clean the countertops and interiors and exteriors of cabinets and drawers. Clean the interior and exterior of the refrigerator. Defrost it if necessary. Clean the dishwasher inside and out. Vacuum and scrub the range hoods and vents.

By this time the oven cleaner will have had time to act. Clean the oven, following directions on the package. Clean and replace the oven parts.

Using scouring powder, clean the sink and faucets.

Finally, pull appliances away from wall. Sweep up where appliances were. Scrub floor and wash all walls. Replace appliances. Resweep and mop.

Bathroom(s). Put bowl cleaner in the toilet, following the instructions on the package.

Spray and clean the shower tile walls with a product designed for this purpose.

Using an all-purpose cleaner, clean the medicine cabinet, vanity, light fixtures, walls, and toilet bowl.

Using scouring powder and a spray cleaner, scrub sink, tub, and chrome fixtures.

Vacuum and scrub exhaust vent.

Finally, sweep and scrub the floor.

Closets. Vacuum the shelves, doors and tracks. Scrub if necessary. Be sure door handles or knobs and door tracks and hinges are tightened.

Lighting. Clean the light globes. Replace bulbs as needed.

Heating and air conditioning. Clean or replace filters in heating and air-conditioning units. Vacuum, wipe, or scrub the units if necessary.

Windows. Clean trim and tracks; make sure windows open and close freely. Use a razor scraper to remove dried paint on glass surfaces. With a spray window cleaner, clean interior window panes (also exterior, if possible).

Floors. Sweep and/or vacuum all hard-surface floors and carpeting. For tile floors, mop with all-purpose cleaner and apply liquid wax. For hardwood floors, clean and wax with products designed for hardwood floors. Use a wax finish that minimizes slippery surfaces.

Carpet cleaning. Carpet cleaning is the last step in apartment preparation. This job is often performed by outside contractors. The best results are obtained with a process that employs water extraction equipment.

If you decide to do the job yourself, follow the instructions that accompany the carpet-cleaning equipment. Prespotting heavily stained areas will improve the final result. Do not use too much shampoo. This is a common mistake, and it makes the job of rinsing the carpet next to impossible.

When you have finished, cover the wet carpet with an absorbing paper that is available at most hardware stores. If no one will be entering the apartment for a few days, you can omit the paper and let the carpet dry in the open air.

After the carpet dries, vacuum it to pick up any residue. At this point the apartment should be ready for new tenants.

Using Outside Contractors

Certain maintenance functions are best handled by outside contractors. You may have to hire a contractor for snow removal; landscaping; garbage removal; roofing; painting (interior and exterior); tuckpointing; pest control; carpet cleaning; and electrical, plumbing, heating, and air-conditioning repairs.

Compile a list of recommended service companies for various types of mechanical problems, including plumbers, electricians, heating and air conditioning contractors, and appliance repairers. If you cannot get a recommendation for a particular job, look in the Yellow Pages™ and take a chance with a company that can give you a reference list of satisfied customers. You may want to check it out with the Better Business Bureau.

Some owners of small apartment buildings hire a local janitor, possibly someone who lives nearby, to perform daily or weekly housekeeping tasks. Inquiries of neighbors and property owners in the area may result in a few good recommendations.

When using an outside contractor, refer to the contractor guideline (Figure 10.2) to avoid problems.

Condominiums

The governing association of a condominium may have a maintenance staff that can perform routine maintenance tasks, charging the owner for time and materials. Association rates usually are less expensive than calling in an outside contractor. The property's maintenance personnel are generally better prepared to deal with problems particular to your building.

Pest and Insect Control

Almost every apartment building will have problems with pests and/or insects from time to time. The most common nuisance is the cockroach. Others are mice, rats, ants, and termites.

Pest control is best left to professional exterminators. At the first sign of trouble, have the building treated, and set up a regular schedule of follow-up treatments. If tenants see that you have a regular extermination program, they will not panic if they see an occasional cockroach.

There are several things you and your tenants can do to help control pest problems; however, these practices are not a substitute for a good, ongoing, professional pest-extermination program. Caulk cracks and openings around windows, foundations, drains, and pipes to prevent pests from entering the building.

Enforce good housekeeping and sanitation practices: Garbage and trash must be covered and removed promptly. Kitchens should be scrubbed regularly to minimize grease buildup. Debris and junk should be thrown out—even accumulated newspapers can harbor pests.

When screening prospective tenants, try to find out if their old building had roaches. If so, the roaches will probably move in with the tenants.

Cutting Costs

Often the difference between a positive and negative cash flow is simply a matter of prudently monitoring controllable expenses. Your biggest costs are usually fixed: mortgage payments, real estate taxes, and insurance. There is not too much you can do about these costs except to file a tax protest or refinance the mortgage.

Other expenses, such as utilities and maintenance costs, can be substantially reduced. For example, if you are paying for common-area lighting, you can install timers to turn off the lights during the day. If you pay for heat, air conditioning, and hot water, installing programmed thermostats and timers can control the output and keep costs down.

Make sure all mechanical equipment is in peak operating condition. Boilers and air conditioners will run more efficiently if you have them inspected and adjusted annually.

Always be on the lookout for more ways to cut costs. Are you paying for certain routine services that you or one of your tenants can perform? Can you make some of the minor repairs or do your own painting?

Use the Cost Cutting Checklist (Figure 10.3) for suggested ways to save money on maintenance.

Figure 10.2: Contractor Guidelines

Contractor Guidelines

The following was prepared to inform you of our procedures and expectations regarding your business relationship with us.

Insurance

All contractors that perform work on our property are required to carry appropriate insurance coverage. A certificate of insurance must be provided before work begins. See the attached page for the specific coverage required.

Proposals

Proposals, when required, should be submitted to the appropriate individual. The proposal must be as specific as possible containing the job address, description of work, type of materials to be used, any warranty/guarantee information, and the dollar amount. If specific payment terms are required, they should be specified (see also payment terms).

Purchase Orders

Prior to starting any work you must get a purchase order or purchase order number. The purchase order should contain all pertinent information regarding the job. You will receive the white copy for your records. All correspondence regarding a job must contain the purchase order number.

Invoices

All invoices should be sent directly to _____.
Invoices must contain the following information:

1. Job address
2. Purchase order number
3. Description of work as per the Purchase Order
4. Dollar amount

Payment Terms

Immediately upon completion of work you should send in your invoice. It will be processed and paid within 30–45 days upon completion and acceptance of work and upon receipt of invoice.

If you do not receive payment in 45 days, provided there are no discrepancies, you should contact us at _____.

Quality of Work

All work is expected to be done, according to specifications, in a professional and workmanlike manner in accordance with accepted practices.

Work Area

Upon completion of work or at the end of each work day the work area must be left clean or in the same condition it was prior to the work starting.

Damage to Property

In the event that your company causes any damage to any property, personal or otherwise, your company will be held liable and be expected to resolve the matter immediately.

Figure 10.2: Contractor Guidelines, continued

Extras
Any extra work not included in the original price must be approved in advance, in writing, prior to the commencement of such extra work.

Keys
If you must use a key to gain access to a work area, you will be required to sign for the key. All keys must be returned at the end of each work day.

Discrepancies
If there are any discrepancies regarding the terms and conditions of the services rendered, you are expected to resolve them immediately.

Business Conduct Policy
The intent of the policy is to preclude the development of any situation or relationship which might compromise good business judgment or create or appear to create the image of unethical practices. Accordingly, this policy prohibits our company's employees, or their family members, from accepting gifts, loans, or use of accommodations from anyone with whom we do business. Gifts of inconsequential value may be accepted in circumstances where such minor gifts are of customary industry practices.

Insurance Requirements for Contractors
All contractors that do work for us must have a certificate of insurance on file.
The requirements are as follows:

General Liability	$100,000 minimum
Property Damage	50,000 minimum
Workers' Compensation*	100,000 minimum
Auto Liability and Property Damage	100,000 minimum

*The only people exempt from Workers' Compensation are sole proprietors and partners and corporate officers. All policies must contain the following clause:

Cancellation: Should your policy be cancelled before the expiration date, the issuing company will endeavor to mail ten (10) days written notice to the certificate holder, but failure to mail such notice shall impose no obligation or liability of any kind upon the company.

The certificate must be mailed to:

_____

_____

_____

_____

Any questions regarding this should be directed to _____

at _____

Thank you.

Figure 10.3: Cost Cutting Checklist

Cost Cutting Checklist

General

Bring in utility companies to explain present rate structure and revise to the most favorable rate.

Heating/Air Conditioning

Check boiler efficiency.

Maintain the boiler regularly to ensure the highest efficiency.

Lower daytime and nighttime thermostat settings for heat. (Follow local ordinances.)

Clean radiators and air registers.

Repair all leaks.

Reduce water temperature in hot water systems.

Check operation of automatic controls.

Balance heating system.

Check operation of all electric heating units.

Install indoor/outdoor controls.

Tune up heating plants.

Install flue restrictors.

Reduce air-conditioning and/or heat in unoccupied units.

Keep doors closed as much as possible when the heating and air conditioning is in operation (specifically service and fire doors).

Leave thermostat on a desired temperature rather than adjusting it all the time.

Maintain thermostat controls for heating public areas at not more than 68° from October to April.

Increase moisture in air to increase tenant comfort and at the same time reduce use of heating fuel.

Check out motors and pumps on heating systems for cleanliness; investigate the possibility of using a lower wattage motor.

Keep air filters clean, change them often.

Do not block registers or ducts.

If the building has window air-conditioning units and a central heating furnace, cover or close the floor or sidewall registers and low return air grills while air-conditioning is on.

With a forced-air system, keep the return-air grills and warm air ducts clean.

If laundry facilities are available in the building, keep dryer lint filter clean.

Eliminate humidity controls for all but certain circumstances.

Insulation

Install heat-absorbing and heat-reflecting glass to reduce heat from direct sunlight by 40 to 70 percent.

Repair broken glass.

Repair window putty.

Replace caulking.

Figure 10.3: Cost Cutting Checklist, continued

Adjust door closers.

If feasible, redo roofing and sidewalls to provide insulation.

Use storm windows and doors or double-pane glass to reduce the loss of heat.

Waterproof foundations to minimize heat loss.

Install weather stripping and caulking to seal cracks around windows and doors.

Electricity

Reduce lighting levels.

Clean bulbs and fixtures.

Investigate the most efficient light sources that can provide the illumination required:

- High pressure sodium vapor (most efficient)
- Metal halide
- Fluorescent
- Mercury
- Incandescent (least efficient)

Replace two 60-watt lamps with one 100-watt to save 12 percent of previous usage and provide the same amount of light.

Put reflective covers or backers on fluorescent lights to maximize light refraction.

Reduce hall lighting to minimum safe levels.

Reduce exterior lighting (around building and parking areas) by removing every other bulb.

Repaint dark-colored areas (lobbies, halls) white to increase reflected light.

Install photocells in place of electric timers.

Install fluorescent light in place of incandescent.

Locate refrigerators away from heating equipment and direct sunlight.

Keep refrigerator coil surfaces clean to provide maximum cooling.

Notify tenants to defrost their refrigerators when frost in the freezer compartment is about 1/4 inch thick.

Water

Reduce water heater temperature.

Repair leaks.

Check boiler water level.

Check combustion efficiency of boiler.

Ask utility company to check the efficiency of the hot water tanks being used.

Instruct tenants to use cold water when operating a garbage disposal. This solidifies the grease, reduces hot water usage, and cuts down on maintenance.

Insulate pipes so that less energy will be wasted in running until it "warms up."

Repair dripping faucets.

Investigate use of smaller water-saving nozzles and spray heads on water fixtures to increase pressure but reduce total gallons of water used.

Property Taxes

CHAPTER 11

Carole Bilina is employed as an assistant director in a social service agency. Her position entails writing, public relations, and administration. Carole, with her mother/partner, owns and manages two six-flat buildings. Her mother resides in one apartment; Carole in another. They share the management tasks.

In 1976, we bought our first property in a neighborhood known as Uptown, an area that was generally perceived as being less than desirable. Uptown was one of the few communities we could afford and we gambled the area would improve in time. Two years later we acquired a second building in nearby East Ravenswood.

In the beginning, the area was so bad you would not want to live there, but we did much of the property rehabbing work ourselves. As work progressed, and as the neighborhood improved, we attracted better tenants. Our communities steadily got better over the years, bringing increases in property values and equal increases in property taxes.

When we discussed rehabbing the Uptown building, we planned on saving the exterior work until last. Our hope was to avoid triggering a sequence of events that would result in our property being prematurely reassessed because of improvements. Another factor we considered was the quadrennial reassessment and the date it was due. If we could schedule the cosmetic work for completion after the reassessment, we might minimize the tax increase for another four years.

Regardless of our efforts to minimize increases, property taxes have gone up each year. We have offset these increases with equal increases in rents. Our renewal letters to tenants cite taxes as one of the major reasons we have to increase rent. We escrow money each month for taxes and insurance with our bank and they pay the bill from our account, although now I think it would be better to earn interest on the money and pay the bills ourselves.

How to Read a Tax Bill

The following discussion is intended to help you understand how your tax bills are calculated. Local laws may vary; consult your local tax authority.

Market Value

The public assessor or appraiser has the responsibility of determining a market value for each property in a jurisdiction (county, township, borough, or parish). The market value of a property is the price the property would probably sell for in a competitive market. If there has not been a recent sale of a property comparable to yours, the assessor uses other methods to determine a market value.

One method that could be used—especially on newer or special-use buildings—is the cost approach, which determines the current cost of replacing the building, less depreciation from all causes, plus the value of the land.

Another method, used for income-producing property, is the income approach. It establishes market value by determining the income the property either produces or is expected to produce.

Assessors usually do not inspect each building. They determine a market value for a representative building, determine the value per square foot for that building, then multiply that value by the square footage of other buildings.

Public assessors are required by law to reassess property at mandated intervals. A reassessment period may be every year, every three years, every fours years, or even longer.

Our example 12-unit apartment building has been determined to have a market value of $240,000 (see Figure 11.1).

Assessed Value

Once the market value is determined, the assessed value can be calculated. The assessed value is a legal term denoting on what value a property will be taxed. (It is not necessarily the sale value of a property.) Assessed value is a percentage of the market value. It varies between states, within a state, and/or by type (or classification) of property. The assessed value is set by the same body that determined market value. It can be 100 percent of the market value or some fraction thereof. This percentage of market value is known as the assessment rate. In our example, the assessment rate is 33.33 percent of the market value. Therefore, our property has an assessed value of $79,992.

Figure 11.1: How to Read and Calculate a Tax Bill

Example 12-Unit Apartment Building		Your Tax Bill Your Building	
Market Value	$240,000	Market Value	$_____
Assessment Rate	x 33.33%	Assessment Rate	x ? %
Assessed Valuation	$79,992	Assessed Valuation	$_____
Equalization Factor (multiplier)	x 1.4153	Equalization Factor	x (multiplier)
Equalized Assessed Valuation	$113,212.68	Equalized Assessed Valuation	$_____
Tax Rate	x 8.785*	Tax Rate	x (tax rate)*
Tax Bill	$9,945.73	Tax Bill	$_____
*For each $100 of Equalized Assessed Valuation		*For each $100 of Equalized Assessed Valuation	

Multipliers

Between reassessment years, some assessed values may need to be adjusted. As an example, there may be times when sales in a given area indicate a property value change, either upward or downward. Or inflation may bring about substantial increases in property values. Sometimes values between taxing jurisdictions get too far out of line, and it may be necessary to make them more uniform so taxpayers are paying proportionately. In any case, making a reassessment adjustment saves the assessor a lot of time and work—saving the taxpayers money in the cost of running the assessor's office.

The assessor may perform a reassessment on a property-by-property basis, or the state, county, and/or other supervisory body may step in and adjust all the values in a given jurisdiction. Instead of reassessing each property in a given area, adjustments are made by applying a multiplier to each property. When an intervention like this takes place, the adjustment to the assessed values is accomplished by applying a multiplier, or equalization factor, to the assessed value. The multiplier is applied to the assessed value, and either increases or decreases the assessed value by the percentage of the multiplier. The process produces the adjusted, or equalized, assessed value of the property.

In our example, because the multiplier is more than 1, the assessed value will increase. Our assessed value of $79,992 times the 1.4153 multiplier results in an equalized valuation of $113,212.68.

Tax Rate

Once the adjusted assessed value is determined, the tax rate (in many states called the millage rate) is calculated. Local taxing bodies (schools, municipality, county, etc.) add up assessed values on all properties in their jurisdictions. The total operations budgeted amount for those bodies is divided by the total adjusted assessed value base to determine the tax or millage rate. Multiplying the equalized assessed value by the tax or millage rate gives you your total taxes due (tax bill). The tax rate for our building has been set at 8.785 per $100 of equalized assessed valuation. To see how much we owe, we would divide the valuation of $113,212.68 by 100, getting $1,132.12 which is then multiplied by the tax rate of 8.785 to calculate a tax bill of $9,945.73. (You can save a step by turning the tax rate into a percentage [.08785] and multiplying the equalized assessed valuation by that number.)

Are You Overassessed?

Your property may be either over- or under-assessed even though the assessors have done their jobs properly.

Assessors have many properties to assess at any given time; and they tackle this problem by using a mass appraisal approach. The assessor takes comparable properties in comparable areas and places comparable market values on them and, therefore, comparable assessed values on them. Since the assessors are not inspecting properties for their unique features, the values they place are almost always inexact. An individual appraisal is much more accurate for determining market value because it focuses on the unique characteristics of the property.

Purchase prices are not always good indicators of true market value. When purchasing property in a state that does not tax personal property, it is generally a good idea to allocate a reasonable portion of the purchase price specifically to the personal property (ask your accountant for details). This amount should be specified on the closing statement and also, if possible, in the contract. Another factor skewing the value of a property is below-market financing. If below-market financing is involved, the selling price may be inflated and, if so, it should be adjusted downward to reflect the effects of the financing. The assessed value should not indicate a market value higher than what was paid for the property after the adjustments for personal property and financing.

There may be comparable properties near your property that are assessed lower than your building. Photographs of these properties may be helpful when filing a complaint with the assessor. In some cases the assessor may either lower your assessed value or raise the assessed value on the comparable properties.

When using an income approach (rental property), keep in mind that assessors usually employ guideline percentages in determining normal operations of a property. They follow these guidelines when looking at vacancies, expenses, and taxes as percentages of taxes of gross possible rents, and taxes per unit, or per square foot.

If your percentages are higher than the guidelines used by the assessor, it is up to you to prove that these problems should be considered in assessing the property, and that they are not the result of poor management. Assessors do not have to lower the value on a property simply because the owner or manager is not doing an adequate job. Be ready to justify and support variances from the guidelines, especially major, unexpected, and necessary expenses. Also, be ready to give reasons why you are experiencing higher-than-normal vacancies.

Any natural disaster, such as flood, fire, tornado, and so on, that causes major damage to the property, should be brought to the attention of the assessor immediately. Documentation should be submitted to the assessor supporting the cost of the damages. Any problem with the property that would have a negative effect on value should be documented for the assessor.

Valuation Complaints

As noted above, by law all property must be reassessed at certain intervals. However, the assessor may reassess your property each and every year. Also, you may file a complaint every year, even if your property has not been reassessed that year.

A call to the local assessor will inform you of the proper forms that are required to be filed, the date by which the complaint must be filed, the documents that must be filed with the complaint, and the number of copies of each document. If you have trouble finding the proper office, as may happen in some rural areas, a call to the town hall may provide the answer. Some jurisdictions are not as formal and may just require that you send the pertinent documents by a certain date. These assessors will work with you to determine the value of your property before formally issuing a notice. By working in this manner with the assessor, you may be able to avoid the appeal process altogether.

Some assessors will not accept a complaint if it is not on their specific forms. It is very important that the taxpayer work with the assessor and know the filing deadline. These filing deadlines may vary from year to year, and if one is missed, it may be very difficult to file a complaint for the given year.

Legal representation is not required to work with the assessor concerning an assessed value. You may file the required information on your own behalf. If you and the assessor do not reach a mutually satisfactory decision, however, the next step will be to appeal to a supervisory board. The name of the supervisory board may vary between states, and even within states. It may be known as the Board of Appeals, Board of Review, Board of Equalization, Board of Assessors, and any number of other titles. In some jurisdictions you may represent yourself before the board. In others, a lawyer may be required. Complaint forms are required and filing deadlines must be met. A hearing or meeting will be arranged at which the taxpayer may present the pertinent information about the property to the board and questions and answers may pass back and forth. A decision is rendered by the board within a specified period of time.

In most cases, if you are not satisfied by the decision of the board, a court remedy is available. This requires hiring an attorney to represent you.

Tax Rate Protests

Some states allow tax rate protests or at least have some type of procedure for protesting the tax rate. The basis for a tax rate protest is that the tax rate being levied, or some portion of it, is excessive and/or illegal. Normally, you would hire a local law firm to determine what portion of the tax rate is illegal and/or excessive, and to file the lawsuit for you. There may be forms that need to be filed at the time the taxes are paid, and other procedures that must be followed. The local treasurer should be able to guide you concerning the necessary procedures, and perhaps provide you with the names of law firms that would assist you in the process. Be advised though, that tax rate protests are allowed only in some areas of the country.

Special Assessments/Incentive Programs

Before contracting to purchase a property, check if there are any special assignments on the property. Sidewalk or street light installation, or the construction of a new sewage treatment plant, are examples of special assessments which would be passed on to the property owner. This could lead to significantly higher taxes for a number of years. Taxes attributable to special assessments or special service areas cannot be reduced through the appeal process. The payment of these taxes is something you would want to negotiate with the seller at the time of purchase.

On the other hand, if the property needs major rehab work, you may want to see if there are any incentive programs, tax credit programs, or exemptions offered. Check with the local assessors office or with the state to find out if any of these things are available and how you qualify your property for them. Programs vary from state to state, between types of properties, and between local jurisdictions.

Before you start upgrading, it is prudent to inquire about anything that might reduce the assessed value during the work period and even for several years after the work is completed. If a landfill is going to open near you or the city is going to rebuild the streets (eliminating parking spaces for a period of time), you may want to reconsider purchasing, purchase price, or upgrading.

Choosing a Reliable Attorney or Tax Consultant

There are many property tax consulting firms as well as law firms that represent taxpayers before the various assessors, boards, and courts. Their degree of success can vary significantly based on their level of expertise, their diligence, and their reputation with the various assessing bodies. It is a good idea to speak to several different consultants or attorneys. Look for one who is established in the field, preferably one who works exclusively in the field of property taxes and has a reputation for being honest, reliable, and imaginative. Request examples of the types of cases they have handled, a list of references, and then call several. Request that they explain the steps in a typical appeal process, your role in the process, what information you would need to provide, as well as anything that you do not understand about the appeal process. Do not hesitate to contact the assessor to determine if the information provided by the consultant or attorney is accurate.

Ask about fees. Call as many different firms as possible to determine the normal fees in a given area. Some firms work on contingency fees while others work on flat fees. A contingency fee is a percentage of the tax savings, usually payable over two or more years. A flat fee is exactly what it implies. The fee will be a specified amount per year for the term of the agreement. Flat fees are normally employed in situations where it is difficult to determine actual savings or where a contingency fee would be outrageously high due to the size of the property. Fees are usually negotiable.

It is also usually preferable to hire a consultant or attorney in the area where the property is located. However, if you own property in many different locations, such as in several different states, a national firm may be the answer. Question how long the firm has worked in these different locations; the type of relationship they have with the different assessors';

what, if any, professional designations they possess; and to what local, national, and international professional organizations they belong. Preferably the firm belongs to organizations that work with assessors in these areas. This will usually signal that the consultant or attorney has a good rapport with the local assessor.

For More Information

If you have questions but are not quite ready to hire a consultant or attorney, there are several organizations that you can contact. All states have their own organizations formed for assessor education and interaction. These almost always allow nongovernment members to make inquiries. Ask the local assessor for the name and location of the organization for your jurisdiction.

You can also contact the *International Association of Assessing Officers* (IAAO), 13013 East Randolph Street, Suite 850, Chicago, IL 60601-6217, 312-819-6120. This is the foremost authority on assessment practices worldwide. It accepts nongovernment members and offers several professional designations. It may be able to provide a list of associate members in the taxpayer's areas. It also is an excellent source for reference materials covering every aspect of assessment practices and procedures. Classes are also offered.

The *Institute of Property Taxation*, 3350 Peachtree Road, NE, Suite 280, Atlanta, GA 30326, 404-240-2300 is an organization of nongovernment members only. It has its own education programs and professional designations. The members are very willing to exchange ideas, give referrals, and to explain the property tax system in areas where they own property.

Accounting

CHAPTER 12

Ronald Fliss is a full-time, self-employed accountant and a part-time real estate investor. He has purchased several condominiums that he rents with the option to buy. He believes that renters take better care of the property if they have an option to own it.

I like to have my tenants take care of their own units and call me only when major problems arise. For the most part, the lease-option arrangement allows me to treat them as owners.

I visit the units monthly to collect rents, observe conditions, and determine how the tenants are doing. If there is something wrong, I want to know before it becomes serious.

I believe that good recordkeeping on each condo is essential. I keep a ledger book with pages on each property, recording income and expenses that occur monthly. Keeping records indicates how each property is doing financially and serves as a basis for reporting to the IRS.

Tenant relations are usually friendly. I try to find good, responsible people to rent my units and treat them as friends. I believe people respond better to consideration than to general rules. There are times, however, when I must be firm in a situation to force proper compliance with the agreement. It takes some experience to know when to be cordial and when to be firm.

I believe that if tenants feel they are in a well-kept, desirable property, they will really try to maintain that situation by paying rent on time, observing condo rules and being fair with the owner-landlord.

Bookkeeping

The bookkeeping for your rental property can be as simple or sophisticated as you like. However, the type of accounting system you use will depend greatly on the size of your income portfolio. A personal computer or computer service company may be helpful if you operate more than 24 units. On the other hand, a simple receipts-disbursements bookkeeping system is adequate for managing a few units.

The Internal Revenue Service requires that taxpayers be able to substantiate rental income and expenses reported on their tax returns. By using a bookkeeping system such as the one illustrated in this chapter, you will not only satisfy IRS requirements, but also determine your cash flow or deficit on a month-by-month basis.

Operating income property is a business. Just as in any other business, you will want to make intelligent decisions based on sound economic reasoning and facts. Maintaining adequate records will enable you to monitor the expenses of your property, allowing you to determine if any of the expenses can be reduced, thereby increasing your cash flow.

Your accountant will be able to prepare your tax return more easily if the history of the past year is readily available. Funds received and cash disbursed as part of a business need to be treated with a little more sophistication than your personal checkbook transactions. Even if your accountant or computer service bureau keeps your records, you need some knowledge of bookkeeping.

Using a Ledger to Produce a Monthly Financial Statement

Checking Accounts

The IRS does not require that you maintain a separate checking account for each building you own (unless the property is not owned by you personally; for example, owned by a partnership), but keeping separate accounts facilitates recordkeeping. By keeping the cash receipts and cash disbursements separate from your personal transactions, it is much easier to prepare the monthly operating statement because all of your transactions are in one checking account.

If you use a separate checkbook for each building, and the building account does not have sufficient cash to pay a certain bill, you will have to put your personal funds into the checkbook. If you have to do this, be certain to indicate in your building checkbook where the money came from, for example: "transfer from personal checkbook." Later, when the building checkbook has sufficient cash, you can write a check reimbursing yourself from the building account.

Rent Schedules

As you receive the monthly rental checks, deposit them into the appropriate building account checkbook. Next, record the rental receipt on a rent schedule (Figure 12.1) for the appropriate building. By recording this when you receive the rent, you can determine at a glance which tenants still owe you money. As your number of units increases, this rent schedule becomes very important; without it you might overlook a non-paying tenant due to the high number of units you own. Your rent schedules function as a cash receipts journal.

Record cash disbursements in the building checkbook when they occur. At the end of each month, complete the cash disbursements journal (Figure 12.2). Record each month on a new sheet. Keep all sheets for your accountant to review at year-end.

To prepare the monthly cash disbursements journal, go through the building checkbook, recording each disbursement by check number, payee, and description. In the sample journal, six columns are used for types of disbursements (mortgage, supplies, utilities, and so on). The building and the number of checks written each month will determine the number of columns you will need to record the transactions. Thirteen-column accountant's worksheets, which can be purchased at most office supply stores, are recommended.

Figure 12.1: Rent Schedule

Building Location or Name _____ 19 _____

Security Deposit	Tenant Name	Apt. No.	Jan.	Feb.	Mar.	Apr.	May	June	July	Aug.	Sept.	Oct.	Nov.	Dec.	Total
$550	Smith	1	$ 550												
600	Jones	2	600												
575	Adams	3	575												
575	Johnson	4	600												
	Total rents		$2,325												
Plus laundry income			50												
	Total income		$2375												

Cash Disbursements Journal

If you pay cash for a supply or service instead of writing a check, get a receipt and indicate on the receipt what type of service was performed or supply purchased from whom, the date, and for which building. You can then reimburse yourself from the building checkbook for the cash you spent, or on the cash disbursements journal write "cash" in the check number column. Attach all receipts to each month's cash disbursements journal. By doing this, you will leave an "audit trail." Should you ever have to substantiate the building operation numbers, all of the paid receipts will be attached to the appropriate month's disbursements journal.

Operating Statement

At the end of each month, tally the income and expenses from your journals and enter the figures on the cash flow statement (Figure 12.3). The operating statement shows a summary of activity during the month and is broken down by line items.

Figure 12.2: Cash Disbursements Journal

Building Location or Name _____   For the Month of _____, 19___

Check Number	Payee	Mortgage Payment	Supplies	Utilities Gas	Utilities Water	Office Supplies	Other
101	Citizens Mortgage	$1,250.00					
102	Ace Supply Store		$13.31				
103	Utility Co.—Gas			$192.72			
104	Water Company				$39.41		
Cash	Smith Hardware		10.00				
105	Ace Supply Store		15.00				
106	All-Office Supply Store					$22.00	
		$1,250.00	$38.31	$192.72	$39.41	$22.00	

Figure 12.3: Cash Flow Statement

Building Location or Name _____ 19 _____

Cash Receipts (table 1)	Jan.	Feb.	Mar.	Apr.	May	June	July	Aug.	Sept.	Oct.	Nov.	Dec.	Total
Rent	$ 2,325.00												
Laundry	50.00												
Other													
Total Receipts (a)	$ 2,375.00												

Cash Disbursements (table 2)													
Mortgage payment	$1,250.00												
Accounting													
Advertising													
Cleaning and maintenance													
Insurance													
Legal													
Repairs													
Supplies	38.31												
Real estate taxes													
Utilities													
Electric	192.72												
Gas													
Water	39.41												
Scavenger													
Landscaping													
Snow removal													
Wages and taxes													
Carpeting													
Appliances													
Office supplies	22.00												
Other (describe)													
Total disbursements (b)	$1,542.44												
Net Cash Flow (Deficit) (a – b)	$ 32.56												

Line Item Definitions for the Cash Flow Statement

Cash Receipts

- *Rents*: all monies received as rent, not including security deposits or other deposits. Security deposits received from tenants are not considered income for tax reporting purposes. It is a good idea to maintain these in a separate checkbook (or an interest bearing account) until the tenants vacate the units. If you use some or all of the security deposit to pay for past due rent or damages to the apartment, it becomes taxable.
- *Laundry*: income received from laundry equipment.
- *Other*: such items as application fees, late fees, and credit-check fees.
- *Total receipts*: equals total of above items.
- *Fees*: application fees, credit check fees, cleaning fees, etc.

Cash Disbursements

- *Mortgage payment*: principal, interest, tax escrow, and insurance escrow. Get an amortization schedule from your lender for your mortgage payments. Using the amortization schedule you will be able to record each month's principal and interest payments. If your real estate taxes and insurance are included in your monthly mortgage payments, the lender also can provide you with the specific amounts.
- *Accounting*: fees paid to accounting companies or individual accountants for services rendered.
- *Advertising*: signs, print ads, promotions, printing of fliers, and so on.
- *Cleaning and maintenance*: labor only (does not include supplies).
- *Legal*: fees paid for legal services.
- *Repairs*: parts and labor for appliances, electrical, plumbing, air-conditioning, and heating, including do-it-yourself maintenance or contractor work.
- *Supplies*: cleaning, janitorial, maintenance, and so on.
- *Landscaping*: service contract or new purchases.
- *Snow removal*: service contract.
- *Wages and taxes*: administrative and janitorial.
- *Carpeting*: new purchases.
- *Appliances*: new purchases.
- *Other*: miscellaneous.
- *Total disbursements*: total of above expenditures.
- *Net cash flow (or deficit) from property*: total cash receipts less total cash disbursements.

Analyzing and Using Operating Statement Data

To further refine your operating statement, determine the rental income and other items on the operating statement on a per-unit basis. You do this by dividing each income and expense category by the total number of units in your building. You can use this information to determine relationships that may help you increase your cash flow.

Operating statements provide historical data for preparing your annual budget and detail important information that is useful when you purchase more investment property.

For example, suppose you own a four-flat apartment building with utility costs of $14 per unit. You are considering purchasing a 12-flat. By using information from your other properties, you can project a per-unit utility cost for the building you are considering buying.

However, do not arbitrarily use the data without giving thought to the details of the potential building. For example, if your four-flat building is gas heated and the 12-flat building for sale has electric heat, the heating costs are not comparable.

In addition to per-unit totals, income and expenses can be expressed as a percentage of gross rents and other values such as vacancy-loss comparisons of the properties. Maintaining good records makes preparing your tax return easier and helps you analyze your building operations on a monthly and annual basis.

When you are ready to sell your real estate investment you will have information readily available to show a potential buyer.

Computer Software

If you own and operate at least six units, you may want to consider using a personal computer to keep track of your tenants, and to perform all your accounting and bookkeeping functions. (If this is your only use, you can buy a reliable used system inexpensively.) Many of the electronic spreadsheet programs (for instance, Lotus 1-2-3, or Quicken) can be used to create your basic functions, along with several canned programs that come pre-loaded on some newer model computers. Beyond these basic spreadsheets you can also purchase a software package designed specifically for property management.

Using a computer will allow you to generate graphs and tables that will make analyzing the details of your investment easier.

As of this writing, there were at least three software packages reasonably priced for the individual owner/operator of rental properties. These, or any other good software systems, should have the following minimum characteristics:

- Make it easier to manage daily and monthly routines.
- Be easy to install or to use.
- Be cost effective.
- Have free technical support.
- Handle all the accounting, record-keeping, and file maintenance.
- Be customizable.
- Handle multiple properties.
- Come with a good set of manuals or instructions.
- Allow for future updates and be expandable.
- Be backed by a reputable company.

Tenant Pro 100, Property Automation Software Corporation, Richardson, Texas, 800-964-2792, www.property1.com, mail@property1.com, $395.00 as of June, 1997. A user-friendly and menu-driven system, designed to handle all aspects of managing 100 units. Features include: general ledger, work orders, rent statements, payables, receivables, multiple properties, digital imaging (photographs), and form letters. Whenever you enter data about one item, it automatically updates throughout the program. A video training program is available for an additional fee. Can be upgraded to handle 500 units.

Tenant File, WG Software, Austin, Texas; 800-398-3904, www.wgsoft.com, $129.95 for the Windows version. Designed to handle 100 units, it has the ability to upgrade to unlimited units. Tenant File is menu-driven with pop-up screens. It offers automatic posting and check writing. Same standard features as most others. Go to their web site to download a demo version.

Easy Landlord, Outlook Software, 800-526-5588, $99.95 up to 50 units (also known as Landlord 97 in the Windows 95 version). Designed for owners and managers, Easy Landlord handles single-family dwellings, apartments, condos, offices, or light commercial buildings. Includes complete accounting and information systems designed specifically for managing up to 50 units. Also available in a 150-unit version. Instantly prepares over 30 professional financial and management reports to help evaluate property performance. Generates checks, tenant billing, and late notices. Up to eight separate checkbooks. Comprehensive user manual, online help, and unlimited free technical support.

For a complete listing of real estate software, order a catalog from *Z-Law Software, Inc.*, 800-525-5588, e-mail at ZLAW1@aol.com, or visit their web site at http://www.z-law.com.

Income Taxes

Tax reform has significantly changed real estate as an investment. Real estate experts believe it will be good for real estate in the long run.

The following information only touches the surface of the changes affecting real estate investing. Contact your own tax adviser for a more in-depth analysis of how this tax law affects you personally.

Active Owners

Tax reform eliminated many tax shelters associated with real estate investments. However, the revisions did leave a substantial portion available to active owners who make less than $150,000 per year in earned income and are actively involved in the management of their real estate.

Owner-operators of income property who have less than $100,000 per year in earned income can still deduct up to $25,000 for depreciation and operating losses to reduce their taxable income from all sources. The $25,000 tax loss is phased out in stages for income between $100,000 and $150,000. If your adjusted gross income stays below $100,000, you could purchase several properties before reaching the $25,000 limit. The elimination of tax incentives for builders has caused a reduction in the construction of new apartment units. This should result in increased rents as the demand for rental units is unfulfilled.

Passive Owners

The following advantages still exist for passive real estate investors (those who are not involved in the management of their real estate).

- *Limited liability*: The mortgages are nonrecourse (only the specific property is at stake) and you have no personal responsibility for any bills or operating expenses of the building.
- *Professional management*: A professional management company handles all of the day-to-day concerns. A passive investor enjoys worry-free ownership.

Depreciation

Depreciation is defined as the allocation of the cost of an asset to the periods benefited, in a rational and systematic manner. What this means to you is a noncash deduction on your tax return.

For example, suppose you purchased a four-unit apartment building for $150,000, of which $30,000 is allocated to the land. Land is a nondepreciable asset, so the higher the land allocation, the lower the amount remaining that you can depreciate. The building value is then $120,000, and, for simplicity's sake, let's assume you depreciate this using the straight-line method for a period of 30 years. You can then deduct $4,000 annually from your rental income as an expense, but you did not pay $4,000 in cash. On your tax return, you would claim a deduction of $4,000 for depreciation expense. This is what is meant by a noncash expense.

Tax reform increased the life over which you would depreciate the building from 19 years to 27.5 years (319.5 years for commercial property). In addition, you are now required to use the straight-line method of depreciation as opposed to using the accelerated method, that was used in the past.

Active versus Passive Income

There are three different types of income and they are reported differently on your tax return. Wages are earned income; dividends and interest are considered portfolio income; and real estate investment is classified as passive income.

In general, if you own the building personally (as opposed to a limited partnership investment), you will be able to deduct any losses you may incur against your other income. For example, you earn $50,000 from your job and your apartment investment has a $10,000 loss (remember depreciation is a noncash expense, so it is not unusual to report a loss on your tax return). You would be able to deduct the $10,000 rental loss on your tax return, in effect decreasing your earned income from $50,000 to $40,000. Depending upon your individual tax bracket, this could save you up to $3,850 in taxes.

Congress has limited the deduction you can claim from real estate losses to a maximum of $25,000. So, if you have more than $25,000 in passive losses, you cannot deduct any amount over the $25,000 limit. Also, if your earned income is more than $100,000, you start to lose 50 percent of the loss. At $150,000 of earned income you cannot deduct any losses from your building. These nondeductible losses become "suspended" losses, to be used when the property is sold. You do not lose these rental losses; it merely becomes a difference in timing—changing from a current deduction to a deduction that will decrease your gain on the sale of the property in the future.

Alternative Minimum Tax

The alternative minimum tax, or AMT, is like a separate set of rules for determining your tax liability. Its purpose, as the name implies, is to ensure that taxpayers who have tax preference income, deductions, or credits will pay at least a minimum tax. Tax preference items were given special treatment under the regular tax laws, so it was possible for taxpayers to take advantage of this special treatment and avoid paying any federal income tax. Congress deemed this unfair, so it implemented the concept of a second tax system to make sure that taxpayers who benefited under the regular tax laws would not escape taxation altogether. The taxpayer would pay the greater of the regular income tax or the AMT.

The alternative minimum tax concept is not new with the most recent tax law change, but its scope is increased so that more taxpayers will be subject to this tax than in the past. The more common tax preferences a real estate investor will encounter, or has encountered in the past, is the excess of accelerated depreciation over the straight-line method.

Passive losses deducted against earned or portfolio income are not allowed for AMT purposes. The entire gain is considered in calculating the alternative minimum taxable income.

Resources

Organizations

Institute of Real Estate Management (IREM). 430 North Michigan Avenue, Chicago, IL 60611-4090, 312-329-6000. IREM is a professional group of Certified Property Managers (CPM), Accredited Resident Managers (ARM), and Accredited Management Organizations (AMO). It offers educational programs, seminars, and conferences for property managers and management companies. It also publishes books, and periodicals.

National Apartment Association. 201 N. Union Street, Suite 200, Alexandria, VA 22314, 703-518-6141. This nonprofit association is the largest broad-based organization dedicated solely to multifamily housing, with 25,000+ members in approximately 160 state and local affiliated associations. It lobbies for the apartment rental industry, publishes magazines and forms, and conducts an annual educational conference and exposition. It offers four programs for apartment management: Certified Apartment Manager (CAM), Certified Apartment Property Supervisor (CAPS), Certified Apartment Maintenance Technician (CAMT), National Apartment Leasing Professional (NALP). It also offers a Rental Owners Course (ROC) for owners of fewer than 100 units.

National Association of Home Builders, Multifamily Council. 1201 15th Street, N.W., Washington, DC 20005, 800-368-5242 x 209. The council offers a Registered in Apartment Management (RAM) program, as well as sponsoring an annual multihousing conference and trade show.

National Association of REALTORS®. 430 N. Michigan Avenue, Chicago, IL 60611, 312-329-8200. The national organization is composed of thousands of local associations and REALTOR® boards. It has more than 730,000 individual members. It operates the largest real estate library in the world (NARLIBRARY@aol.com)

Books and Magazines

Multifamily Executive. MGI Publications, Inc., 301 Oxford Valley Road, Suite 903A, Yardley, PA, 19067 800-422-2681. Subscription free of charge to qualified individuals.

RAM Digest. NAHB/RAM, 1201 15th Street, N.W., Washington, DC 20005, 800-368-5242, ext. 215. Official magazine of Registered In Apartment Management certificate holders. The program is offered by the National Association of Home Builders.

Journal of Property Management. Institute of Real Estate Management (IREM), 430 N. Michigan Avenue, Chicago, IL 60611, 312-661-0004 six times a year. Caters to property managers of large apartment communities, but their articles about managing multifamily properties are very useful for the owner/operator.

Dictionary of Real Estate Terms. Third Edition, 1993, $11.95, Published by Barrons Educational Services, written by Jack Friedman, Jack Harris, and Bruce Lindeman. This is a must-have book that contains definitions, graphs, illustrations, tables, and explanations about everything in real estate.

MultiHousing News. Published six times a year by Miller Freeman, Inc., 600 Harrison Street, San Francisco, CA 94107, 800-250-2430. Caters to the property manager of large apartment communities, but has lots of articles useful for owner/operators as well.

Index